DATE DUE

Biography Today

Profiles of People of Interest to Young Readers

1998
Annual
Cumulation

Laurie Lanzen Harris
Executive Editor

Cherie D. Abbey
Associate Editor

Omnigraphics, Inc.

Penobscot Building
Detroit, Michigan 48226

Laurie Lanzen Harris, *Executive Editor*

Cherie D. Abbey, *Associate Editor*

Helene Henderson, Kevin Hillstrom, Laurie Hillstrom,
Sue Ellen Thompson, and John Wukovitz
Sketch Writers

Barry Puckett, *Research Associate*

Joan Margeson, *Research Assistant*

Omnigraphics, Inc.

* * *

Matt Barbour, *Production Manager*

Laurie Lanzen Harris, *Vice President, Editorial Director*

Peter E. Ruffner, *Vice President, Administration*

James A. Sellgren, *Vice President, Operations and Finance*

Jane Steele, *Marketing Consultant*

* * *

Frederick G. Ruffner, Jr., Publisher

Printed in the United States

Indexed in
CHILDREN'S
MAGAZINE
GUIDE

Contents

4

Preface

Biography Today is a magazine designed and written for the young reader—ages 9 and above—and covers individuals that librarians and teachers tell us that young people want to know about most: entertainers, athletes, writers, illustrators, cartoonists, and political leaders.

The Plan of the Work

The publication was especially created to appeal to young readers in a format they can enjoy reading and readily understand. Each issue contains approximately 10 sketches arranged alphabetically; this annual cumulation contains 28 entries. Each entry provides at least one picture of the individual profiled, and bold-faced rubrics lead the reader to information on birth, youth, early memories, education, first jobs, marriage and family, career highlights, memorable experiences, hobbies, and honors and awards. Each of the entries ends with a list of easily accessible sources designed to lead the student to further reading on the individual and a current address. Obituary entries are also included, written to provide a perspective on the individual's entire career. Obituaries are clearly marked in both the table of contents and at the beginning of the entry.

Biographies are prepared by Omnigraphics editors after extensive research, utilizing the most current materials available. Those sources that are generally available to students appear in the list of further reading at the end of the sketch.

Indexes

To provide easy access to entries, each issue of *Biography Today* contains a Name Index, General Index covering occupations, organizations, and ethnic and minority origins, Places of Birth Index, and a Birthday Index. These indexes cumulate with each succeeding issue. The three yearly issues are cumulated annually in a hardbound volume, with cumulative indexes. The indexes also include references to individuals profiled in the **Biography Today Special Subject** volumes, explained below.

Our Advisors

This magazine was reviewed by an Advisory Board comprised of librarians, children's literature specialists, and reading instructors so that we could make sure that the concept of this publication—to provide a readable and accessible biographical magazine for young readers—was on target. They evaluated the title as it developed, and their suggestions have proved invaluable. Any errors, however, are ours alone. We'd like to list the Advisory Board members, and to thank them for their efforts.

Sandra Arden, *Retired*
Assistant Director
Troy Public Library, Troy, MI

Gail Beaver
Ann Arbor Huron High School Library
and the University of Michigan School
of Information and Library Studies
Ann Arbor, MI

Marilyn Bethel
Pompano Beach Branch Library
Pompano Beach, FL

Eileen Butterfield
Waterford Public Library
Waterford, CT

Linda Carpino
Detroit Public Library
Detroit, MI

Helen Gregory
Grosse Pointe Public Library
Grosse Pointe, MI

Jane Klasing, *Retired*
School Board of Broward County,
Fort Lauderdale, FL

Marlene Lee
Broward County Public Library System,
Fort Lauderdale, FL

Judy Liskov
Waterford Public Library, Waterford, CT

Sylvia Mavrogenes
Miami-Dade Public Library System
Miami, FL

Carole J. McCollough
Wayne State University Library and
Information Science Program and
Associate Dean of University Library
Systems, Detroit, MI

Deborah Rutter
Russell Library, Middletown, CT

Barbara Sawyer
Groton Public Library and Information
Center, Groton, CT

Renee Schwartz
School Board of Broward County
Fort Lauderdale, FL

Lee Sprince
Broward West Regional Library
Fort Lauderdale, FL

Susan Stewart, *Retired*
Birney Middle School Reading
Laboratory, Southfield, MI

Ethel Stoloff, *Retired*
Librarian, Birney Middle School,
Southfield, MI

Our Advisory Board stressed to us that we should not shy away from controversial or unconventional people in our profiles, and we have tried to follow their advice. The Advisory Board also mentioned that the sketches might be useful in reluctant reader and adult literacy programs, and we would value any comments librarians might have about the suitability of our magazine for those purposes.

Special Subject Series

In response to the growing number of suggestions from our readers, we have decided to expand the *Biography Today* family of publications. So far, we have published special subject volumes in these categories: **Authors, Artists, Scientists and Inventors, Sports Figures, and World Leaders**. Each of these hardcover volumes is approximately 200 pages in length and covers about 15 individuals of interest to readers ages 9 and above. The length and format of the entries is like those found in the regular issues of *Biography Today*, but there is **no duplication** between the regular series and the special subject volumes.

Your Comments Are Welcome

Our goal is to be accurate and up-to-date, to give young readers information they can learn from and enjoy. Now we want to know what you think. Take a look at this issue of *Biography Today*, on approval. Write or call me with your comments. We want to provide an excellent source of biographical information for young people. Let us know how you think we're doing.

And take a look at the next page, where we've listed those libraries and individuals who received a free issue of *Biography Today* for 1998 for suggesting people who appeared this year.

Laurie Harris
Executive Editor, *Biography Today*
Omnigraphics, Inc.
Penobscot Building
Detroit, MI 48226
Fax: 1-800-875-1340

Congratulations!

Congratulations to the following individuals and libraries, who received a free copy of *Biography Today* for suggesting people who appeared in 1998:

Nathan Adams, Canton, OH
Sadia Ali, Springfield, VA
Fang An, Manhattan, KS
Sophy Ang, Phoenix, AZ
Champion R. Avecilla, San Jose, CA
Avondale High School,
    Auburn Hills, MI
Kelly Ann Baskins, Holland, PA
Tiffany Bates, Machesney Park, IL
Elaena Bennett, Mooresville, IN
Alexandria Benoit, Raleigh, NC
Bixby Spartan Media Center,
    Bixby, OK
Allison Boyer, Klingerstown, PA
Brownsburg Public Library,
    Brownsburg, IN
Central Junior High School,
    Oklahoma City, OK
    Bobbie Frisk
Central Junior High School,
    Sand Springs, OK
Central Middle School, Dover, DE
    Brenda Maxon
Central Middle School, Waukesha, WI
Shannon D. Charney, Trenton, MI
Cherokee Attendance Center Library,
    Cherokee, KS
Kayla Courneya, Bay City, MI
Andrea Cushing, Concord, CA
Stephanie Davis, Toledo, OH
Sylvia Do, Gilroy, CA
Lynn Douangpangna, Ft. Smith, AR
Sonja Durham, Dover, DE
Rachael Ann Dymanski,
    Cleveland, OH
Jenna Ferguson, Millersville, MD
Rebecca Ferraro, Mahomet, IL
Adam Finkel, Bloomfield Hills, MI
Forest Park School Library,
    Albany, NY

Lise Forestal, Albany, NY
Caitlin Frates, Los Altos, CA
Erica Freeburg, Brookfield, IL
Jessica Gottschalk, Imlay City, MI
Allen Graves, Indianapolis, IN
Greenwood Elementary School,
    La Grande, OR
Jamie Groh, North Branch, MI
Melissa Haacke, Riverton, UT
Howards Grove Middle School,
    Howards Grove, WI
Megan Hunt, Fishers, IN
Erica Hunter, Camp Springs, MD
Jimmy and Linda Huynh, Portland, OR
Alexis Kasperek, Suisun, CA
Amanda Kelley, Terre Haute, IN
Meghan Kelly, Jamesport, NY
Tiffany Kosolcharoen, Cupertino, CA
Katherine Kromidas, Carlton, OR
Lafayette District Library,
    Higginsville, MO
Lake Dolloff Elementary, Auburn, WA
Rebecca Lawson, Noblesville, IN
Randall Lewis, Coram, NY
Sara Lewis, Kentwood, MI
Lincoln School, Brookfield, IL
Kathy Ly, San Jose, CA
Mui Ly, Charlotte, NC
Lynbrook Elementary, Springfield, VA
Connie Mahautmr, Bartlett, TN
Augusta Malvagno, Glendale, NY
Brenda Maxon, Dover, DE
Ramsey Meitl, Oberlin, KS
Helen Mengstu, Florissant, MO
Molalla Middle School, Molalla, OR
Giota and Natalie Momtsios,
    Framingham, MA
Natalie Momtsios, Framingham, MA
Northeast Hamilton School,
    Blairsburg, IA

North Whitfield Middle School,
  Dalton, GA
Perryton Junior High School,
  Perryton, TX
M.J. Porter, Stoughton, WI
Aarika Robinson, Dayton, OH
Raychel Rondez, Milpitas, CA
Rivera Library, Pico Rivera, CA
Roosevelt Middle School,
  Coffeyville, KS
  Martha Tilton
Rossman Elementary School,
  Hartford, WI
Saratoga Public Library, Saratoga
  Springs, NY, Children's Room
Frances and Jo-Lin Shih,
  Woodhaven, NY
Jessie Simmon, East Machias, ME
Heather Snead, Oxon Hill, MD
Spring-Ford Middle School,
  Royersford, PA
St. Clair Shores Public Library,
  St. Clair Shores, MI
  Rosemary Orlando

St. Johns Public Library,
  St. Augustine, FL
Sunrise Middle School, Scottsdale, AZ
Alyssa Tapps, Des Moines, IA
Jacinda Treadway, Nashville, TN
Twin Beach Elementary School
  Library, West Bloomfield, MI
Allison Vesely, Darien IL
Washington Elementary School,
  Mt. Clemens, MI
Washington School, Caldwell, ID
Korin M. Weber, Waterford, WI
Willow Springs Elementary School,
  Fairfax, VA
Shalia Wills, Brandywine, MD
Joanna Wong, San Francisco, CA
Theresa Wong, Saratoga, CA
Sarah Woodard, Florissant, MO
Woodmore Elementary School,
  Woodville, OH
Jared Yecker, Lancaster, PA

Bella Abzug 1920 - 1998

American Feminist, Lawyer, Activist, and Politician
Former Congresswoman from New York

BIRTH

Bella Abzug was born Bella Savitzky on July 24, 1920, in the
Bronx, a borough of New York City. Her parents, Emanuel
Savitzky and Esther (Tanklefsky) Savitzky, were Jewish immi-
grants from Russia. Her father, Emanuel (called Manny), was a
butcher who ran a meat market in Manhattan; her mother,
Esther, was a homemaker when Bella was young, although she

also helped out at the meat market when she was needed. Later, Esther went to work as a cashier in a department store. Bella was their second child; she had one older sister, Helene.

Both Manny and Esther had left Russia with their families because of persecution against Jews. They had seen Russian soldiers come into their villages and beat and kill Jewish people simply for the crime of following their religion. Both Manny and Esther came to the United States looking for freedom. After World War I ended in 1918, Manny was disheartened to see people disagreeing over what seemed like small issues during the peace negotiations. So he described his plan for world peace in the name that he painted over his butcher shop: the Live and Let Live Meat Market. Manny failed to see the humor in using that name on a butcher shop, because it perfectly expressed his philosophy of life. Bella would later say that her parents' experiences as immigrants searching for freedom had a profound influence on her, inspiring her to become an activist for social justice.

WOMEN'S LIVES IN THE EARLY 20TH CENTURY

Bella Abzug grew up at a time when most women's lives were very different than they are today. In fact the year that she was born, 1920, was the year that American women won the right to vote. Up until that time, only men had been allowed to vote. During the first half of the 20th century, most American women simply had very few choices. They grew up, got married, had children, and took care of their husbands and kids. Educational opportunities for women were limited — an education was wasted on a woman who was just going to stay home and raise kids, many people felt. Career opportunities were equally limited. Most people believed that women were capable of doing only a few types of jobs, like secretaries, nurses, and teachers. It was extremely rare for women to become doctors, bankers, lawyers, or politicians. And it was practically unheard of for a woman to combine raising a family and working in a career. It was in this environment that Bella Abzug grew up, went to school, got married, had children, and started her career as a lawyer, activist, politician, and feminist.

Choices for women that we take for granted today didn't exist when Bella Abzug was young — and in fact, she worked throughout her life to guarantee these choices for all women.

YOUTH

Bella grew up in an apartment in the Bronx in a loud, loving family that included her parents, her sister, her grandparents, and an uncle. They encouraged Bella to be intelligent, strong, religious, and involved with the world. As a child, she was a natural leader and competitor and a talented athlete. When the neighborhood kids would line up to make teams for a game of stick ball or red rover, she was always one of the first kids picked. She'd play any sport — volleyball, basketball, track and field — but her first love was swimming. Roaming the streets of her neighborhood in the Bronx, she also enjoyed playing checkers, climbing trees, and beating all comers at marbles. At home, family life was filled with music. Her father had a beautiful singing voice and her sister played the grand piano that filled their parlor. Bella started taking violin lessons, and soon she was joining them on violin.

Bella's grandfather, Wolf Tanklefsky, used to babysit for her and her sister Helene while their mother was working at the meat market. "He was a very religious man," she recalled, "and I used to go to synagogue with him a lot."

She also went to Hebrew school, where she learned how to read and speak Hebrew. She had a wonderful memory for the Hebrew prayers, and she delighted her grandfather and others with her ability to *daven*, or pray aloud in Hebrew with feeling. But she became frustrated, as she got older, with certain customs. Bella and her family were Orthodox Jews, a branch of Judaism that rigorously follows ancient Jewish customs and laws. In Orthodox Judaism, women and men are not permitted to sit together during religious services. Men sit on the main floor of the synagogue

"I came from a home where there was a clear sense of social justice. And I really believed that if I could become a lawyer, I could set things straight."

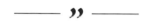

and conduct the services, and women sit in the balcony. For Bella, who had never felt inferior to boys, this was a frustrating experience. "Many people have suggested," she later said, "that it was those early days up in the balcony that got me interested in women's rights."

Through her Hebrew school teacher, Bella got involved in raising money to establish a Jewish homeland in Palestine, in what is now Israel. At that time, Israel didn't exist yet — the country was founded in 1948, after World War II and the horrors of the Holocaust. But in the 1930s, with Jewish people being persecuted around the world, many felt that a separate country that would be safe for Jews should be created in Palestine. At age 11, Bella began collecting money for a Jewish homeland. With a group of similarly committed young people, Bella would ride on the New York subways. As a train would pull into a station and prepare to stop, she would give a brief, impassioned speech while the other members of her group went around collecting coins from all the passengers. People seem moved to give generously to this dedicated, articulate girl.

EARLY MEMORIES

Bella's father died when she was just 13. In the Jewish tradition of mourning, a son or close male relative will say prayers, or *kaddish*, every day for a year after a death. Manny's relatives lamented that there was no close male relative to say the memorial prayer for him. Although Jewish law dictates that this should be done by a male relative, Bella didn't let that stop her. She went to synagogue that first morning, stood in front of the alter, bowed her head, and began to pray. For a full year, she went to synagogue each morning before school to pray. Although people didn't approve, they didn't try to stop her, either.

After her father's death, money was a little tight. There was some insurance, but not enough to cover all the family's expenses. So her mother, Esther, took a job as a cashier in a department store, and Helene helped out by giving piano lessons. Within a few years, Bella was able to help too, by teaching beginner's classes in Hebrew language, history, and customs at the Jewish center during the school year and by working with the swimming counselor at camp during the summer.

EDUCATION

Early Education

Growing up, Abzug attended the New York public schools, including Walton High School, an all-girls school that was considered one of the best in the city. She did well in her classes and earned good grades, but she was equally interested in sports. She spent most of her time running around the school in her gym suit and tennis shoes. Abzug was also active in student government and was elected class president for several semesters, including her senior year. In addition to her regular high school activities, she continued her study of music and Hebrew. She took lessons on the violin and attended a special Hebrew school, Florence Marshall Hebrew High School, after finishing classes each day at Walton. "[My mother] used to meet me after school and take all my books so I could go to Hebrew school. She'd bring me my Hebrew books [in exchange]. If I got in trouble in school and was scolded by the teacher, I'd come home and tell my mother. She would go to school and scold the teacher!" Abzug graduated from Walton High School in 1938.

By this point, Abzug had already decided that she wanted to be a lawyer. "I came from a home where there was a clear sense of social justice," she said. "And I really believed that if I could become a lawyer, I could set things straight." Most of her extended family was adamantly opposed to the idea. Being a lawyer was work for a man, they would argue with her. A girl might dream about *marrying* a lawyer, but she couldn't *become* one. Bella disagreed, of course, and her mother encouraged her. "My mother was always support-

Elizabeth Taylor, Bella Abzug, and Shirley MacLaine

ive," Abzug once said. "She thought I could do anything." Esther Savitzky had arrived in this country from Russia unable to speak a word of English. She had attended school, worked hard, and studied to be a teacher. She had to quit school, though, to help out in the family business. After her husband died and she went back to work to support her two daughters, Esther regretted that she hadn't been able to become a teacher. She was determined to see both her daughters get a good education.

College Years

So after finishing high school, Bella entered Hunter College in New York City. There, she majored in political science and spent much of her time working in student government. She was president of her class and president of the student council, active in the American Student Union, and a champion of issues related to civil rights and civil liberties. At Hunter, Abzug became part of a circle of women who would become lifelong political activists and friends. She also continued her Hebrew studies, now at the Teachers Institute at the

Jewish Theological Seminary. Abzug graduated from Hunter College in January 1942.

Determined to study law, Abzug applied to Harvard Law School, which she considered the nation's top school. Despite her excellent credentials, she was turned down by Harvard—"We take no females," they told her. Harvard Law School didn't accept women until ten years later, in 1952. She was enraged, but her mother convinced her to apply to Columbia Law School, another excellent school that had the advantage of being in New York City, so she could save money by living at home. Abzug accepted this plan when Columbia offered her a generous scholarship that covered most of her expenses.

Meeting Martin

Abzug had several months off between graduating from Hunter in January and starting law school at Columbia in September, so she took a vacation in Florida to visit her aunt and uncle. While there, she went with a friend to a concert by the violinist Yehudi Menuhin to raise money for Russian war relief. During the intermission, she noticed a few guys watching her and her friend. Then on the bus ride home after the concert, one of the guys that she had noticed earlier started quoting poetry to her. That's how she met her future husband, Martin Abzug. He asked her out several times, then he had to go back to New York. He wrote to her while she was staying in Florida, then called her as soon as she returned to New York. Soon afterward, he went into the service to fight in World War II, and they began corresponding.

For a while, Bella thought she should help the war effort, too. After Martin left for the service, she worked in a couple of defense-related office jobs. But the jobs were boring and tedious and she felt that she wasn't making much of a contribution to the nation's defense, so she decided to continue with her plans to attend law school.

Law School

Abzug started law school at Columbia in the fall of 1942. For Bella, who had routinely earned good grades without too much effort, law school was very tough at first. But she worked hard, spent long hours in the law school library, and soon learned what was required and how to do the work. While many of the other women in the class acted meek, Abzug developed a reputation as tough, combative, diligent, and dedicated. By the end of her first year, she was named an editor of the *Columbia Law Review*, a journal that publishes important articles about legal issues. It's considered a very prestigious honor to be named an editor of the law review.

While Bella was still in law school, Martin was discharged from the army for medical reasons—he had eczema, a skin condition. He returned to New York and started working in the family's shirt-manufacturing business; he later became a novelist and a stockbroker. Martin liked going out on the town each night, seeing Broadway shows or new movies. But Bella was too busy with her law studies to join him. So he would go out with others, then show up at the library around midnight to see Bella. He would pick up any writing she had done, type it up over night, and deliver it to her the next morning. From the beginning, Martin respected her ambitions, her integrity, her dreams, and her plans to be a working woman. He encouraged and supported her in every way. Bella and Martin were married while she was in her second year of law school. Bella Abzug finished law school and earned her LL.B. in about 1945.

Her first challenge after law school was finding a job. The 1940s were a tough time for a woman to be a lawyer. Abzug had been very successful in law school, editing the *Columbia Law Review* and graduating as one of the top students in her class, so she hoped to have her pick of jobs. But instead, prospective employers would ask her questions about her typing skills and offer her salaries that were much lower than what a male lawyer would earn. Sexism was widespread and blatant.

"When I was a young lawyer, I would go to people's offices and they would always say: 'Sit here. We'll wait here for the lawyer.' Working women wore hats. It was the only way they would take you seriously. After a while, I started liking them."

Even after she got her first job it was tough. People weren't used to female lawyers, and judges, other lawyers, and even her clients didn't take her seriously. Most women in offices worked in secretarial or other clerical positions, and people assumed she did, too. But Abzug discovered that wearing hats made all the difference in earning people's respect as a professional woman. As she later recalled, "When I was a young lawyer, I would go to people's offices and they would always say: 'Sit here. We'll wait here for the lawyer.' Working women wore hats. It was the only way they would take you seriously. After a while, I started liking them." Wearing a hat became Abzug's trademark, and she continued to wear them throughout her life.

CAREER HIGHLIGHTS

Abzug was a lawyer, activist, and politician for about 50 years, from the 1940s through the 1990s. She fought passionately for the issues that she believed in, including peace, civil rights, and the environment. She was one of the pioneers of the feminist movement, fighting for equality for women in the U.S. and around the world. But Abzug was as well known for the image she presented as for the issues she supported. A passionate crusader with a belligerent, brash, and confrontational manner, she developed a reputation for abrasive activism. Her flamboyant style, both in dress and speech, always commanded attention—from loyal supporters as well as outspoken opponents.

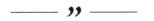

"They call me Battling Bella, Mother Courage, and a Jewish mother with more complaints than Portnoy. There are those who say I'm impatient, impetuous, uppity, rude, profane, brash, and overbearing. Whether I'm any of these things or all of them, you can decide for yourself. But whatever I am—and this ought to be made very clear at the outset—I am a very serious woman."

"I've been described as a tough and noisy woman, a prizefighter, a man hater, you name it," Abzug wrote in *Bella! Ms. Abzug Goes to Washington,* her account of her years in Congress. "They call me Battling Bella, Mother Courage, and a Jewish mother with more complaints than Portnoy. There are those who say I'm impatient, impetuous, uppity, rude, profane, brash, and overbearing. Whether I'm any of these things or all of them, you can decide for yourself. But whatever I am—and this ought to be made very clear at the outset—I am a very serious woman."

Early Career

During her early career, the period from the 1940s to the 1960s, Abzug devoted herself to her legal practice and to political and social activism. Her first job was with a law firm that specialized in labor law. Many unions and other employee groups had avoided asking for wage increases during World War II, as their way of helping the war effort. But with the war over, unions were ready to fight for better pay and working conditions for their members. Abzug's firm took cases helping workers who were being treated unfairly by their employers. She represented individuals as well as union groups, including fur workers, restaurant workers, auto workers, and longshoremen. Later, Abzug left the law firm to set up her own individual law practice.

In addition to her legal practice, Abzug also worked as an activist on political and social causes. On civil rights issues, she worked as a lawyer for the American Civil Liberties Union, defending people who were treated unfairly because of their race. Abzug was a brave and dedicated legal defender of civil rights. One of her most famous cases involved a black man in Mississippi named Willie McGee. He had had a long-term affair with a white woman, and then he was falsely accused of raping her. At that time, it was illegal for blacks and whites even to date each other in many states, and a black man convicted of raping a white woman could get the death penalty. When the relationship between McGee and the woman became public, people accused him of raping her because they couldn't believe that a white woman would be involved with a black man. The accusation of rape was false, but McGee was convicted anyway. The woman presumably went along with it because she was afraid for her own safety if she admitted the truth.

Abzug got involved with this internationally celebrated case when it was up for appeal. With the level of racism that existed in the South at that time, it was dangerous for her to defend McGee. The Ku Klux Klan and other white supremacist groups threatened to kill her. Local newspapers ran editorials threatening to lynch McGee and his "white lady lawyer." At one point she traveled to Mississippi and discovered after she arrived that no hotel would rent a room to her. Abzug spent the whole night in a brightly lit bus station, even though she was pregnant at the time. "She slept sitting up," her husband said with pride years later. "That woman has more guts than the whole damn Army." Despite her efforts, McGee was executed.

In the 1950s, Abzug also worked as an activist in defending people accused of Communist tendencies by the McCarthy committee. At that time, the United States was in the middle of the Cold War, a period of tremendous political tension between the two great superpowers, the United States and the Soviet Union. There was great fear in the U.S. that there would be a war between the two countries, possibly even nuclear war. There was also fear that Communism would spread throughout the world. In this tense environment, Senator Joseph McCarthy began a series of Congressional committee hearings. Often with very little evidence, he used these hearings to accuse people of being Communists and taking part in subversive activities. It was like a witch hunt. There was no way for people to defend themselves against the unsubstantiated accusations. Many people's careers were ruined on the basis of sensationalist innuendo and malicious rumor. Abzug was one of very few independent attorneys who was willing to defend the artists, writers, teachers, and others who were fired from their jobs or even faced jail when they were accused by Senator McCarthy of being Communists. It took great political courage for Abzug to stand up to the McCarthy committee.

Beginning in the 1960s, Abzug also worked as an activist to promote peace. In 1961, the United States and the Soviet Union were testing nuclear bombs by exploding them in remote locations. Scientists discovered that radioactive fallout from the bombs included Strontium-90. This dangerous chemical, which

Poster for Abzug's 1970 campaign for U.S. Congress

causes cancer, was eventually ingested by cows and was getting into the milk supply, thereby endangering people. Abzug and a group of other women, including many of her friends from Hunter College, banded together to create Women Strike for Peace (WSP). They fought to put an end to testing nuclear bombs and to stop the arms race between the U.S. and the Soviet Union, in which each country tried to develop an arms supply that was bigger and more deadly than the other's. With the support of people from around the world, WSP lobbied for an international treaty to ban all nuclear tests. In 1963, leaders in the U.S., the Soviet Union, and Great Britain signed the first of many treaties to stop testing nuclear bombs. With Women Strike for Peace, Abzug also became active in other peace issues, particularly in protesting U.S. involvement in the war in Vietnam.

Getting Elected to Congress

In addition to these activities, Abzug was also involved in politics, particularly for Democratic candidates. She pressured candidates on issues, won their support for her ideas, then encouraged people to vote for them. She was particularly active in Eugene McCarthy's 1968 campaign for president and in John Lindsay's 1969 campaign for mayor of New York City.

In 1970, on the advice of her supporters, Abzug decided to run for a seat in the U.S. Congress, using the slogan, "This woman's place is in the House . . . the House of Representatives!" She faced a tough campaign, first in the Democratic primary election against incumbent Leonard Farbstein and then in the general election against Barry Farber in November 1970, but she won. In 1972, she faced an even tougher reelection campaign. New York had gone through redistricting, and her Congressional district was eliminated. Abzug ran in a different New York district against William Fitts Ryan, an incumbent Democratic Congressman with similar views. She lost in the primary, and Ryan won the Democratic nomination and the right to run in November against the Republican challenger. But Ryan died in September, before the

November election, and the Democratic committee selected Abzug to take his place. Ryan's wife also entered the race, as an independent, and the election turned into a heated and personal battle. Abzug won that contest, and then easily won reelection in 1974 to another two-year term.

Abzug served in the U.S. House of Representatives for six years, from 1971 through 1976. On her first day, after taking the oath of office, she went out to the Capitol steps and took a second oath, administered by Congresswoman Shirley Chisholm, while thousands of women from Women Strike for Peace cheered, "Give 'em hell, Bella." That same day, she introduced a resolution calling for the withdrawal of all U.S. troops from Vietnam.

Abzug was a forceful presence in the U.S. House. She took stands on issues years ahead of many other politicians, long before such positions became fashionable. She fought to end the war in Vietnam, to abolish the draft, to impeach President Richard Nixon, to create national health insurance, to finance housing for the poor, and to fund urban public transportation. She spoke out on a number of issues for women, including the need for day care centers, shelters for battered women, job training for former homemakers, Medicare funding for abortions, and fair Social Security benefits. She argued for equal employment, education, and credit opportunities for women. She spoke on behalf of the Equal Rights Amendment, in the Congress and around the country. She battled against the entrenched male leadership and the rigid seniority system in the Congress, which preserved power for members with the most seniority and prevented new members from having much impact. She also battled against the interests of big business and the military establishment, fighting with members of Congress who were willing to fund military programs and weapons systems but wouldn't pay for the many social programs the country needed. She introduced the first bill protecting the civil rights of homosexuals and pushed through the Freedom of Information Act, which gave U.S. citizens the right to see files the government had kept on them. She also joined with leading feminists Shirley Chisholm, Betty Friedan, and Gloria Steinem in founding the National Women's Political Caucus (NWPC). This organization worked to elect women to public office and to support women's issues.

Abzug was considered an effective, knowledgeable, and influential legislator. But she was also considered brash, abrasive, pushy, obnoxious, and belligerent. She was often rude, loud, angry, impatient, and foul-mouthed, with a raspy voice that author Norman Mailer said "could boil the fat off a taxicab driver's neck." Her infuriating confrontational style won her many enemies, in Congress and throughout political circles. But no one ever doubted her integrity, her principles, and her commitment to helping her constituents.

The year 1976 was the beginning of a series of political setbacks for Abzug. That year, she declined to run again for her seat in the U.S. House of

Representatives. Instead, she decided to run for the U.S. Senate. She lost that election to Daniel Patrick Moynihan by less than one percent. A year later, she ran for mayor of New York City; she lost that election to Edward Koch. Then she announced that she would run for the seat Koch had held in the House; she lost that election, too. Despite all these losses, Abzug remained sanguine about her political career: "I'm a politician—I run for office," she once said. "That's my profession."

Abzug returned to her career as a lawyer and activist in New York, but she later made two more bids for political office: in 1986, she again ran for a seat in the U.S. House, and in 1992 she announced her candidacy for the House, to replace a representative who had died. Abzug was unsuccessful in both these attempts to win political office.

Later Career

Abzug never again held elective office after 1977. But for the next 20 years, she continued to work as a lawyer and to serve as an activist and policy maker on political and social issues. Her very first action outside Congress resulted in controversy. In 1977 she presided over the group planning the National Women's Conference to be held in Houston, Texas. The conference was part of the United Nations Decade for Women. First, Abzug oversaw the planning of public meetings in each state to discuss strategies for achieving equality for women. Then, she oversaw the national meeting as well. The resolutions adopted at that conference became a national plan of action that became the first agenda for U.S. policy on women's issues. After those meetings, President Jimmy Carter appointed Abzug co-chair of a new National Advisory Committee for Women. The group was to advise the president on women's issues and to work on the plans made in Houston. In 1979, the group issued its first report, which criticized the president's economic policies as harmful to women. President Carter fired Abzug from the committee, and most of its members immediately resigned in protest.

In 1979, Abzug helped to found an organization called Women U.S.A. This group tried to reach out to mainstream American women who weren't involved in politics. It sponsored lobbying, letter-writing campaigns, and boycotts. She continued her work with this group, as well as lectures and legal work, through the 1980s. An outgrowth of this group was the Women's Environmental and Development Organization (WEDO), a worldwide group. Through her involvement in the United Nations conferences for women in Mexico City (1975), Copenhagen (1980), Nairobi (1985), and later Beijing (1995), Abzug had become a respected leader in the international women's movement. With the formation of WEDO, she transformed herself from an activist within the U.S. political system to one organizing women around the world to fight for their rights and to combat oppression. With WEDO, she

Bella Abzug with women's rights activist Gloria Steinem

worked with international agencies on issues related to human rights, economic justice, population, development, and the environment. WEDO became an important means for women around the world to bring their concerns before the United Nations and its agencies and to force their way into the power structures of these predominantly male groups. The group challenged the thinking and the policies of the UN community. With WEDO, Abzug's view of feminism grew to include all women around the world and all issues that affected the quality of their lives. Many consider Abzug's work with WEDO to be her greatest contribution to political and social activism that improves people's lives.

Throughout the 1990s, Abzug had battled several health problems, although she hadn't let them slow her down. She had breast cancer, heart disease, and circulatory problems; the latter forced her to use a wheelchair to help her get around in her last few years. Bella Abzug died of complications following heart surgery on March 30, 1998.

MARRIAGE AND FAMILY

Bella Savitzky and Martin Abzug were married on June 4, 1944. They had two children, Eve Gail (called Eegee) and Isobel Jo (called Liz). Over the years they lived in several areas of New York: in the Bronx, a borough of New York City; in Mount Vernon, a suburb just north of the city; and in Greenwich Village, a section of Manhattan.

It's not unusual today for a woman to combine a career with raising children, but it certainly was when Bella did it. Her daughters were born in 1949 and 1952, when Bella was just getting her start as a lawyer and civil-rights activist. She worked throughout their lives, although she didn't run for political office until they were in their late teen years. And she always had the loving support of her husband, Martin, who encouraged, supported, and helped her in everything she did.

WRITINGS

Bella! Ms. Abzug Goes to Washington, 1972 (edited by Mel Ziegler)
Gender Gap: Bella Abzug's Guide to Political Power for American Women, 1984
    (with Mim Kelber)

HONORS AND AWARDS

Women's Hall of Fame: 1994
Bradford Morse Memorial Gender and Development Award: 1995

FURTHER READING

Books

Abzug, Bella, with Mel Ziegler, ed. *Bella! Ms. Abzug Goes to Washington,* 1972
Abzug, Bella, with Mim Kelber. *Gender Gap: Bella Abzug's Guide to Political Power for American Women,* 1984
Chamberlin, Hope. *A Minority of Members,* 1973
DeLeon, David, ed. *Leaders from the 1960s: A Biographical Sourcebook of American Activism,* 1994
Faber, Doris. *Bella Abzug,* 1976
Fireside, Bryna J. *Is There a Woman In the House . . . or Senate?* 1994
Gilbert, Lynn. *Particular Passions,* 1981

Hyman, Paula E., and Deborah Dash Moore, eds. *Jewish Women in America: An Historical Encyclopedia*, Vol. 1, 1997
Stineman, Esther. *American Political Women*, 1980
Who's Who in America, 1998
World Book Encyclopedia, 1997

Periodicals

Baltimore Sun, Apr. 1, 1998, p.A1
Current Biography Yearbook 1971
Harper's, Nov. 1983, p.69
Ms., July/Aug. 1990, p.94; Jan./Feb. 1996, p.62
New York, June 20, 1977, p.54
New York Times, Apr. 1, 1998, p.A1
New York Times Biographical Service, Aug. 1977, p.1040; Feb. 1978, p.147; Dec. 1978, p.1145; Sep. 1995, p.1346
New York Times Magazine, Aug. 21, 1977, p.14
Philadelphia Inquirer, Apr. 1, 1998, p.A1
Washington Post, Apr. 1, 1998, p.B6; Apr. 2, 1998, p.B1

Kofi Annan 1938-

Ghanaian International Civil Servant
First Black African Secretary General of the
United Nations

BIRTH

Kofi Annan (KO-fee ANN-en) was born April 8, 1938, in
Kumasi, the capital city of the Ashanti Province of Ghana. His
father, Henry, was governor of Ashanti Province and a heredi-
tary paramount chief of the Fante people, who are closely related to the Ashanti people in Ghana. His mother, Victoria, was a
homemaker. He had a twin sister, Efua, who died in 1990.

Little has been published about Kofi Annan's early years growing up in Ghana, though his mother has been quoted as saying that he was a mischievous child who nonetheless was always able to get out of trouble.

EDUCATION

Annan attended the University of Science and Technology in Kumasi in 1958-59, where he served as vice-president of the national student union in Ghana. In that capacity, he attracted the attention of a representative from the Ford Foundation who was scouting out talented students for its Foreign Students Leadership Project. The Ford Foundation is a nonprofit organization founded by the Ford Motor Company that provides aid to developing nations and cultural institutions around the world to foster world peace and economic development. The Foundation awarded Annan a scholarship to continue his education in the U.S. So in 1959 he went to the U.S. to attend a summer program at Harvard University in Massachusetts before enrolling in Macalester College in St. Paul, Minnesota, in the fall. There he majored in economics. During his undergraduate years he participated in speech competitions and set a state record in track. He recalls that "it was an exciting period. I had come from Ghana, and we had just gone through our own struggle for independence [the country became independent in 1957]. . . . People of my generation, having seen the change that took place in Ghana, grew up thinking all was possible. When I came to the States, the social upheaval [of the 1960s] reminded me of some things that had gone on there."

It was also his first experience with the changing of the seasons. And the bitterly cold winters of Minnesota overrode his sense of vanity: "I resisted as long as I could, until one day, going to get something to eat, my ears nearly froze. So I went and bought the biggest pair [of earmuffs] I could find." That experience taught Annan a lesson that undoubtedly served him in his career as an international civil servant "You never walk into a situation and believe that you know better than the natives. You have to listen and look around. Otherwise you can make some very serious mistakes."

During the summer of 1960, after his first full year at Macalester, Annan took a cross-country road trip with a member of the college faculty and some other foreign students. One of the highlights, Annan recalls, was the night they tried to stay in a jail in Dodge City, Nevada, but the jailer wouldn't allow it. The group, consisting of Annan along with students from Britain, Sri Lanka, and Greece, experienced discrimination in some of the southern states. For example, in Las Vegas, he remembers, "the Sri Lankan was told he couldn't use the pool."

After earning his bachelor of arts degree in 1961, Annan did graduate work in economics at the Institut des hautes etudes internationales in Geneva,

Switzerland, in 1961-62. After beginning his career at the UN in 1962, he attended the Massachusetts Institute of Technology, where he was a Sloan Fellow in 1971, and earned his master of science degree in management in 1972. Over the years, as part of his educational and vocational training, Annan has learned English, French, and a number of African languages

CAREER HIGHLIGHTS

The United Nations

Since 1962, when he finished his graduate studied in Switzerland, Annan has worked at the United Nations. He has continued working there to this day, serving in various departments throughout the international organization. The UN was created at the end of World War II by representatives of 50 countries around the world. The Preamble of the United Nations Charter from 1945 describes the mission of the UN: "To save succeeding generations from the scourge of war, which twice in our lifetime has brought untold sorrow to mankind, and to reaffirm faith in fundamental human rights, in the dignity and worth of the human person, in the equal rights of men and women and of nations large and small, and to establish conditions under which justice and respect for the obligations arising from treaties and other sources of international law can be maintained, and to promote social progress and better standards of life in larger freedom."

Within the UN are several main bodies with different functions. The General Assembly is the largest body, composed of the 185 member countries. It discusses problems around the world, approves the budget, and determines policies and programs. Decisions are made with a majority vote. The Security Council has 15 members, five of which are permanent: China, France, the United States, the United Kingdom, and the Russian Federation. In addition, ten countries are elected for two-year terms in the Council. It is the Security Council that decides whether to intervene in national or international conflicts. It decides whether to deploy peacekeeping missions, whether to impose sanctions on a country, and whether to deploy military coalitions as it did in response to Iraq's invasion of Kuwait and recent crises in Somalia, Rwanda, and Haiti. The Economic and Social Council deals with the UN agencies that focus on eco-

———— **"** ————

Of that UN peacekeeping mission that failed in Yugoslavia, Annan reflected, "we should all recall how we responded to the escalating horrors of the last four years . . . each of us must ask, what did I do? Could I have done more? . . . Above all, how would I react next time?"

———— **"** ————

nomic development and such issues as human rights and the environment. The International Court of Justice, or World Court, settles legal questions between countries. The Secretariat administers the above bodies of the UN and is led by the secretary general. In addition, the UN runs such specialized agencies as the UN Children's Fund (UNICEF) and the UN Environment Programme (UNEP). Some of these programs are run from the UN's main headquarters in New York City, while others are located in Geneva, Switzerland, and elsewhere around the world.

The role of the UN has changed over the years. The UN has operated during most of its history in the context of the Cold War between the U.S. and the U.S.S.R. During the years after World War II, the U.S. and the former U.S.S.R. were enemies. Each nation tried to build up its sphere of influence by winning the allegiance of different countries. The greatest fear was that war would break out between the allies of the U.S. and the U.S.S.R., and ultimately involve those two nations also. Nuclear war was a deadly possibility.

The sovereignty of a country used to be respected above all before the UN would get involved in conflicts. Since the collapse of communism began in 1989, however, world crises have taken on a decidedly different character. Yet most of the world's hot spots in recent years have involved ethnic strife and civil wars in countries without secure governments, rather than wars between countries. As Annan put it, "the greatest threat to world stability today is crises like Rwanda and Somalia and Bosnia. It is not one of nuclear war . . . but rather a rising tide of ethnic and regional conflicts that could eventually engulf us all." Annan has stated "that is it no longer acceptable for . . . cruel leaders to hide behind sovereignty and national boundaries and brutalize the population."

Annan got his first job at the UN in 1962 as an administrative officer and budget officer at the World Health Organization (WHO) in Geneva. Since that time, he has worked for the UN for most of his career. His various jobs within the organization have taken him around the world, to Addis Ababa, Ethiopia; Cairo and Ismailia, Egypt; Geneva, Switzerland; and New York. He worked for WHO in Switzerland from 1962 to 1971, then worked in an administrative position in New York for the UN from 1972 to 1974. From 1974 to 1976, Annan lived in his native Ghana to work as a managing director for the Ghana Tourist Development Company and serve on the Ghana Tourist Control Board. Returning to the UN in 1976, he worked as the deputy chief of staff for the Office of UN High Command for Refugees. From 1981 to 1983 Annan was governor of the UN International School in Geneva, which his children attended when they were younger. From 1987 to 1995 he served as chairman of the board of trustees of the UN International School in New York.

In 1990, Annan was sent on a diplomatic mission to the Persian Gulf. He was sent by then-Secretary General Boutros Boutros-Ghali after Iraq invaded

Kuwait to negotiate for the safe return of Western hostages and more than 900 international staff members. He also negotiated on behalf of up to 500,000 Asians who had become stranded in the area due to the outbreak of the war. The 1996 agreement between Iraq and the UN, in which Iraq agreed to sell oil and use the money to fund humanitarian aid, grew out of Annan's 1990 negotiations with the Iraqi government.

Peacekeeping

In 1992 Kofi Annan took on the position that would begin to bring him into the public spotlight. He became assistant secretary general of the Department of Peacekeeping Operations at the UN. The UN's peacekeeping missions are made up of troops from all the member nations. Their goal is to bring peace to war-torn areas, such as Bosnia and Somalia, and to foster negotiations leading to the end of conflict. Annan believes that peacekeeping operations can be successful in stemming regional violence: "The assets are there. What is lacking is the will."

From March 1993 until his election to secretary general, Annan served as under-secretary general for Peacekeeping Operations. In 1995-96, he served as special representative of the secretary general in the former Yugoslavia. Of that UN peacekeeping mission that failed, Annan reflected, "we should all recall how we responded to the escalating horrors of the last four years . . . each of us must ask, what did I do? Could I have done more? . . . Above all, how would I react next time?"

During the time Annan was head of peacekeeping, the number of operations the UN undertook increased dramatically. There have been 41 such operations in the UN's history, and the majority have been initiated since 1993. To cope with the increase, Annan oversaw the creation of a "Situation Centre," which provides 24-hour communications between the various peacekeeping operations around the world and UN headquarters. He also created a "Lessons Learned" unit to help the UN improve its peacekeeping operations by studying past mistakes. Peacekeeping Operations under Annan's tenure was considered one of the UN's best-managed departments.

Secretary General

On December 14, 1996, Kofi Annan was elected the seventh secretary general of the UN. Those who previously served in the post were Trygve Lie of Norway (1946-53), Dag Hammarskjöld of Sweden (1953-61), U Thant of Burma (1961-71), Kurt Waldheim of Austria (1972-81), Javier Pérez de Cuéllar of Peru (1981-91), and Boutros Boutros-Ghali of Egypt (1991-95). Annan is the first black African to serve as UN secretary general and the first to come up from the ranks of UN personnel.

The role of the secretary general is to present problems and situations warranting action to the different bodies and agencies within the UN, such as UNESCO, the World Health Organization, and the Food and Agricultural Organization. The secretary's duties include the administration of a large staff, which is made up of a diverse group of individuals from around the world who work exclusively in the interests of the UN.

The secretary general is elected by the General Assembly, after being recommended by the 15-member Security Council. In Kofi Annan's case, the recommendation was unanimous, though the circumstances that led to his election were politically stormy. His predecessor, Boutros Boutros-Ghali was the first secretary general to serve only one five-year term and not be reelected for the traditional second five-year term. Led by then-U.S. Ambassador to the UN Madeleine Albright, the U.S. vetoed the Security Council's recommendation to reelect Boutros-Ghali. The U.S. believed that he mismanaged the UN and that he did not undertake reforms the U.S. believed to be critical.

During his 30 years at the UN Kofi Annan has become known among co-workers and diplomats for his personal integrity, likability, and calm manner. At the party his staff held after he was elected secretary general, the only evidence of excitement Annan reportedly displayed was slightly shifting his weight from one foot to the other. According to a member of his staff,

33

"That's what he does when he shows emotion." Another official who worked for Annan likes to tell the story of when he got in trouble over a remark he made to the press. Annan called the man, who feared he was about to lose his job, into his office and told him, "Don't let the turkeys get you down." Annan can also be quite frank and outspoken. He once aroused anger when a French newspaper quoted him as saying that he has trouble getting peacekeeping troops from Africa because African governments "probably need their armies to intimidate their own populations."

Plans for the Future

Annan has several long-term goals to achieve during his tenure as secretary general. Two of these goals are to "encourage Member States to develop the sustained will to support the Organization" and to "demystify the United Nations and not make it so bureaucratic and distant from the average person." More specifically, he says, "we need to do a lot of work in sustainable development and the environment. And we need to work on intolerance." Annan concluded his election-acceptance speech to the General Assembly, "I accept the high post you have entrusted to me, humbled by the formidable challenges that lie ahead, but filled with confidence in the nobility of our common goals, in the determination of our common spirit, and in the success of our common effort. Alone, I can do nothing. Together, we can irreversibly advance the frontiers of peace, dignity and justice for all humankind."

Some of those challenges are financial. The UN is currently dealing with the worst financial crisis in its history. In order for the UN to operate, it relies on dues paid by member nations and private contributions. Each country pays according to its gross national product. The U.S. is the largest debtor, owing about $1.5 billion. The U.S. Congress, which is responsible for allocating funds to pay its membership dues to the UN, refuses to pay until the UN agrees to several management

> ——— " ———
>
> *Annan concluded his election-acceptance speech to the General Assembly, "I accept the high post you have entrusted to me, humbled by the formidable challenges that lie ahead, but filled with confidence in the nobility of our common goals, in the determination of our common spirit, and in the success of our common effort. Alone, I can do nothing. Together, we can irreversibly advance the frontiers of peace, dignity and justice for all humankind."*
>
> ——— " ———

reforms and conditions, including decreasing the amount of the U.S.'s dues. For his part, Kofi Annan has instituted cost-cutting reforms in the administration of the UN that will save more than $100 million in 1997. He has also been lobbying wealthy people around the world for donations. Ted Turner, founder of the CNN network, gave the largest charitable gift ever in September 1997 when he donated $1 billion to the UN.

MARRIAGE AND FAMILY

Kofi Annan has been married twice. His first wife was a Nigerian woman whose name is unavailable. They had two children, a son, Kojo, and a daughter, Ana. Annan's second wife is Nane Annan-Cronstedt, whom he married in 1984 at the UN Chapel in New York. They met in 1981 while both worked for the UN High Commissioner for Refugees in Geneva. Nane is now an artist, though she was formerly a lawyer and judge in her native Sweden. Nane is also the niece of Raoul Wallenberg, the diplomat who rescued thousands of Jewish people from the Nazis during World War Two. Nane has one daughter, Nina, 27, from a previous marriage.

Although Annan had spent time in Europe and Nane had traveled around Africa, they had some cultural adjustments to make in their life together. One difference between them, in fact perhaps their most difficult cultural difference, was in their perception of time. Nane grew up always striving to be early to social events, while Kofi was accustomed to being late. Since his election to secretary general, they are now adjusting to life with bodyguards. As Kofi complained to one reporter, "you always have to have somebody babysitting you . . . it's a bit tough."

HOBBIES AND OTHER INTERESTS

Annan enjoys tennis, photography, appreciating art, and taking walks with his wife, Nane. He serves on the board of trustees of Macalester College and on the board of trustees of the Institute for the Future in Menlo Park, California, a nonprofit research and consulting firm.

WRITINGS

Essay in *Preventive Diplomacy: Stopping Wars Before They Start,* edited by
  Kevin M. Cahill, 1997

HONORS AND AWARDS

Trustee Distinguished Service (Macalester College Board of Trustees): 1994,
  for service to the international community

FURTHER READING

Books

Who's Who in the United Nations, 2nd edition, 1992
Who's Who in the World, 1996

Periodicals

Financial Times (London), Dec. 19, 1996, p.4
Los Angeles Times, Dec. 14, 1996, p.A1
New York Times, Dec. 14, 1996, p.7; Jan. 7, 1997, p.3; Sep. 19, 1997, p.1
St. Paul Pioneer Press, Dec. 13, 1996, p.A10
Toronto Star, Dec. 23, 1996, p.A19
UN Chronicle, 1996, p.5
USA Today, Dec. 18, 1996, p.A6
Washington Post, Dec. 14, 1996, p.A22; Jan. 7, 1997, p.A1

ADDRESS

Office of the Secretary General
United Nations
New York, NY 10017

WORLD WIDE WEB SITE

http://www.un.org

Neve Campbell 1973-

Canadian Actress
Star of the Hits "Party of Five" and *Scream*

BIRTH

Neve (rhymes with Bev) Campbell was born on October 3, 1973, in Toronto, Ontario, and grew up in the nearby town of Guelph. Her mother, Marnie Neve, is a psychologist; her father, Gerry Campbell, is a high school drama teacher. They divorced when Neve was still a baby, and both went on to remarry and get divorced again. Neve's father remarried a third time. She has one brother, Christian, who is 18 months older. She also has two younger half-brothers, Damian and Alex. Neve's unusual first name is taken from her mother's last name, which is Dutch.

YOUTH

Campbell comes from a family with many ties to the theater. Her mother once owned a dinner theater, and her father directs a Scottish theater group in Toronto, in addition to being a drama teacher. Her grandparents on her father's side performed for soldiers during World War II, and her mother's parents ran a theater company in Holland. Her older brother Christian, who is also an actor, played Teddy on NBC's "Malibu Shores."

Campbell and her brother grew up watching their father direct plays put on by his amateur theater group, and both developed a love of the theater at a very early age. Christian remembers being given a small role in their father's production of Gilbert and Sullivan's *H.M.S. Pinafore* when he was ten. "I came into the living room all dressed up in my little costume," he recalls. "Neve broke into tears because she felt so left out."

When Campbell was six, her father took her to see *The Nutcracker* ballet. She decided that her dream was to become a ballerina, and she later attended Toronto's National Ballet School. In her first year at the school, she performed in *The Nutcracker* with the National Ballet of Canada.

EDUCATION

Campbell remembers herself as being "pretty geeky" as a kid. She was very insecure about herself and had a difficult time relating to people her own age. She describes herself as "the loser of my class" throughout her elementary school years at Vista Heights Public School in Mississauga. She also recalls a particularly painful memory from her school years. When she was nine, Campbell remembers cookies being distributed at her school for Valentine's Day. Students could buy them and send them to their friends. The teacher would call students up to the front of the class each time their name was drawn out of the Valentine's box. Campbell's name was never called, until finally the teacher gave her a cookie. "I was devastated," she says. "No one would spend five cents to send me a cookie."

At age nine, Campbell entered the prestigious National Ballet School in Toronto, which has a reputation for training some of the world's top dancers. The school takes only 150 students. The rigorous training there requires tremendous self-discipline and three to five hours of practice each day. Campbell found the intense competitiveness and the back-stabbing attitudes of the students to be overwhelming. "I got to a place at that school where I hated dance, and that was really tragic for me," she recalls. "I had no friends, I didn't fit in, and I was living in residence [at the school dormitories]. When you live with people you don't fit in with, you're in trouble." Plagued by injuries and on the verge of a nervous breakdown, she left the school at age 14. Even though she was unhappy at the National Ballet

School, Campbell believes that her experiences there taught her self-discipline and self-reliance. The physical stamina that she developed there also proved to be very valuable later, in her career as an actress.

When she left the National Ballet School, all she wanted was a normal high school life. She enrolled in a public high school in 10th grade, only to discover after a year that she missed performing. So she transferred to Interact, an alternative school with a flexible schedule that catered to young artists, actors, and athletes.

At 15, while attending Interact, Campbell won a role as one of the Degas girls in the Toronto production of Andrew Lloyd Webber's *Phantom of the Opera*. She was the youngest member of the cast. Her role as a ballet dancer in *Phantom* also gave her an opportunity to use her years of dance training. She performed the show 800 times over the next two years, but soon realized that she couldn't be on stage and keep up her academic studies at the same time. She dropped out of school for good when she was 16 and moved in with her brother Christian, who was already living on his own.

When Campbell was 13, she went to a sleep-over and saw **The Changeling***, a horror movie she claims gave her nightmares for a year. "I couldn't sleep a wink that night. I couldn't lie down. . . . That movie still haunts me. Maybe it's because I believe in ghosts and spirits."*

EARLY MEMORIES

When Campbell was 13, she went to a sleep over and saw *The Changeling*, a horror movie she claims gave her nightmares for a year. "I couldn't sleep a wink that night," she recalls. "I couldn't lie down. . . . That movie still haunts me. Maybe it's because I believe in ghosts and spirits." Even though she went on to star in one of the most successful horror movies of all time, Campbell still avoids watching such films because she takes them too seriously.

FIRST JOBS

Campbell's success in *Phantom of the Opera* led to commercials and other acting opportunities in Canada. She tried modeling for a couple of months, but she didn't like standing in front of a camera and being paid for how she looked. After her years of professional training in ballet, she was accustomed to using her talents rather than her appearance to get ahead.

In 1993, Campbell won her first television role in "Catwalk," a Canadian dramatic series about a young, undiscovered rock band struggling to win fame and fortune. She quit the series after a year because she felt that her character, Daisy, was becoming too much of a sex symbol. Even though she was only 17, Campbell was already concerned with how the public perceived her. Even then, she was developing a reputation for being very disciplined, focused, and mature for her age.

CAREER HIGHLIGHTS

"Party of Five"

After working on an NBC-TV movie called *I Know My Son Is Alive*, Campbell decided to move to Los Angeles. Within a few weeks she had landed the role of Julia Salinger in "Party of Five," beating out 300 other actresses for the part. Campbell signed a six-year contract with the show in 1994.

"Party of Five" is a weekly television series on the Fox network about five San Francisco siblings trying to raise themselves after their parents are killed in a car accident. Julia is the middle child in the Salinger family, an average teenager who is pretty but insecure. The oldest of the Salinger kids is big brother Charlie, played by Matthew Fox. Charlie was put in charge of the family through a guardianship agreement that says they have to prove they can make it on their own. Next in line is Bailey, a college student, played by Scott Wolf. The younger sister is Claudia, played by Lacey Chabert. Owen, the baby of the family, was first played by twins Brandon and Taylor Porter and is now played by twins Andrew and Steven Cavarno.

"Party of Five" debuted in 1994. During its first two seasons, the show was praised by critics but largely ignored by viewers. Its small audience, however, was very loyal. When the show was threatened with cancellation near the beginning of its run, viewers mounted a letter-writing campaign. They sent thousands of letters to Fox executives, who were persuaded to save the series. "Party of Five" solidified its reputation when it won a Golden Globe Award in 1996 for "Best TV Drama Series," beating out "ER" and other top-rated shows.

Since the debut of "Party of Five," its loyal audience has grown in size. Viewers respond to the realistic plots, emotional story lines, and good writing. They appreciate the focus on tough topics like racism, mental illness, suicide, alcoholism, pregnancy, and failed relationships. The strong cast is a big part of the show's appeal as well. The characters often seem naive, selfish, and fearful—above all, realistically human. The fact that the cast actually looks as though they might be related to each other in real life solidified the appearance of family bonds. Campbell says that they even acted like a family off-screen, cooking dinner at each other's houses on weekends.

The cast of "Party of Five"

Julia's character is particularly popular among teenage girls. "People respond to Julia mainly because she's very confused about life and doesn't have it all together," Campbell explains. "She's insecure about herself, friendships, and relationships. And who isn't?" Many reviewers describe Campbell as vulnerable, saying that's why viewers relate to her so well. In fact, *Time* magazine called Julia "television's most believable teenager." In the show's most controversial episode, she got drunk, lost her virginity, and ended up pregnant at the age of 16. At first she planned to have an abortion, although she eventually had a miscarriage. More recently, she has had to struggle with an unstable marriage and a gravely ill sibling.

With two more seasons before her contract runs out, Campbell no longer worries about the show being canceled. If anything, she worries about outgrowing her character. "I do not want to [play a teenager much longer]. Julia will be 20 when I'm 26. [Julia's] been in high school for a long time—

and I didn't even graduate high school. I didn't like it then! I want to play my age, and I've started doing that in my other roles now. . . . No matter how good you are as an actor, you grow up. Your face grows up. I have a sophistication about me now."

The Craft

In 1996, during a break from filming "Party of Five," Campbell starred in *The Craft*, a black comedy and supernatural thriller about four teenage girls. Bonnie, the character played by Campbell, was in a bad car accident as a child that left her with scars all over her body. She is very insecure about her appearance and never really fits in with her peers. She gets together with three other girls who are also misfits at their Catholic school, and together they form a witches' coven. They discover that they can cast spells to get the love and attention they've always been denied, and they use their power to seek revenge on their classmates, parents, and boyfriends.

> *Craven, the director of* Scream, *credits much of the film's success to Campbell. "The whole film depended on her. We agonized over who to cast because her role was instrumental. But ultimately she was the linchpin without whom the movie wouldn't work. She's very wry and witty."*

Scream and Scream 2

The movie for which Campbell is best known is *Scream*, a 1996 parody of horror movies that also starred Drew Barrymore, Courteney Cox, and Skeet Ulrich It was directed by Wes Craven, famous for his "Nightmare on Elm Street" series. Even though Campbell was terrified of horror movies as a child, she says she went to work for Craven because she respected him.

The film tracks a series of brutal murders among high-school students in the small town of Woodsboro, California. Campbell plays Sidney Prescott, one of a group of students who are terrorized by a knife-wielding killer in a cape and Halloween mask. But *Scream* is different than earlier horror movies. It pokes fun at the "slasher" movie genre, and Sidney Prescott is a survivor rather than a helpless victim. Campbell describes it as "a very scary and funny story about teenagers who've been desensitized to violence by horror films. It's almost as if my character doesn't realize she's in a horror film."

Scream was a huge hit with teen audiences, who enjoyed its humor, suspense, and realism. It became the first movie of its kind to gross more than $100

Campbell in Scream 2

million. The film earned Campbell her nickname, "The Scream Queen," since she spends most of her time on screen either terrified or on the verge of tears. Fans often come up to her on the street and ask her to shriek for them. "I love screaming," she admits, "so I usually do it." Craven, the film's director, credits much of the film's success to Campbell. "The whole film depended on her," he said. "We agonized over who to cast because her role was instrumental. But ultimately she was the linchpin without whom the movie wouldn't work. She's very wry and witty."

Scream 2, the 1997 sequel to *Scream*, takes place two years after the Woodsboro murders. Sidney is now a Midwestern college student majoring in drama. *Scream 2* features a movie-within-a-movie: the opening scene takes place at a movie theater. Students have come to see "Stab," a movie made from the best-selling book by journalist Gale Weathers (Courteney Cox) on the Woodsboro killings. The mask-wearing murderer who first stalked Sidney in *Scream* shows up at the movie theater where "Stab" is being shown. *Scream 2* is a spoof on sequels as well as on horror movies in general. The movie-within-a-movie scene makes fun of the original *Scream* while at the same time setting the mood for the murders that follow.

Filming the movie was tough, though. They did a lot of the filming at night, so they could work in the dark. For part of the time Campbell would work on *Scream 2* all night until 6:00 a.m., take a quick shower to get rid of the fake blood, spend the whole day on the set of "Party of Five," and then return to *Scream 2* at night. Her character spent much of the movie in a high-pitched state of terror, which is difficult for an actor to maintain for weeks at a time. The process was exhausting for Campbell, but it paid off: *Scream 2* has also proved to be a huge hit with teen audiences.

Current and Future Projects

Campbell's most recent film is *Wild Things*, a suspenseful thriller released in 1998 in which she co-stars with Matt Dillon and Kevin Bacon. Other upcoming projects include *Hair Shirt*, a low-budget independent film that she and her brother, Christian, have recently produced. She just finished playing a soap opera star in the movie *54*, due to be released in 1998, about the Studio 54 disco in Manhattan. She is also expected to co-star in *Three to Tango*, a romantic comedy with Matthew Perry, and she is considering appearing in *Scream 3*, to be filmed in late 1998. As soon as her contract with "Party of Five" runs out, Campbell wants to play more mature characters, and perhaps take on a role that enables her to use her background in ballet. In addition to acting, her future plans include writing as well as producing and directing movies and TV shows. Above all, Campbell says, "I would like to sleep more. I would like to have more of a life. I would like to have stronger relationships with the people I love."

MARRIAGE AND FAMILY

When Campbell came to Los Angeles in 1994 to be in "Party of Five," she wanted her Canadian boyfriend, Jeff Colt, to join her. They had met in Toronto when she was performing in *Phantom of the Opera* and Colt was bartending in the same theater. Because he couldn't stay in this country without a green card, they ended up getting married on April 4, 1995. The wedding took place near Wimbledon, England, where she was filming the ABC-TV movie, *The Canterville Ghost*. Neve and Jeff were married for two-and-a-half years before they separated. They are currently in the process of divorce.

HOBBIES AND OTHER INTERESTS

Campbell still loves to dance. She's built a studio in her Hollywood Hills home, and she tries to dance for 90 minutes a day when she isn't off shooting a movie. "That's my way of venting any kind of problem that I have, or just escaping from the busy-ness of my life," she explains. She occasionally takes a ballet class, but she doesn't have time to train consistently.

In addition, Campbell has been involved in fighting discrimination against those with Tourette's Syndrome. She got involved in this because one of her brothers has Tourette's. People with this neurological problem often have uncontrollable facial and body tics. They might make grunting noises or shout out obscenities, but they have no control over this behavior. People with Tourette's Syndrome face a lot of misunderstanding and discrimination. Campbell is the national spokesperson for the Tourette's Syndrome Association of America and the youth spokesperson for the Tourette's Syndrome Foundation of Canada.

CREDITS

"Catwalk," 1993 (TV series)
I Know My Son Is Alive, 1994 (TV movie)
"Party of Five," 1994- (TV series)
Northern Passage, 1995
The Canterville Ghost, 1996
The Craft, 1996
Scream, 1996
Scream 2, 1997
Wild Things, 1998

FURTHER READING

Periodicals

Cosmopolitan, Jan. 1997, p.80
Los Angeles Times, Dec. 7, 1997, Calendar section, p.5
People, May 27, 1996, p.79 and 80; May 3, 1997, p.78
Rolling Stone, Sep. 18. 1997, p.57
TV Guide, Feb. 8, 1997, p.23
US, Sep. 1997, p.12

ADDRESS

1940 Westwood Blvd.
Suite 295
Los Angeles, CA 90025

WORLD WIDE WEB SITES

http://www.foxworld.com
http://www.spe.sony.com/tv/shows

Sean Combs (Puff Daddy) 1969-

American Music Producer and Recording Company
Executive
CEO of Bad Boy Entertainment
Rap Artist and Creator of *No Way Out*

BIRTH

Sean John Combs was born in New York City, probably on
November 4, 1969. His birth date is the subject of question; it is
sometimes given as 1970 or 1971, but the 1969 date is believed
to be correct. His parents were Melvin and Janice Combs. He
has one sister, Keisha, who is three years younger.

Combs uses the stage name Puff Daddy, but his nickname ever since childhood is Puffy. There are several different stories about how he got that name. In one version, he got the name when he played football in school because he would puff out his chest to try to look bigger. In another version, the name came about because others would taunt him for being a cream puff. He has also said that he had a temper as a child, and his friends would call him Puffy because when he got mad he would huff and puff. It's unclear which of these versions, if any, is the real reason for the name.

YOUTH

Combs started out living in Harlem, a predominantly African-American section of New York City. When he was three, his father died. The cause of his death is unclear. In some accounts, Combs says that his father died in a car accident. In other accounts, Combs says that he was a street hustler, running numbers or selling drugs, who died in a shooting near New York's Central Park. Sean Combs and his younger sister, Keisha, were raised by their mother. Janice Combs was a devoted and strong-willed mother who worked hard to provide a good life for her children. They were never poor, but they were never very well off, either. A school teacher, Janice Combs worked several jobs to pay the tuition for Puffy's education at a private Catholic school. She valued education and religion, and she made sure that both were important parts of her children's lives.

Perhaps his mother's example was the source of Combs's dedication to hard work. His first job, at about 11 or 12 years old, was delivering the newspaper. But he wasn't content to handle just one newspaper route. Showing the determination and commitment that he would demonstrate in his later work life, Combs used multiple names and fake ages so he could manage several paper routes—and make more money, of course.

When Combs was 12, his family moved to Mount Vernon, an integrated middle-class suburb of New York City. Known as Money Earnin' Mount Vernon, this suburb was viewed as a way out by many Harlem residents. Here is how one neighborhood friend recalled those days. "In Mount Vernon—it's only four square miles—everybody kind of knows each other if you are around the same age. We all played ball, went to parties, chased girls. Puffy liked being outrageous. It was just the way he carried himself, like needing to be the center of everything."

EARLY MEMORIES

Music was also an important part of Combs's life. He was lucky enough to grow up around New York in the early 1980s, just when hip-hop music was getting started. "I grew up in the prime time of hip-hop," he boasts, "when it was just getting off the ground. From Run-DMC to KRS-One to the

Beastie Boys to LL Cool J, I was there. I seen that. I would be 12 years old, and sometimes I'd be out until 3, 4 in the morning, seeing the music. I had to sneak out to do it, but I was doing it. . . . New York is the mecca of hip-hop. It's where it started. But it was mostly underground. It was word-of-mouth," Combs recalls. "See, there was gangs in New York during the time. Our gang problem wasn't as big as L.A., but we had some gangs. And hip-hop, break dancing, all that was a way for the gangs to battle without violence, and it was working. There wasn't that violence in the early stages of hip-hop. It was a bunch of fun, people hanging out in the park, plugging their system into the light post and having a block party right there. Killing somebody was unheard of back then. Kids didn't even have that on their minds. Punching somebody in the eye, maybe. But killing somebody? No."

EDUCATION

Combs attended Mount St. Michael's Academy, an exclusive all-boys' Catholic school in Mount Vernon. He did well in his studies there. According to Combs, "I was scared to death to bring home any grade below a B." Yet listen to his description of how he earned his lunch money. "[Every] day I used to do the same routine in the lunchroom: I saved the money my mother gave me, and I would ask everybody for 50 cents. That's how I got my money." It was at Mount St. Michael's, the story goes, that his goofing on the football field earned him the nickname Puffy. Combs graduated from Mount St. Michael's Academy in about 1987.

In the late 1980s Combs attended Howard University, a prestigious predominantly black university in Washington, D.C. In his class work, he majored in business administration. But outside the classroom, he majored in hustling. During his two years at Howard, Combs sold term papers, operated an airport shuttle bus, and promoted and hosted weekly rap and dance parties. The *Washington Post* explained his influence at Howard like this. "As a harbinger of the effect he would have on black popular culture, Puffy was a ringleader of a crew of friends that infected the Howard campus with New York style. They brought their baggy pants, oversize leather belts, rayon shirts, and big shoes with ribbons in the laces. They brought high-top fade haircuts, some with the tops dyed brown or blond. Puffy was sometimes seen in what would become his trademark sunshades and black derby. They brought a nonsense saying, 'Naa-Naa-No!" which they would boom over parties and popular campus gathering spots as a private signal for the hip." According to one classmate, "It would mean anything. Heads up, party over here, beef over here. Hey, I'm here and who else here is down with me?" Another classmate said this about Puffy and his friends, "I don't know what it was, but everyone wanted to be down with the New York crew. I think it was because we thought they were really, really cool."

While still in college, Combs got a job in New York City as an intern at Uptown Records, a division of MCA Records that was run by Andre Harrell. New York City is several hundred miles from Washington, D.C., where Combs was attending school, so he commuted back and forth between the two cities. He paid other students to take notes for him in classes and convinced his professors to let him skip class. "I started working for Andre," he recalls, "when I was going to Howard University. I would get on the train Wednesday night, work at Uptown Thursday and Friday, and then get back on the train." Combs soon became known as the hardest working intern anyone at Uptown had ever seen. He was determined to make the most of his experience there. "I did everything. I drove Andre's car; if they needed something delivered, I would take a cab instead of the subway and pay for it out of my own pocket. I knew it was the place to be."

> ## "
>
> *"I'm not going to go down in history as a black music maker," Combs says.*
> *"I'm going to go down as a music maker that was so incredible that he represented all of culture. You're not going to be able to label me. You can't keep on underestimating me and what I can do."*
>
> ## "

For Combs, working at Uptown Records fueled his ambition to get out of school and move on. "I was serious about my studies in the beginning, but my mind was moving too fast for it. My dreams were bigger. I was like, 'Four years? That's holding me back. I can't wait that. I got to get my hustle on now.'" Combs dropped out of Howard University without finishing his degree.

CAREER HIGHLIGHTS

Combs worked at Uptown Records between about 1988 and 1993, although the exact dates for each position are unclear. His first full-time position at Uptown was in A & R, or artists and repertory. A & R is the section of a record company that finds and develops talent. Combs eventually became director and then vice-president of A & R at Uptown Records. He also began sponsoring hip-hop parties at clubs around New York City. Called "Daddy's House," his parties were always big successes, drawing celebrities along with hundreds of fans. Combs was making a name for himself, both in the music business and among hip-hop fans.

A Tragedy Occurs

During that time, though, Combs was involved in a tragic event. He organized a basketball game between competing squads of rappers that was to be played at a gym at the City University of New York on December 28,

1991. The event was heavily promoted on radio ads on a popular rap station. But too many people showed up to watch the game, far more than could fit into the small gym. Despite the presence of New York police officers and private security guards, the crowd quickly got out of control. People continued pushing into the building without realizing that the doors into the gym had been closed. A big crowd on a stairwell surged forward, and the people at the bottom of the stairs were trapped. Nine people were crushed to death by the crowd. They were suffocated. Combs was down in the gym when it happened, and he helped to pull out the people who were injured. He tried to give artificial respiration, but he was unable to revive them.

An inquiry conducted by city officials found enough blame to cover all those involved in the event. The official report blamed university officials for failing to ensure that all security procedures were followed, to provide adequate security, and to adequately oversee those from student government who sponsored the event. It blamed the student government for failing to cooperate fully with university officials in organizing the event. It blamed the crowd for demonstrating a total disregard for others. It blamed the police for failing to respond as the event escalated out of control. It blamed the Emergency Medical Service (EMS) for failing to respond quickly to the urgent calls for help. For the most part, these groups were found to be primarily at fault, with the police earning the greatest share of the blame.

But the report blamed Combs, too. He was blamed for failing to provide adequate security and insurance. He was also blamed for allowing inexperienced assistants to plan the event and for over-publicizing it, leading to the over-capacity crowd. The report also noted that Combs had called it a charity event and claimed that proceeds would benefit an AIDS program, even though no arrangements had been made.

Combs was cleared of any criminal negligence, but he was devastated by the event. Over the next several months he suffered periods of severe depression. He spent most of his time sleeping—he had days when he couldn't even get out of bed. With time, though, he recovered. Combs has said that it was his deep faith in God that helped him through that terrible time.

Working at Uptown Records

Working at Uptown in the A & R department, Combs was able to get involved in all parts of the artists' careers—selecting the songs, creating an image with clothing and hair styles, directing the videos, and producing the music. Combs has had no formal musical training, and he doesn't know how to play a musical instrument. What he does have is a talent for producing records with just the right sound. Here is how he describes the process of producing a record. "I'm more like an orchestrator [conductor]. You know, those guys don't actually play the violin. They just tell the violinist

what they want to hear. Same with me. I say to my programmer, 'Make the drums go ba boom ba boom.' And he sets the computer up to do it. I sing the chords I want to the piano player and hum a rhythm to the bass player. Pretty soon, we got a song. That's the way I started and that's still the way I work." But the music itself is just one part of the package, as Combs explains here. "I'm hearing the music and seeing how the kids are going to dance to it in the clubs. I'm thinking how it's going to look on video, how it's going to sell. I'm looking forward to 40 or 50 years' time when people will still be listening to it on the radio. I'm selling the whole lifestyle."

For a while, Combs was doing great at Uptown. He had a string of successes, starting with Jodeci and Mary J. Blige. With Andre Harrell, the president of Uptown, Combs is widely credited with creating hip-hop soul, a musical hybrid of rap lyrics mixed with rhythm-and-blues-based soul. In *Rolling Stone* magazine, Mikal Gilmore described his approach like this. "[He] was quickly developing a wide-ranging style as a producer who mixed a taste for hard-edged, radical rhythms with strong melodies and familiar pop samples. In the process, he helped formulate a highly successful sound that became known as hip-hop soul." Combs went on to produce hits by TLC, Michael Jackson, and Mariah Carey.

Bad Boy Entertainment

But soon he was having problems with Andre Harrell. Combs had set up his own company, Bad Boy Entertainment, which was to be distributed by Uptown. Tensions between Combs and Harrell rose as they clashed over the creative direction of Combs's new label. Despite being his mentor, Harrell fired his young protégé in July 1993. Many observers have said that it just became too difficult for these two strong-willed people to continue to work together.

Despite losing his job, Combs came out OK. He took his new label, Bad Boy Entertainment, to Arista Records. There he got a deal worth $10 to $15 million for three years; it has gone up considerably since then. In addition to his work for Bad Boy, he also produced records for artists on other labels. Here is just a partial list of some of the top artists with whom he's worked: Boyz II Men, LL Cool J, Toni Braxton, Johnny Gill, Craig Mack, Lil' Kim, Faith Evans, 112, Total, Keith Sweat, Mase, and the Queen of Soul, Aretha

—— *"* ——

"I'm more like an orchestrator [conductor]," Combs says. "You know, those guys don't actually play the violin. They just tell the violinist what they want to hear. Same with me. I say to my programmer, 'Make the drums go ba boom ba boom.' And he sets the computer up to do it. I sing the chords I want to the piano player and hum a rhythm to the bass player. Pretty soon, we got a song. That's the way I started and that's still the way I work."

—— *"* ——

Franklin. Combs would often rap on the records of his top acts, and he would pop up in their videos as well. For many observers outside of Bad Boy, this was evidence of an astounding arrogance on Combs's part. Still, his approach seemed to work. By 1997, his label was responsible for 60% of the year's top pop songs. In just a few short years, Bad Boy has sold more than $100 million worth of music.

The Notorious B.I.G.

The artist with whom Combs was most closely associated was the Notorious B.I.G., or Biggie Smalls, whose real name was Christopher Wallace. When he hooked up with Combs, Wallace was a street hustler and a drug dealer with a talent for constructing rhymes about the world he lived in. Combs heard Wallace on a demo tape and decided to sign him to a contract with Bad Boy. "He had so much melody in his voice," Combs recalls. "It was like he was rapping, but it was so catchy, it was almost like he was singing. And he was such a clever poet, the way he put his words together, the way he saw things. He saw things so vivid. If you sat and listened to a Biggie Smalls record in the dark, you'd see a whole movie in front of you. And the amazing thing is, Biggie never wrote down his lyrics. He'd sit and compose them in his head."

Wallace soon became one of the most successful acts at Bad Boy. He also became Combs's closest friend. "Biggie was somebody who came into my life right on time," Combs says. "When I met him, I had this dream of a company, and all he wanted to do was be a rapper. I thanked God, not because he sent me a dope rapper, but because he sent me somebody who cared for me. I needed that."

In early 1997, they were just putting the finishing touches on Wallace's latest record, *Life after Death*. Both he and Combs were excited and pleased with the record, sure that it would be his most important release yet. But on March 9, 1997, Wallace was killed in a drive-by shooting after leaving a party in Los Angeles, California. The killer has not been found, although gang involvement is suspected. Many fans have questioned whether his death was somehow related to the shooting death of Tupac Shakur in September 1996 (see the entry on Shakur in *Biography Today*, April 1997). There have been longstanding rumors of an ongoing feud between East Coast rappers affiliated with Bad Boy and West Coast rappers affiliated with Death Row Records (Shakur's record company). Harsh words, threats, and accusations have been exchanged between those associated with the two studios. But Combs adamantly denies that he or anyone at Bad Boy Entertainment had anything to do with Shakur's death. Combs also claims that he has no idea why Wallace was killed, or by whom. He says that he wants to put an end to any sort of animosity between the two groups and concentrate, instead, on his business and on making music.

No Way Out

The loss of his best friend had a devastating effect of Combs. At first, he was so depressed that he seriously considered quitting the music business. He had been working on what was to be his own first album, full of party songs and hit singles. After Wallace's death Combs lost all interest in finishing it. "I did not want to do the album after Biggie died," he said. "I didn't really want to make music, and honestly, I didn't even want to be the president of this company. But me and him, we started this together, and you have to finish what you started. I can't stop making music. I can't stop being me. There's no way out." So Combs went back to work on his new album, but he changed its direction. "I wanted it to be more of a story, more of a tale of what I go through — from the party stuff to the happy stuff to stuff with girls to the way I feel about Biggie. I put songs on there like 'Pain,' about the way I feel about my father, who died . . . when I was a kid, and the way I feel about people not liking me at times."

On *No Way Out* (1997), Puff Daddy's first release, he was joined by a wide range of established and up and coming hip-hop stars, including Faith Evans, 112, Lil' Kim, Mase, the Lox, Busta Rhymes, Foxy Brown, and tracks from the Notorious B.I.G. recorded before his death. Many of the songs address his grief and rage at the loss of his friend, and the album has been called a meditation on death and mortality. But there are also funky party records that mix rap and rhythm and blues. "The work of a man who doesn't need the money but can't help making it," Touré wrote in *Village Voice*, "a man of insurmountable resilience faced with an unbearable loss, *No Way Out* is filled with brilliant exhilarating party records — smashes — like 'Victory,' 'It's All about the Benjamins,' and 'Been Around the World,' and personal, poignant, anti-commercial moments like 'Pain,'' 'If I Die Tonight,' and the prelude to 'I'll Be Missing You.'"

———— " ————

"Five years from now,"
Combs says,
"Bad Boy is going to be a
Fortune 500 company.
In 10 years, we're going to be
big, like Coca-Cola — giant,
everywhere, all over the
world. Music, films, clothes,
politics. Bad Boy is not just a
company, it's a lifestyle."

———— " ————

Despite the success of *No Way Out*, Combs has had his critics. Many call its quality uneven. Some give credit to the record's producers, rather than the artist. They fault his style, calling his voice thin and his delivery flat. They say he can't sing or play an instrument, and he can't rap. They also say he relies too heavily on sampling. Some of the record's biggest hits are remakes of other tunes: "I'll Be Missing You" is based on "Every Breath You Take" by the Police; "Can't Nobody Hold Me Down" is based on "The Message" by Grandmaster Flash and the Furious Five; and "Been Around the World" is based on "Let's Dance" by David Bowie. As one critic wrote in *Rolling Stone*, "[There's] a difference between rappers who make something new out of the music they sample and artists who merely bask in the reflected glory of the songs from which they draw. Combs—though he credits every songwriter he borrows from—is in the latter group." Many observers believe that, ultimately, Combs is more talented as an entrepreneur than an artist.

OTHER INTERESTS

People around Combs often joke that he is the hardest working man in show business. He sleeps very little, often working until 4:00 in the morning and then starting over again by 10:00 the next day. In addition to his record label, he is involved with many other projects. He founded and provides financial support for Daddy's House Social Programs, Inc., a non-profit organization that works with disadvantaged kids around New York. Its executive director is rapper Sister Souljah. Daddy's House conducts computer camps, summer camps, ethics classes, and boys' and girls' clubs, all for inner-city kids. Combs has said that he wanted to create this group to give back to the community that has supported his business. He also donated $3 million to a fund for the children of Christopher Wallace. In addition, he recently opened a restaurant in New York City, Justin's, which is named after his young son. He is developing a clothing line called Sean John and a sneaker named after his initials, PD. He has talked about becoming an agent for professional sports. He has expressed interest in creating a movie division at Bad Boy Entertainment, and has even said that he might like to try acting himself. There have been rumors that he would appear in the next *Lethal Weapon* movie with Mel Gibson, Danny Glover, and Chris Rock.

While Combs is clearly enjoying the success he has now, he has even bigger plans for the future. "I'm not going to go down in history as a black music maker. I'm going to go down as a music maker that was so incredible that he represented all of culture. You're not going to be able to label me. You can't keep on underestimating me and what I can do," Combs has said. "Five years from now, Bad Boy is going to be a Fortune 500 company. In 10 years, we're going to be big, like Coca-Cola—giant, everywhere, all over the world. Music, films, clothes, politics. Bad Boy is not just a company, it's a lifestyle."

MARRIAGE AND FAMILY

Combs, who is unmarried, lives in New York City. He used to be involved with Misa Hylton, although they split up several years ago. He has one son from that relationship, Justin, born in 1993. Combs is currently involved with Kim Porter, whom he first met in 1991 when they both worked at Uptown Records. They've been involved now for about four years. She currently works as the marketing director for his restaurant, Justin's. Combs and Porter are expecting a baby in April 1998.

HONORS AND AWARDS

ASCAP Award (American Society of Composers, Authors, and Publishers): 1997, Songwriter of the Year, for "No One Else," "Only You," and "Soon As I Get Home" (with Jermaine Dupri)

MTV Music Video Award: 1997, Best R & B Video, for "I'll Be Missing You"

Grammy Awards: 1998 (2 awards): Best Rap Album, for *No Way Out*; Best Rap Performance by a Duo or Group, for "I'll Be Missing You" (with Faith Evans)

FURTHER READING

Periodicals

Essence, Nov. 1997, p.111
Jet, Jan. 12, 1998, p.32
Los Angeles Times, June 27, 1995, p.D4; May 25, 1997, Calendar section, p.8
New York, Oct. 23, 1995, p.36
New York Times, July 20, 1997, p.28; Dec. 3, 1997, p.E1
Newsweek, Oct. 7, 1996, p.58
Rolling Stone, Aug. 7, 1997, p.50; Dec. 25, 1997-Jan. 8, 1998, p.78
Teen People, Apr. 1998, p.38
USA Today, July 22, 1997, p.D1
Vibe, Dec. 1997-Jan. 1998, p.102
Washington Post, Mar. 28, 1997, p.C1

ADDRESS

Bad Boy Entertainment
8 West 19th
9th Floor
New York, NY 10011

WORLD WIDE WEB SITE

http://www.badboy-ent.com

Dalai Lama (Tenzin Gyatso) 1935-
Tibetan Religious and Political Leader
Winner of the 1989 Nobel Peace Prize

BIRTH

The Dalai Lama (DAHL-eye LAHM-uh), the spiritual and political leader of Tibet, was born on July 6, 1935, in the village of Takster, in the province of Amdo, in what was then northeastern Tibet. His name when he was born was Lhamo Thondup, although he later also took a longer name that's abbreviated as Tenzin Gyatso. He was the sixth of seven children born to his father, Chokyong Tsering, and his mother, Tekyi Tsering. His brothers were named Gyalo Thondup, Takster Rinpoche,

Lobsang Samten, and Tenzin Choegyal, and his sisters were named Tsering Dolma and Jetsun Pema. The children in the family were born over many years. Lhamo Thondup's oldest sister, Tsering Dolma, was 18 years older than he, and the youngest member of the family, Tenzin Choegyal, was 12 years younger.

EARLY LIFE

Lhamo Thondup spent his first two years in the farming village of Takster, where his parents raised sheep and grew barley, buckwheat, and potatoes. Although Tibet is a large country, some 470,000 square miles, it is sparsely populated, with only 6 million people at the time of Lhamo Thondup's birth. His family was one of only 20 families in the area around Takster.

A BRIEF HISTORY OF TIBET

Tibet is one of the most remote regions on Earth, sometimes called the "Roof of the World." It is bordered in the south by the Himalayan Mountains and the countries of India, Nepal, Sikkim, Burma, and Bhutan. China lies to the east, and East Turkestan and the Kunlun mountain range border the country to the north. Surrounded largely by mountains, the country is one vast plateau, with an average elevation of 16,000 feet.

The country of Tibet is an ancient one, emerging as an independent kingdom during the seventh century. From the 13th to the 18th centuries it was under the influence of Mongolian leaders from the north. China invaded Mongolia in the 18th century, and for the next several hundred years China also influenced Tibetan politics. In the early 20th century Tibet declared its independence from China. The influence of other nations on Tibet's political life remained marginal, however, because it was so physically isolated from the rest of the world. In fact, it was largely left alone until the advent of 20th-century technology. With the coming of cars, trucks, airplanes, and modern weapons, Tibet was at last accessible to the outside world.

When Lhamo Thondup was growing up, Tibet was still isolated from the rest of the world, both geographically and culturally. The terrain was so formidable that there were hardly any roads in the entire country. The majority of the people lived in mountain valleys, accessible only by steep, treacherous mountain paths. There was no official currency, and people bartered their crops and livestock for staples like tea, sugar, and cloth. All aspects of life, from birth to death, were informed by the Tibetans' deeply held belief in Buddhism. It was into this remote culture, self-sufficient and virtually unknown to the outside world, that the future Dalai Lama was born.

TIBETAN BUDDHISM

The vast majority of Tibetans believe in a faith called Tibetan Buddhism. So pervasive is the religion that one in five men were Buddhist monks at the beginning of the 20th century. It is derived from the teachings of an Indian named Siddhartha Guatama, called Buddha, who lived 2,500 years ago. The body of teachings of the Buddha are contained in a work called the "dharma." One of the central precepts of Buddhism is that life is suffering and that beings must live through cycles of birth, death, and rebirth, called "samsara." The birth, death, and rebirth cycle is related to the concept of "karma." Buddhists believe that all people live through a series of lives, or "incarnations." They believe that the collective actions and

The Dalai Lama at about age three

thoughts of each individual, the good and the bad, are rewarded or punished in these successive lives, or "incarnations." Thus, they believe that every human being is a "reincarnation," or reborn being, who has lived before in another form, perhaps as another animal, or as another human being. Buddhists strive for "nirvana," a state of being in which all the good and bad deeds of many lifetimes have been lived out and all worldly attachments eliminated, preparing the individual for a life of the spirit. Buddhists also believe in the sacredness of all life, human and animal, and nonviolence is a central part of their faith.

THE DALAI LAMA

By the 14th century, the leaders of Tibetan Buddhism had established the position of the Dalai Lama. The Dalai Lama is the spiritual and temporal leader of the people of Tibet. The Dalai Lama is considered to be a living god, and a manifestation of the "bodhisattva" (boh-dee-SUT-vah) of compassion. Tibetan Buddhists believe that bodhisattvas are beings of great compassion who choose to stay in the temporal world as helpers to humankind, rather than entering nirvana.

According to Tibetan tradition, the first Dalai Lama was born in 1351. There have been 14 Dalai Lamas so far, and each is considered to be a reincarnation of the previous Dalai Lama. The current Dalai Lama, born as Lhamo Thondup in Takster in 1935, was discovered following the death of the 13th Dalai Lama in 1933.

How He Was Discovered

After the death of a Dalai Lama, Buddhist high priests, called lamas, begin a search for a successor. They look for signs and clues in visions or dreams. When the 13th Dalai Lama died in 1933, a senior lama had a vision in which he saw a house with strange gutters, a monastery, and several Tibetan letters. The lamas thought that the vision suggested that the new Dalai Lama had been born in the northeastern province of Amdo, near the monastery at Kumbum. So a search party journeyed to Amdo and the village of Takster, where they looked for a house with strange gutters. In the house, they found a family with a two-year-old boy. The leader of the party, Kewstang Rinpoche, and other lamas spent the evening observing and playing with the boy. In his autobiography *Freedom in Exile*, the Dalai Lama describes the visit:

"The child recognized him and called out 'Sera Lama, Sera Lama.' Sera was Kewstang Rinpoche's monastery. Next day they left—only to return a few days later as a formal deputation. This time they brought with them a number of things that had belonged to my predecessor, together with several items that did not. In every case, the infant correctly identified those belonging to the 13th Dalai Lama saying, 'It's mine, it's mine.' This more or less convinced the search party that they had found the new incarnation. . . . It was not long before the boy from Takster was acknowledged to be the new Dalai Lama. I was that child."

So at the age of two, Lhamo Thondup was acknowledged as the 14th Dalai Lama, the reincarnation of the spirit of compassion who has been the spiritual leader of Tibet for centuries. He was taken from his home and sent to the monastery at Kumbum, where he spent the next two years. He recalls that "there now began a somewhat unhappy period of my life." He was alone, and he was lonely. "It is very hard for a child to be separated from its parents," he recalled. His older brother, Lobsang Samten, was a monk at the monastery, so he did have some family and companionship. Yet his life had changed forever, as he began the training for the leadership of his people and their faith. After his selection as the Dalai Lama, he became the responsibility of a select group of Tibetan Buddhist monks whose job it was to prepare the Dalai Lama for his role. Thus, he no longer saw his family or anyone from the outside world on a regular basis. His life was devoted to his education and development as the head of his religion and his country.

Official portrait of the Dalai Lama on the Lion Throne, 1942, at age seven

JOURNEY TO LHASA

When he was four, he and his family journeyed to Lhasa, the capital of Tibet, in a large caravan of lamas and government officials, where he would be installed as the Dalai Lama. The journey took three months, and during his travels the young Dalai Lama saw "some of the most remote and beautiful countryside in the world: gargantuan mountains flanking immense flat plains which we struggled over like insects."

In Lhasa, he was greeted in a ceremony of which he remembered "a great sense of homecoming and endless crowds of people." For a year, he lived at the Dalai Lama's summer palace at Norbulingka, a lovely home surrounded with gardens. There, over the next year, the young Dalai Lama enjoyed occasional visits with his parents, who had acquired noble status after his own divinity had been discovered. As a young monk in training, he was forbidden to eat certain foods, like pork and eggs. He would steal over to visit his parents and eat those forbidden foods. That year would be, in his words, "the last temporal liberty I was ever to know."

In the winter of 1940, the Dalai Lama was taken to the Potala palace, the ancient home of the Dalai Lama. It is a huge, imposing structure with over 1,000 rooms, built into the side of a mountain above Lhasa. His only memory of the ceremony marking his installation at the Potala was that "it was the first time I sat on the Lion Throne, a vast, jewel-encrusted and beautifully carved wooden structure that stood in the *Si shi phuntsog* (Hall of All Good Deeds of the Spiritual and Temporal World), the principal stateroom in the east wing of the Potala."

He also received his full name, Jetsun Jamphel Ngawang Lobsang Yeshi Tenzin Gyatso Sisunwangyur Tshunpa Getson Mapal Dhepal Sango. Translated, his name means Gentle Glory, Holy Lord, Eloquent, Compassionate, Ocean of Wisdom, Pure in Mind, Learned Defender of the Faith. Then as now, his name was often abbreviated to Tenzin Gyatso. He is also referred to as "Kundun," an honorary title given to the Dalai Lama.

Next, he was taken to the Jokhang temple in Lhasa, one of the holiest shrines in Tibetan Buddhism, and there he had his head shaved, in accordance with his monk's training. As a monk, the Dalai Lama took the four root vows of Tibetan monasticism: "a monk must not kill, steal, or lie about his spiritual attainment. He must also be celibate. If he breaks any one of these, he is no longer a monk."

EDUCATION

Shortly after his installation, the Dalai Lama began his education, studying with tutors in religion and in academic subjects. Although he was not allowed to have friends of his own age, he spent his first years studying with his brother Lobsang Samten. He remembers that the room in which they learned to read had two whips on the wall, one in yellow satin, for the Dalai Lama, one in leather, for Lobsang Samten. The Dalai Lama was never struck, but Lobsang Samten was, when his brother misbehaved. Lobsang Samten was, according to the Dalai Lama, "made to suffer on my behalf."

When the Dalai Lama was eight, his brother was sent away to school, and he lost his last regular contact with his family. He did still see his mother and sisters occasionally, visits he looked forward to, especially when his mother would bring him fresh bread. At night, he would be especially lonely, for he slept in the ancient bedroom of the fifth Dalai Lama, left much as it was when he died in 1682. For company, the young 14th Dalai Lama would play with the mice that would look for food left in front of the little butter lamps at the Buddhist shrines in the palace. His only other playmates at the time were the sweepers who swept the rooms of the dusty palace. The Dalai

Lama remembers them with great affection; outside of his tutors, they were the only other people he saw on a daily basis.

The Dalai Lama continued his studies, which included penmanship, the memorization of religious texts, and attendance at meetings of the government. When he got older, he began to train with tutors for his degree, a Doctorate of Buddhist Studies. There were major and minor areas of study for the degree. The major categories included logic, Tibetan art and culture, Sanskrit, Tibetan medicine, and Buddhist philosophy. The minor categories covered poetry, music, drama, astrology, meter and phrasing, and synonyms.

One of the most important aspects of the training of a Tibetan Buddhist monk is learning to debate. These debates take the form of questions and answers between the debaters, given with stylized gestures and rendered with wit and humor. Training in this activity continued throughout the years of the Dalai Lama's education.

——— **"** ———

The Hobbies of a Young Dalai Lama

After a day of study, the young Dalai Lama would often go to the roof of the Potala palace and observe the outside world through his telescope. He was forbidden to meet with and talk to people outside the palace, and the telescope offered one way of contact with the world. He would often train his telescope on the prisoners in the yard of the local prison.

As a monk, the Dalai Lama took the four root vows of Tibetan monasticism: "a monk must not kill, steal, or lie about his spiritual attainment. He must also be celibate. If he breaks any one of these, he is no longer a monk."

——— **"** ———

He also loved to learn how simple mechanisms worked, and he enjoyed taking apart clocks and watches, then putting them back together. He also developed a passion for movies, after discovering a movie projector and several old newsreels among the things of the previous Dalai Lama. These old films featured the coronation of England's King George V and a documentary about mining. They offered a glimpse into a world the Dalai Lama had never seen, and rarely heard about.

In 1948, when he was 13, the Dalai Lama met his first "inji," or Westerner. He was an Austrian mountain climber named Heinrich Harrer, who had escaped from a British prisoner of war camp in India, which was then controlled by Great Britain. At the start of World War II, Harrer was trying to climb the Himalayas. He had been captured and imprisoned because Austria was part of the German empire, and was thus an enemy of the British and the Allies during the war. Harrer and the Dalai Lama became close friends, as Harrer described in his book *Seven Years in Tibet* (1954); which later became a film starring Brad Pitt (see entry in this issue). Harrer taught him about the outside world, including the geography and history of Europe and the background of World War II. The Dalai Lama, who had never seen blond hair before, nicknamed his new friend *Gopse*, meaning "yellow head."

Among the belongings of the 13th Dalai Lama were three cars — three of only four cars that were in Tibet at that time. The 14th Dalai Lama loved them, and tried to fix them up and drive them. Harrer helped out in this task, too, but the Dalai Lama's driving skills were pretty rough. He managed to smash one of them into a tree.

CHINA INVADES TIBET

The idyllic, isolated life of the Dalai Lama and all Tibetans changed forever in 1950, when the Chinese army invaded Tibet. Claiming that they were "liberating" the people of Tibet, 80,000 Chinese soldiers stormed the country from the east, taking towns and provinces as they pushed toward Lhasa. China had become a Communist nation in 1949, under the leadership of Mao Zedong. Mao's early programs to modernize Chinese industry and agriculture had proved to be disastrous. After just a few years, some 20-30 million Chinese people had died from famine. In invading Tibet, China hoped to exploit the people and resources of the country.

The Tibetans' response was immediate. They demanded that the Chinese withdraw and respect their sovereignty as a nation. Up until this point, the Dalai Lama had not been made head of the government of Tibet, which had been run by a regent during his youth. It was decided that it was time for the Dalai Lama to become both the "spiritual and temporal leader," meaning the religious and governmental leader, of Tibet. The ceremony marking his enthronement took place on November 17, 1950. At the time, he was only 15. "When eventually the proceedings drew to a close," the Dalai Lama wrote in his autobiography, "I found myself undisputed leader of six million people facing the threat of full-scale war."

The Dalai Lama immediately appealed to the nations of the world to intervene on behalf of Tibet. He sent delegations to the U.S., Great Britain, and Nepal, and another to China to try to begin negotiations leading to a withdrawal. The Dalai Lama himself was also in personal danger. The Chinese had made his brother Takster Rinpoche, a monk in Amdo, a virtual prisoner in his monastery. They tried to indoctrinate him and to force him to persuade the Dalai Lama to accept Chinese rule. If he couldn't, the Chinese had ordered Takster Rinpoche to kill his brother. Secretly, he met with the Dalai

The Potala Palace, Lhasa, Tibet

Lama and urged him to contact the American government for their help. Sadly, neither the U.S. nor any of the other nations contacted offered any help to Tibet.

In order to insure his safety, the Dalai Lama moved to the south of the country, to be prepared to go into exile if necessary. While staying in the southern town of Dromo, he heard a radio broadcast that stated that an "agreement" had been reached in which Tibet consented to become part of China. "I could not believe my ears," the Dalai Lama recalled. "The speaker described how 'over the last hundred years or more' aggressive imperialist forces had penetrated into Tibet and 'carried out all kinds of deceptions and provocations'." He remembered feeling "physically ill as I listened to this unbelievable mixture of lies and fanciful cliches."

"But there was worse to come," he continued. "Clause One of the 'Agreement' stated that 'The Tibetan people shall be united and drive out imperialist aggressive forces from Tibet. The Tibetan people shall return to the big family of the motherland—the People's Republic of China.' . . . The idea of Tibet returning to the 'Motherland' was a shameless invention. Tibet had never been part of China."

Thus began the occupation of Tibet by China that continues to this day. Deprived of all autonomy and authority to control its internal and external affairs for itself, Tibet even lost its place on the maps of the world, depicted as within the boundaries of China. Many religious and governmental leaders of Tibet encouraged the Dalai Lama to flee the country immediately, but he felt he had to return to Lhasa. There, he tried to negotiate with the Chinese general in charge of Lhasa, and he learned, to his horror, about atrocities against Tibetans in the far eastern provinces. The Chinese had murdered Tibetans who resisted their rule, and destroyed sacred temples and monasteries. This was particularly horrific for a people who practiced nonviolence as a way of life, and whose religion forbid the killing of any being.

The occupation of Tibet by the Chinese continued, as they forced the Tibetans to abandon their former ways of farming and utilize the "collective farming" techniques favored by the Communists. In the collective farming of the Communist Chinese, people with little or no experience were forced to work on farms run by the state, utilizing techniques that had never been proven to increase crop yields. As it had in China, the collectivization techniques resulted in the massive failure of crops and the death by starvation of hundreds of thousands of Tibetans. They also forced Tibetans into road crews, where many more perished from hunger and exposure.

In 1954, the Dalai Lama decided to travel to Beijing, capital city of China, to meet with Mao and other Chinese leaders in an effort to win freedom for his people. Mao impressed him as a savvy political leader, but the Dalai Lama soon realized that his visit was carefully choreographed to include only the positive aspects of life in Communist China, with no contact with the common Chinese people. And, in one of his final encounters with Mao, the Chinese leader clearly described his plans for Tibet and Tibetan Buddhists. As the Dalai Lama recalled, "he drew closer to me and said, 'Your attitude is good, you know. Religion is poison. Firstly it reduces the population, because monks and nuns must stay celibate, and secondly it neglects material progress.' At this I felt a violent burning sensation all over my face and I was suddenly very afraid. 'So,' I thought, 'you are the destroyer of the *Dharma* after all'."

Upon returning to Tibet, the Dalai Lama learned of further barbaric atrocities by the Chinese. There was continued resistance to Chinese rule throughout the country, some of it organized into alliances of freedom fighters. These groups, when discovered by the Chinese, were publicly and barbarically tortured. The Chinese also began the systematic abuse, torture, and murder of Buddhist monks and nuns. The Dalai Lama's pleas on behalf of his people went unanswered. And Tibet's powerful neighbor to the south, India, signed an agreement with China at this time that signaled its acknowledgment of China's annexation of Tibet.

In the late 1950s, during a visit to India, the Dalai Lama began to seriously consider seeking political asylum in that country. Upon his return to Lhasa from his trip, he decided to devote himself to the completion of his degree, a Doctorate of Buddhist Studies, for which he took his final exams in March 1959. Soon after, he learned that the Chinese had plotted to attack Lhasa and to kidnap and probably kill him. As word of the plot spread among the people, thousands came to the city of Lhasa to protect their leader.

ESCAPE TO INDIA

It became clear to the Dalai Lama that the time had come to leave Tibet and go into exile. "Not only was my own life in danger, but the lives of thousands upon thousands of my people now seemed certain to be lost." In disguise, the Dalai Lama, his closest advisors, and members of his family left Lhasa and took a perilous journey into exile in northern India. They traveled for days, over mountain passes and through blizzards,

"I believe that suffering is caused by ignorance, and that people inflict pain on others in pursuit of their own happiness or satisfaction. Yet true happiness comes from a sense of inner peace and contentment, which in turn must be achieved through the cultivation of altruism, of love, of compassion, and through the elimination of anger, selfishness, and greed."

always alert to the danger of being discovered by Chinese soldiers. En route, they learned that the Chinese had shelled the Dalai Lama's Norbulingka palace and machine-gunned the crowds of his loyal followers. At the end of the trip, the Dalai Lama made a formal rebuttal of the "Agreement" between Tibet and China and announced the formation of his own government, a government in exile. Then, he fell ill. Several days later, in April 1959, he left Tibet for the last time. Entering India, he requested asylum from the Indian government, which was granted.

The government and people of India extended a warm welcome to the Dalai Lama, and he was also greeted with messages from people all over the world. He met with the international press to explain his reasons for going into exile and to refute the story being circulated by the Chinese government: that he had been kidnapped and taken by force into India.

LIFE IN EXILE

Thus began the exile of the Dalai Lama, which has lasted almost 40 years. For the first year, he lived in a house in northern India provided by the government. Then, he set up his own government in exile in the city of Dharamsala, in northern India. Refugees from Tibet began to pour into India, eventually numbering more than 100,000. The Indian government settled the Tibetans in areas all over the country, sometimes successfully, sometimes not. The Tibetans were used to the cool mountain climate of their own country, and the heat and humidity of India, as well as diseases for which they had no immunity, decimated the early refugee population.

India was then under the government of Pandit Nehru, who provided for the refugees as best he could, while trying to maintain friendly relations with the powerful Chinese government. Of primary concern to the Dalai Lama was the preservation of Tibetan culture, and Nehru was in full agreement. He set up schools where the Tibetans could be educated in their own language and culture.

The Dalai Lama now began the campaign that has continued to this day to make the world aware of the fate of Tibet and to try to win autonomy for his country and his people. He contacted people in countries all over the world to ask them to speak to the international organizations, like the United Nations and the International Commission of Jurists, to review the record of the Chinese in Tibet and to bring international attention to bear on the issue. In 1959, the UN debated the issue and voted to condemn China's actions. In 1960, the International Commission of Jurists reported that China "had violated 16 articles of the Universal Declaration of Human Rights and was guilty of genocide in Tibet."

Throughout the early 1960s, the Dalai Lama and his advisers worked on a draft of a constitution for Tibet. One of its main issues concerned the Dalai Lama himself. It was his wish that the government change from a "theocracy"—a form of government in which the church and state are one—to a democracy. As such, he made the ruling that gave the power to the democratically elected government to remove the Dalai Lama as head of the government. Many Tibetans were dismayed at this thought, but he insisted that it was following both democratic and Buddhist principles.

The Dalai Lama greets followers in Washington, NJ, in May, 1998

Life for Tibetans under Chines Rule

Meanwhile news of the continued atrocities against the people and the land of Tibet reached the Dalai Lama. The Tibetans organized small and large up risings against the Chinese, and each met with incredible brutality on the part of the Chinese military. To date, the Chinese have murdered, tortured, or starved to death some 1.25 million Tibetans —one-fifth of the population. In addition, they have resettled millions of Chinese onto Tibetan soil, in their efforts to destroy the Tibetan people, culture, and way of life. They have for bidden Tibetans to use their own language, outlawed the practice of religion, and destroyed thousands of Tibetan Buddhist temples, shrines, and monasteries. In all government-provided agencies and services, the occupying Chinese took horrible advantage of the Tibetans. The Dalai Lama received reports that "Many of the schools were nothing more than labor camps for children."

A country that had once been wholly self-sufficient in growing food to feed itself now became a scene of famine. The Chinese planted wheat in place of the traditional barley, which caused soil erosion and flooding. They also mined uranium from the rich mines of Tibet, and placed one-third of their nuclear arsenal on Tibetan land. And in Amdo, the birthplace of the Dalai Lama, the Chinese built the largest prison in the world, big enough to hold 10 million prisoners.

It was the message of this atrocity and abandonment that the Dalai Lama took to the peoples of the world. Over the past 40 years, he has met with virtually every head of state and religious leader, tirelessly pleading the case of his people. Central to his message is his belief that "the most important thing for humankind is its own creativity. I further believe that, in order to be able to exercise this creativity, people need to be free. I have freedom in exile. And, as a refugee, I have learned something of its value." And central to all his efforts is his deep belief in nonviolence. It is against the precepts of Buddhism to harm or kill any being, and the Dalai Lama has never sanctioned violence as a way of restoring autonomy to Tibet.

The Dalai Lama became a regular visitor to the United States, where he met with many people who wanted to help Tibet. In 1985, the U.S. Congress signed a letter to Li Xiannian, the president of the Chinese People's Assembly, that urged the Chinese to "grant the very reasonable and justified aspirations of His Holiness the Dalai Lama and his people every consideration." The letter was ignored. Then, in 1987, the Dalai Lama addressed Congress himself. He discussed a five-point plan for peace, which included "The transformation of the whole of Tibet into a zone of peace; abandonment of China's population transfer policy which threatens the very existence of the Tibetans as a people; respect for the Tibetan people's fundamental human rights and democratic freedoms; restoration and protection of Tibet's natural environment and the abandonment of China's use of Tibet for the production of nuclear weapons and dumping of nuclear waste; and commencement of earnest negotiations on the future status of Tibet and of relations between Tibetan and Chinese peoples."

These concepts have remained central to the Dalai Lama's quest for the freedom of his people. In a similar speech before the European Parliament in 1988, he restated his position, and introduced a proposal stating that "it could be possible for the whole of Tibet to exist in association with the People's Republic of China, with foreign affairs and limited defense directed from Peking until a regional peace conference can take place, after which the whole of Tibet would be designated a Zone of Peace."

The response to his peace initiatives was negative, yet the Dalai Lama continued to make overtures to the Chinese government to begin talks on the issue of Tibet.

THE NOBEL PEACE PRIZE

In 1989, the Dalai Lama was awarded the Nobel Peace Prize. In selecting him, the Nobel Committee noted that the "the Dalai Lama in his struggle for the liberation of Tibet consistently has opposed the use of violence. He has instead advocated peaceful solutions based upon tolerance and mutual respect in order to preserve the historical and cultural heritage of his people.

The Dalai Lama has developed his philosophy of peace from a great reverence for all things living and upon the concept of universal responsibility embracing all mankind as well as nature. In the opinion of the Committee the Dalai Lama has come forward with constructive and forward-looking proposals for the solution of international conflicts, human rights issues, and the global environment."

Since he received the Nobel Prize, the Dalai Lama has continued to travel the world to raise awareness of the plight of Tibet and to promote his message of universal responsibility. "The need for simple human-to-human relationships is becoming increasingly urgent. Today the world is smaller and more interdependent. One nation's problems can no longer be solved by itself completely. Thus, without a sense of universal responsibility, our very survival becomes threatened. Basically, universal responsibility is feeling for other people's suffering just as we feel our own. It is the realization that even our enemy is entirely motivated by the quest for happiness. We must recognize that all beings want the same thing that we want. This is the way to achieve a true understanding, unfettered by artificial consideration."

"Universal responsibility is feeling for other people's suffering just as we feel our own. It is the realization that even our enemy is entirely motivated by the quest for happiness. We must recognize that all beings want the same thing that we want. This is the way to achieve a true understanding, unfettered by artificial consideration."

RECENT DEVELOPMENTS

The life of the Dalai Lama and the fate of Tibet is still very much in the news. In 1997, two high-profile films came out on his life: *Seven Years in Tibet,* a film version of Heinrich Harrer's book of the same name, and *Kundun*, a biography of the Dalai Lama by American director Martin Scorsese. In both cases the Chinese government protested vigorously and tried to stop the filming and showing of the movies. Despite the Chinese threats, the films were produced and viewed around the world. Several famous members of the Hollywood community, notably actors Richard Gere and Harrison Ford and screenwriter Melissa Mathison, have appeared with the Dalai Lama and lent greater publicity to his campaign for Tibet.

As recently as June 1998, Tibet was in the news again. As President Clinton prepared for a trip to China, supporters of a free Tibet held the third annual Tibetan Freedom Concert in Washington, D.C. Some of the bands that performed to show their support for the Tibetan people include the Dave Matthews Band, Sonic Youth, REM, Radiohead, Sean Lennon, Luscious Jackson, Blues Traveler, Wyclef Jean, The Wallflowers, A Tribe Called Quest, Pearl Jam, and the Beastie Boys, who organized the concert. They wanted to draw attention to the plight of Tibet and to encourage people around the world, and Americans, to tell Clinton to urge the Chinese to begin a dialogue with the Dalai Lama.

And in late June, Clinton discussed the issue of Tibet with current Chinese President Jiang Zemin in an unprecedented televised debate, which was broadcast throughout China. The Dalai Lama was delighted with the exchange, not only because it to put the issue of Tibet in front of the world, but also because "Millions of Chinese, especially intellectuals, opinion-formers, and those who are politically conscious, will certainly have taken notice."

At this point in his quest, the Dalai Lama maintains what he calls his "middle-way policy," as he outlined in his five-point plan in 1987: "I've made it very clear that I'm not seeking independence for Tibet; I'm seeking genuine autonomy, and this indirectly recognizes Chinese sovereignty."

He still believes he will live to see the day when Tibet is free and he is able to return to his country. He also believes he is key to any successful negotiations between the Chinese and Tibetans. Over the years, various splinter groups have developed who are impatient with the Dalai Lama's nonviolent methods and who advocate violence on behalf of the liberation of Tibet. "In 20 years time, I'll be 83, just an old man with a stick, moving like a sloth bear," he said recently. "While I'm alive, I am fully committed to autonomy, and I am the person who can persuade the Tibetan people to accept it."

In the meantime, he holds fast to his principles, working for peace for his country and all peoples. "I believe that suffering is caused by ignorance, and that people inflict pain on others in pursuit of their own happiness or satisfaction. Yet true happiness comes from a sense of inner peace and contentment, which in turn must be achieved through the cultivation of altruism, of love, of compassion, and through the elimination of anger, selfishness, and greed." And he remains true to his faith and to his place in the Buddhist order as a being of compassion. He sees his past, present and future purpose articulated in the following prayer: "For as long as space endures/And for as long as living beings remain/ Until then may I, too, abide/To dispel the misery of the world."

HONORS AND AWARDS

Albert Schweitzer Humanitarian Award: 1987
Nobel Peace Prize: 1989
Raoul Wallenberg Congressional Human Rights Award: 1989

FURTHER READING

Books

Dalai Lama. *My Land and My People*, 1962
——. *Freedom in Exile: The Autobiography of the Dalai Lama*, 1990
Demi. *The Dalai Lama*, 1998 (juvenile)
Friese, Kai. *Tenzin Gyatso, The Dalai Lama*, 1989 (juvenile)
Goodman, Michael Harris. *The Last Dalai Lama*, 1986
Harrer, Heinrich. *Seven Years in Tibet*, 1953
Stewart, Whitney. *The 14th Dalai Lama: Spiritual Leader of Tibet*, 1996 (juvenile)

Periodicals

Chicago Tribune, July 28, 1996, p.A3
Current Biography 1951; 1982
Independent (London), Mar. 21, 1991, p.14
Life, Apr. 23, 1951, p.130; Feb. 22, 1954, p.83; May 4, 1959, p.26
Mother Jones, Nov.-Dec. 1997, p.28
New York Times, Oct. 6, 1989, p.A6; Mar. 21, 1996, p.A4; May 11, 1998,
    p.A19; June 29, 1998, p.A1
New York Times Biographical Service, Oct.1989, p.971
New York Times Magazine, Sep. 29, 1996, p.168
Newsweek, Oct. 13, 1997, p.48
Rolling Stone, Aug. 8, 1996, p.20
Time, Apr. 6, 1959, p.24; Apr. 20, 1959, p.26; Dec. 22, 1997, p.72
Times (London), Jan. 5, 1997, July 27, 1997
Vanity Fair, Aug. 1996, p.98

ADDRESS

The Office of Tibet
241 E. 32nd. St.
New York, NY 19916

WORLD WIDE WEB SITES

http://www.tibet.com
http://nobel.se/laureates/peace-1989-1-bio.html

OBITUARY

Diana, Princess of Wales 1961-1997
English Princess

*[**Editor's Note:** Diana, Princess of Wales, previously appeared three times in* Biography Today: *in a regular entry in the July 1992 issue, and in Updates in the 1996 and 1997 Annual Cumulations. However, in view of the many revelations about her life that have been disclosed during the past few years, as well as her recent death, the Editors of* Biography Today *decided to prepare a full, updated entry.]*

BIRTH

Diana Frances Spencer, later known as Diana, Princess of Wales, was born on July 1, 1961, in Norfolk, England. She was born at

Park House, a 10-bedroom country home on the grounds of Sandringham House. Sandringham is a 20,000-acre country estate in Norfolk, in northern England, that is owned by Queen Elizabeth. Sandringham is one of two country estates owned by the British royal family; the other is Balmoral Castle, a 40,000-acre estate in Scotland.

Diana's parents were Edward John and Frances Burke (Roche) Spencer, the Viscount and Viscountess Althorp. Later, Edward became the eighth Earl Spencer. Diana was the fourth of five children in the family. She had two sisters, Sarah, who was six years older, and Jane, who was four years older, and a brother, Charles, who was three years younger than Diana. Another brother, John, born just 18 months before Diana, lived for less than a day.

Diana is descended from a long line of English nobility with many ties to the monarchy. It is traditional in England for members of the nobility to serve the king and queen in various posts. The Spencers, Diana's father's side of the family, have a centuries-long tradition of service to the crown. They acquired their wealth in the 15th century as sheep traders. They received an earldom from King Charles I, acquired a coat of arms and a motto ("God defend the right"), built Althorp House in Northamptonshire, which is one of England's grandest estates, and began amassing a collection of art, antiques, and books. Her father was equerry (officer by appointment) to both the present queen and to the queen's late father, King George VI. Diana's paternal grandmother, as well as four great-aunts, were close members of the court of Queen Elizabeth, the Queen Mother. On Diana's mother's side, her grandfather was Maurice Roche, the fourth Baron Fermoy, who later became a member of Parliament. He was given a grant to Park House, where Diana was born, by King George V in recognition of his service to the king's son. His Scottish wife, Ruth, Lady Fermoy, was a close friend and member of the official household of the Queen Mother.

YOUTH

Diana was born into her family at an awkward time. From the start, her parents were looking for a male heir to carry on the family name and to inherit the family wealth and the family title. All of these assets are traditionally passed down to the first-born male in each generation, not to the females in the family. Just 18 months before Diana was born, her mother had given birth to a boy, John, who had lived for just ten hours. So they were very hopeful that their next child would be a boy, and a bit disappointed to have another girl. Diana was baptized without ceremony at a small church in Sandringham. Three years later, when her brother Charles was born, he was baptized in Westminster Abbey in London, and the Queen was his principal godparent.

A child of privilege, Diana was raised in an aristocratic country lifestyle. She and her siblings were surrounded by servants, and they ate their meals with their nannies instead of their parents. In fact, they had minimal contact with their parents, and the relationship between parent and child was formal and restrained. As her brother Charles described it, "It was a privileged upbringing out of a different age, a distant way of living from your parents. I don't know anyone who brings up children like than any more." Still, there was much for Diana to enjoy in her life at Park House. She and her siblings hiked in the woods and open fields, played hide-and-seek in the gardens, took summer trips to the seaside, swam in the heated pool, played with the animals, hid out in their tree house, and went horseback riding.

Her Parents' Divorce

In 1967, when Diana was six, her life changed greatly. Her parents went through a messy divorce that shattered her world. There was a period of tension, bitterness, and fighting. "The whole thing was very unstable," Diana later recalled. "I remember my mother crying. Daddy never spoke to us about it. We could never ask questions. Too many nannies." Her parents separated, and her mother had an affair with wealthy wallpaper heir Peter Shand Kydd. For that, she was branded an adulteress and denied custody of the children, who stayed with their father, although they did see their mother on some weekends and school holidays. The two older sisters, Sarah and Jane, were off at boarding school by that time, so they were rarely around. Diana was left to be the nurturing older sister to her younger brother Charles, then only three years old. At night, she could hear him in his room way down at the opposite end of their home. He would lay in his bed crying, "I want my mummy. I want my mummy." Diana wanted to get out of bed and go to comfort him. But at only six years old, she was just too afraid of the dark. So she would put her head under the pillow and cry. "I just couldn't bear it," she later said. "I could never pluck up enough courage to get out of bed."

In England in the 1960s, scandalous divorce among members of the nobility was very much an embarrassment, and Diana and her siblings were deeply scarred by their parents' breakup. Among their friends, only they had suffered such painful public exposure. They felt, friends say, "set apart." Family times as they knew them had ended, and they were often shuffled around among grandparents and nannies, and between parents who had difficulty hiding their bitterness toward one another. Many observers have conjectured that the pain that Diana experienced as a result of her parents' divorce later fueled her determination to have a successful marriage and contributed to the devotion and attention she always gave to her own children.

Both of Diana's parents later remarried. In 1969, shortly after the divorce, her mother married Peter Shand Kydd, who was a generous and demonstrative stepfather. Diana's visits to their home, first in England and later on their 1,000-acre farm in Scotland, became relaxed and easy going. Relations were a bit more difficult with her stepmother. In 1975, when Diana was about 14, her grandfather died, her father became Lord (Earl) Spencer, and she became Lady Diana Spencer. He and the children moved to Althorp, the family's 100-room manor set on 550 acres of parkland in the English Midlands. In 1977, he married Raine, Countess of Dartmouth and the daughter of romance novelist Barbara Cartland. Relations between the Spencer children and Raine, whom they called "Acid Raine," were very strained. Their difficulties reportedly stemmed from jealousy, but also from what they considered her overbearing attitude and her mishandling of the family home. Trying to stabilize the financial situation at Althorp, she fired staff, sold off some of the family's priceless treasures that dated back centuries, created a tearoom and a gift shop, and opened the family estate to tourists. None of these decisions endeared her to her stepchildren.

EDUCATION

Diana's earliest education was at home at Park House with a governess. Beginning at age six she attended classes at Silfield School. There, as the only child of divorced parents, she always felt different from the other students. At age nine, an age when many upper-class British children are sent away to boarding school, Diana was enrolled at Riddlesworth Hall Preparatory School, a boarding school for girls in Norfolk. At first she felt betrayed, resentful, lonely, and sad. It was a difficult transition, but she eventually prospered there. As Ingrid Seward explains, "British boarding school is a strange institution. . . . Yet by its very routine and insistence on rules and order it can give a sense of security. Diana, like many children from broken homes, found a stability there she might otherwise have missed." At Riddlesworth, she enjoyed swimming, horseback riding, and other sports. She took ballet lessons and developed a real passion for dance. She was even able to keep her pet guinea pig Peanuts there. Friendly and popular with the other students, she was quiet in class. Diana was only a passable student, but she was known for her athletic abilities, her love of animals, and her exceptional kindness and helpfulness.

At age 12, Diana moved on to the West Heath School, a boarding school in a woodland park in Kent that emphasized character and confidence as much as academics. Her mother had been educated there, as had her sisters, who were remembered as excellent students. Diana did not fare as well academically, although she was a talented athlete. She won swimming and diving cups, was captain of the netball team (a game like basketball), and played a good game of tennis. She loved ballet and tap dancing, but at five feet ten-and-a-half inches she was considered too tall to dance professionally. At

West Heath, she discovered a natural aptitude for compassion while visiting the elderly and the mentally handicapped. It became the start of a life-long habit of public service. It was while Diana was attending West Heath that her father became an earl, moved to Althorp, and married Raine, Countess of Dartmouth. At age 16, Diana left West Heath after twice failing her "O" level exams, which are standardized tests for British students. It was the end of her formal academic schooling.

In 1978 Diana attended the Institut Alpin Videmanette, an exclusive finishing school for girls near Gstaad, Switzerland. There, she took classes in domestic science, dressmaking, and cooking. Although she enjoyed the skiing there, she was unhappy at school. She soon returned to England.

FIRST JOBS

After finishing school, Diana was eager to move to London. But at age 17, she was really a bit young to be on her own. She started out staying in an apartment in London that belonged to her mother. Her mother spent most of her time in Scotland, so Diana was quite independent there. She lived in her mother's apartment for about a year with one of her girlfriends. Then in 1979 her parents bought her an elegant apartment in the fashionable London neighborhood of South Kensington, which she shared with three girlfriends.

Diana later described these few years in London as the happiest time of her life. She took cooking classes and held a series of jobs, despite her parents' wealth and her own comfortable finances, which included a sizable inheritance. She worked as a waitress, cleaned houses, and babysat the children of her sisters' friends. Her final employment was as a part-time teacher's assistant in a kindergarten at the Young England Nursery School, plus two days a week as a babysitter for the child of an American oil executive. There were the last jobs she held before she was engaged to Prince Charles and was discovered by the press.

THE ROYAL COURTSHIP

Lady Diana Spencer and Charles, Prince of Wales, had known each other for some time before they first became involved. They probably knew each other as children — when Diana was growing up at Park House and Charles, who was 12 years older, would visit Sandringham with his family. But they first remember meeting in 1977 at Althorp. Charles was there visiting Diana's sister Sarah, who he was then dating. There was a weekend pheasant hunt, and Charles and Diana met in a plowed field. Though Diana was only 16 at the time, Charles later said he remembered her as "very jolly and amusing and attractive."

Perhaps the real start of their relationship came in July 1980. Diana was invited to watch the Prince and his team play in a polo match and then to a barbecue afterward at a friend's country home. There, Diana was seated next to Charles on a bale of hay. As they were chatting, they discussed the recent funeral of Lord Mountbatten, Charles's uncle and one of the people closest to him. Diana later confided that she said to him, "You looked so sad when you walked up the aisle at Lord Mountbatten's funeral. It was the most tragic thing I've ever seen. My heart bled for you when I watched. I thought: 'It's wrong, you're lonely, you should be with somebody to look after you.'" From that time onward their relationship began to develop.

> *Although she often appeared poised and confident throughout their courtship, Diana later said she felt terrorized by the relentless attention that reporters turned on her. She confided to one friend, "I am terrified of them. Everywhere I turn, they are there, poking their cameras at me, asking me questions, following me whenever I step outside. I don't know how I'm going to cope." Diana was just 19 when she faced this ordeal, which continued for the rest of her life.*

At that point in his life, Prince Charles was under some pressure to find a suitable bride. As the future king of England, it was his duty to marry and to produce an heir. He had had many relationships with women in the past, but none that had led to marriage. At almost 33 years old, Charles was being pressured by his family, by the public, and by the British press. And Diana — young, vibrant, aristocratic, pretty, and with little experience with men — fit the bill perfectly.

At first, Diana and Charles managed to keep their new relationship a secret. But in September 1980, reporters spied Diana and Charles together at Balmoral, the 40,000-acre royal estate in Scotland. At first they didn't know who she was. But a British reporter soon identified Lady Diana Spencer as a romantic interest of the Prince. From that moment onward, until the time of her death, she was pursued by the press. Photographers and reporters followed her every step, trying to satisfy the insatiable demand — in Britain and around the world — for information about Diana.

Although she often appeared poised and confident throughout their courtship, Diana later said she felt terrorized by the relentless attention that reporters turned on her. They waited outside the door of her apartment in packs at all hours of the day and night, followed her every time she went out in her car, tracked down and interviewed all of her friends, and even called her in the middle of the night trying to get a reaction from her. She confided to one friend, "I am terrified of them. Everywhere I turn, they are there, poking their cameras at me, asking me questions, following me whenever I step outside. I don't know how I'm going to cope." Diana was just 19 when she faced this ordeal, which continued for the rest of her life.

Charles and Diana continued to date throughout 1980. In February 1981, Charles proposed to Diana over a candlelight dinner at Windsor Castle. He wanted to give her time to think about it, but she said yes right away. When the engagement was announced, he said "I feel positively delighted and frankly amazed that Di is prepared to take me on." Diana said, "With Prince Charles beside me I cannot go wrong." Prior to the wedding, Diana went to stay first at Clarence House, the home of the Queen Mother, and then at Buckingham Palace, to learn about royal protocol.

A FAIRY-TALE WEDDING

The marriage of Lady Diana Frances Spencer to Charles Philip Arthur George, Prince of Wales, took place on July 29, 1981. They were married in an Anglican service at London's St. Paul's Cathedral, the beautiful edifice designed three centuries earlier by Sir Christopher Wren, one of England's greatest architects. Diana rode with her father from Clarence House in a glass coach. Cheering onlookers lined the Strand along the two-mile route to the church, waiting for a glimpse of the young noblewoman who would one day be their queen. She arrived at St. Paul's to the thunderous applause of hundreds of thousands of British subjects. The ceremony was attended by 2,500 guests, and 750 million viewers around the world watched it on television.

The marriage service was performed by Dr. Robert Runcie, Archbishop of Canterbury, who described the wedding as "the stuff of which fairy tales are made." In a break with royal tradition, prayers were offered by Catholic and other non-Anglican clergymen. Three orchestras, three choirs, and opera singer Kiri Ti Kanawa provided majestic music for the lavish ceremony that came to be known as the "wedding of the century." Diana was attended by five young bridesmaids and two pageboys; Prince Charles was attended by his two brothers, Prince Andrew (now the Duke of York) and Prince Edward. All the bells of London pealed as the newlyweds rode from St. Paul's in an open landau (horse-drawn carriage) to Buckingham Palace. There, they had a private breakfast reception and a public appearance on the balcony of the palace that was widely photographed. With her marriage, Diana's full name became Diana, Princess of Wales, and she earned the right to be addressed as Her Royal Highness.

After the wedding, Diana and Charles lived at Kensington Palace in London and at Highgrove House in Gloucestershire. Diana had two sons within three years—"an heir and a spare"—which endeared her even further to the already enchanted nation. William Arthur Philip Louis (called Wills) was born on June 21, 1982, and Henry Charles Albert David (called Harry) was born on September 15, 1984. The children are second and third in line to the throne, after their father.

TROUBLE IN PARADISE

But by this point there were already serious problems in Diana's marriage. There was a public and a private side to Diana's life, and for many years only that public side was known to her many admirers. Then Andrew Morton, a British journalist, published a biography in 1992 called *Diana: Her True Story*. Morton offered a more intimate look at her life among the royal family. He said that he had spoken with people close to the princess, although he declined to name some of them. After Diana's death, Morton revealed that he had had her full cooperation and that, with the help of an intermediary, he had conducted extensive interviews with the princess herself. He also published transcripts of those interviews at that time, along with corrections that

Diana had made in the margins. Many of the details here about Diana's private life come from Morton's account, published first in 1992 and then republished in 1997 as *Diana: Her True Story, In Her Own Words*.

Beginning with her engagement to Prince Charles, Diana's public and private lives began to diverge. On the outside, it appeared that she was radiantly happy and in love with her prince. Except for her difficulties in dealing with the press, it seemed that she had neither a doubt nor care in the world. Her wedding seemed like a fairy tale come to life, and the births of her two sons confirmed the public view of domestic bliss. These appearances were very far from the truth.

In fact, Diana was having serious misgivings about the marriage well in advance of the wedding. During her engagement, as soon as she arrived at first Clarence House and then at Buckingham Palace, she felt isolated and estranged. She was offered no help by the her future husband's family or by staff members in learning royal protocol and appropriate behavior. She felt entirely unprepared for the role she was about to play. For of course, Diana was not just getting married — she was also becoming a future queen.

Diana was also having trouble coming to grips with the ongoing friendship between Prince Charles and Camilla Parker Bowles, a married woman who had been the prince's mistress. There were several different incidents during the days just before and after the wedding that confirmed her suspicions that Charles still cared for Camilla. For example, Diana once found a parcel that contained a bracelet Charles had selected with the initials F and G on it. Diana knew that F and G stood for Fred and Gladys, Charles and Camilla's pet names for each other. Another time, Diana found Charles wearing new gold cuff links with two Cs intertwined on them. When she confronted him, he admitted that they were a gift from Camilla. A bit later, Diana and Charles were looking through their calendars to compare appointments when two photos of Camilla fell out of his book. But throughout these incidents Charles denied that he and Camilla were still involved and belittled Diana's growing feelings of anger, resentment, betrayal, and hurt. Diana even confided her fears to her sisters, seriously considering whether she should call off the marriage. By that time, though, all the wedding preparations had been made. "Bad luck, Duch," her sisters said, using her family nickname. "Your face is on the tea-towels so you're too late to chicken out."

DEVELOPING BULIMIA AND OTHER EMOTIONAL PROBLEMS

On the night before her wedding, Diana had what was probably her first experience with bulimia. Bulimia is an eating disorder in which the individual, usually female, binges by eating large amounts of food and then purges by inducing vomiting. Often done in secret, binges are followed by mood swings characterized by guilt, depression, and self-hate. Sufferers are often afflicted with feelings of failure and low self-esteem. During dinner with her sister Jane on the night before her wedding, Diana ate everything she could, and then was sick later. This pattern continued for years to come. Soon she was making herself sick as many as five times a day.

Living among Charles's family exacerbated her problems. Neither he nor the other member of his family had any patience for or understanding of this emotionally volatile young woman. The situation worsened when Diana got pregnant with their first child, William, late in 1981. Pregnancy brought acute morning sickness, mood swings, and a continuation of bulimia. In addition, she had royal duties, like making a visit to Wales, that were physically taxing. In January 1982, Diana had an argument with her husband and threatened to kill herself. He didn't believe her and said he was going horseback riding. So she threw herself down a flight of stairs. Despite this desperate act, Charles still went riding. Fortunately, neither Diana nor the baby was hurt. There were several other incidents of this type: she threw herself against a glass cabinet, she slashed her wrists with a razor blade, and she cut her chest and legs with a penknife during an argument with her husband. As Diana later said, "They were desperate cries for help. I just needed time to adjust to my new position."

For Diana, it was a time of intense despair. The birth of each of her sons filled her with joy, but she also struggled with an acute case of postpartum depression. She spent most of the first years of her marriage during the early 1980s struggling with bulimia, depression, misery, and loneliness.

> *When she joined the campaign against land mines, she had this to say. "I am not a political figure, nor do I want to be one. But I come with my heart, and I want to bring awareness to people in distress, whether it's in Angola or any other part o f the world. The fact is, I'm a humanitarian figure. I always have been, and I always will be."*

DIANA'S LIFE AS A ROYAL

Becoming a member of the royal family meant a life of public duty. For Diana, that included many public appearances, both with and without Charles. As a representative of Great Britain, she made overseas trips to Australia, New Zealand, Norway, Italy, West Germany, Fiji, the United States, Austria, Japan, Portugal, France, Kuwait, the United Arab Emirates, Indonesia, Hong Kong, Nigeria, Hungary, and Belgium. At first, she was shy, afraid to speak in public, and uninformed about world events. With time, though, both her confidence and knowledge grew. Soon, she was writing speeches and giving them with confidence and style. The British people responded with devotion. Diana quickly became the most popular member of the royal family, which only added to the tensions in her marriage and in her relationships with the other royals.

Diana was also well known for her charity work. When she got involved with a charity, she didn't just serve as a figurehead. Instead, she would work tirelessly as a fundraiser, promoter, and public spokesperson. Some of her major interests were the children's charity Bernardo's, the Great Ormond Street Hospital for Children, the English National Ballet, the Royal Academy of Music, the Leprosy Mission, the National AIDS Trust, the Royal Marsden Hospital, Help the Aged, the National Meningitis Trust, and Centrepoint, a shelter for young people who are homeless, unemployed, drug addicts, or prostitutes. Diana had a remarkable ability to be genuine despite her lofty position and to connect personally with those she met. She showed deep compassion and personal courage. She reached out to touch a leper and a man with AIDS, when many people mistakenly believed that those diseases could be communicated by touch. She visited cancer patients, the homeless, AIDS sufferers, and others among the world's poor, downtrodden, and desperately ill. It was these works that earned her the tribute "Queen of people's hearts."

During both daytime charity work and evening gala events, Diana was always impeccably groomed and fashionably dressed. Her style evolved greatly over the years. When she first started out, as a very young woman, her clothes were frilly, fussy, and even dowdy. Later, her look became sleek, refined, modern, and glamorous. Her beauty and her personal style made her a favorite with the press, putting her picture on best-dressed lists and magazine covers. But her glamorous image also invited criticism, as many suggested that she was an empty-headed mannequin, concerned only with appearances and not with substance.

Diana combined her public responsibilities with her life as a mother. Both she and Charles had been raised in families where the relationships between parent and child were distant and formal. It was expected that William and Harry would be raised that way also, with an emphasis on tradition and family duty. But that's not what Diana wanted for her children. She was determined to raise her sons her own way. She didn't want to forsake their family heritage as members of Britain's royal family, but she did want to mix it with lots of love and lots of hugs. She didn't want the boys to lead a completely sheltered life; she wanted them to know what life was like for most people. So she took them to visit homeless shelters and hospitals, to see Disney World and McDonalds, and to enjoy amusement parks and white-water rafting.

THE FAIRY-TALE MARRIAGE COMES TO AN END

By the late 1980s, there was widespread speculation about the state of Charles and Diana's marriage. Although they continued their official engagements, they appeared cool and distant in public. British tabloid newspapers gleefully counted up their separate vacations and their rare private moments together. Sources at the palace suggested that they simply pursued different activities, with Charles enjoying life in the country and Diana preferring the city.

Diana talking with land mine victims in Angola

That pleasant image was soon crushed, though, with revelations in the press. The next several years saw a series of disclosures that dispelled the impression of a happy marriage. First came the 1992 biography by Andrew Morton, which discussed Diana's depression, bulimia, and suicidal tendencies throughout her marriage. Reports came out that Charles had resumed his affair with Camilla, and that Diana had had an affair with a military officer. In December 1992, the Prince and Princess of Wales formally separated. But the battle in the press didn't stop there. In an unprecedented move for a future king, Charles gave an interview on television in 1994 in which he confessed that he had cheated on his wife by having an affair with Camilla during his marriage and in which he implied that he never loved his wife. A year later Diana retaliated with her own TV interview. She frankly discussed her eating disorders, the problems in her marriage, and the affairs by both her and Charles. Almost acknowledging that she would never become queen of England, she expressed her desire to become "the queen of people's hearts."

In August 1996, Charles and Diana were officially divorced. In the terms of their divorce decree, she received a one-time payment of $26.5 million, $600,000 a year for her office staff, and an apartment at Kensington Palace. She would continue to be known as Diana, Princess of Wales, but she lost the title "Your Royal Highness." She and Charles were given joint custody of William and Harry, and both parents continued to raise the boys.

Diana went through a painful period immediately after the separation in which she withdrew from public life. After her divorce, she returned to public life, supporting a select group of charities that focused on AIDS, leprosy, homelessness, cancer research, the treatment of sick children, and the English National Ballet. She associated herself in particular with the Red Cross and with the international campaign to ban the manufacture and sale of land mines, a type of explosive device that is buried underground. Land mines are considered an especially deadly type of weapon because they are difficult to find and remove and because they continue to kill people — often civilians — long after the war has ended. Diana traveled to both Angola and Bosnia to bring publicity to her cause. When she joined the campaign against land mines, she had this to say. "I am not a political figure, nor do I want to be one. But I come with my heart, and I want to bring awareness to people in distress, whether it's in Angola or any other part of the world. The fact is, I'm a humanitarian figure. I always have been, and I always will be."

THE ACCIDENT

In the summer of 1997, Diana became romantically involved with Emad (Dodi) al-Fayed, a movie producer. He was the son of Mohamed al-Fayed, a well-known Egyptian multimillionaire who lived in London and who owned the famed Harrod's department store in London, the luxurious Ritz Hotel in Paris, and many other assets. Mohamed al-Fayed was a friend of Diana's father and stepmother, and it was he who first introduced Diana to his son, Dodi. Some observers questioned Dodi's suitability as a partner for the princess because he had had a succession of romantic involvements. Still, their romance blossomed during that summer. There has been speculation that Diana and Dodi were about to announce their engagement, but the truth will never be known.

On August 30, 1997, Diana and Dodi arrived in Paris. They had been vacationing together on a Mediterranean cruise, and they planned to spend one night in the French capital before Diana returned to England the next day to see her sons. After stopping at the Ritz Hotel to freshen up, they planned to go out to dinner at a fashionable French bistro and then spend the night at Dodi's apartment in Paris. Yet when they left the hotel, the French paparazzi (celebrity photographers) followed their every move. So they decided to eat at the hotel instead, where they could be assured of some privacy. After dinner, photographers were still waiting outside the hotel, hoping to get a shot of Diana with her new beau. So they made a fateful decision. One car, a decoy, would leave from the front, while a second car, a black Mercedes containing Diana and Dodi, would try to slip out unnoticed from the back. Diana and Dodi would be driven by Henri Paul, the deputy director of security for the Ritz Hotel, and accompanied by a bodyguard, Trevor Rees-Jones. They left the hotel shortly after midnight. The photographers quickly figured out the ruse, and several followed their car.

Much of what happened next, and why, is unclear. With several photographers in pursuit, Diana and Dodi's car set off on a high speed chase. The Mercedes entered a short traffic tunnel on a road along the Seine, near the Eiffel Tower. The car has been reported as traveling at speeds as high as 80 to 110 miles per hour. In the tunnel, the car went out of control. It hit the right wall, ricocheted

> **"**
>
> *Perhaps it was her brother who best summed up her appeal. In his funeral eulogy, Earl Spencer gave thanks for "the life of a woman I am so proud to be able to call my sister, the unique, the complex, the extraordinary and irreplaceable Diana, whose beauty, both internal and external, will never be extinguished from our minds."*
>
> **"**

diagonally across the road and hit a pillar in the center, and then came to rest facing the wrong way. Henri Paul and Dodi al-Fayed were killed instantly. Both Trevor Rees-Jones and Diana were seriously injured. Only Jones was wearing a seat belt in the crash, and only he survived the accident.

Diana was unconscious when rescue workers reached the scene. They rushed her to a Paris hospital and began providing emergency surgery. For three hours, they worked tirelessly to save her. Despite the excellent care, her wounds were too severe. Diana, Princess of Wales, died in Paris at 4:00 a.m. on August 31, 1997.

The Duke of Edinburgh, Prince William, Earl Spenser, Prince Harry, and Prince Charles outside Westminster Abbey during the funeral procession for Diana

THE AFTERMATH

The reaction to Diana's death was swift and profound. People around the world were shocked at the news of the senseless tragedy. Their thoughts turned in sorrow to her two sons, bereft of their mother. In Britain, the whole nation mourned, united in their grief. In London, Diana's home at Kensington Palace was quickly turned into a shrine as thousands placed bouquets of flowers outside the gates. Many personal tributes, loving notes, and even stuffed animals accompanied the sea of flowers. Prime minister Tony Blair expressed the feelings of many when he said, "She was the people's princess and that's how she will stay, how she will remain, in our hearts and in our memories for ever."

There were many unresolved issues following the accident. One, in particular, is the cause of the accident. French police have been conducting a thorough investigation, and the results have not yet been announced. But some information has been disclosed. Initially, many believed that the photographers following the princess were somehow at fault for the crash, and they were harshly criticized. Yet recent reports contradict this view. Police are looking for a second car, a white Fiat, that may have been involved. But investigators currently believe that the primary cause of the accident was that the driver, Henri Paul, was drunk; his blood alcohol level was three times the legal limit. The accident happened, they say, because the driver got drunk, drove too fast, and lost control of the car. Another devastating accident because of a drunk driver. And to compound the tragedy, both Diana and Dodi might well have survived if they had been wearing their seat belts.

Another unresolved issue is the effect of Diana's death on the future of the British monarchy. The British people are divided in their opinions on whether the monarchy should continue to exist. Recent polls indicate that less than half of the nation currently supports the monarchy. Her death, observers say, focused attention on her criticism of the royal family and inspired a national call for change. According to Polly Toynbee, "Diana the dead may threaten their stability and tranquility as strongly if not more so than the divorced Diana they could not silence. Diana the difficult was a problem the palace could tackle, but Saint Diana is something it can never contend with." Diana was the most popular and most loved of the British royals, and her style was completely original. She was considered warm, accessible, caring, and interested in the lives of regular British people, whereas the other members of the royal family are considered cold, formal, distant, and bound by tradition. Columnist Julie Burchill highlighted the differences between Diana and Charles, saying that she "took to royal life like a champion and for one brief shining moment made sense of it all while her husband with every flinch and faux pas made it painfully obvious that he found it increasingly difficult to love his people or do his duty." But others were cheered by the royal family's response to the tragedy, when Queen Elizabeth made a public statement on television and several members of the royal family, including William and Harry, stopped at Kensington Palace to witness the floral tribute. As the *Times of London* suggested, these actions were "the first glimpse of a monarchy which was at last learning the lesson of the Princess's life: that it should be responsive and spontaneous—and not afraid to show that it, too, has a heart."

The city of London, the nation of England, and the world mourned together for a full week until Diana's funeral at Westminster Abbey on September 6, 1997. A horse-drawn carriage bore her body from Kensington Palace to Westminster Abbey along a three-mile route that was lined with mourners. For part of the way, the carriage was followed by the male members of her family: her sons, Prince William and Prince Harry; her brother, Earl Spencer; her ex-husband, Prince Charles; and her former father-in-law, Prince Philip, the Duke of Edinburgh. About 1,900 people attended the funeral, bringing together people from all parts of her life: members of royalty, movie and rock stars, fashion designers, and representatives of the charities that Diana supported. Millions more gathered in London parks and streets to listen to the service. More than two billion people around the world watched it on TV. In addition to prayers, the funeral included Diana's favorite hymns selected by her sons, poems read by her sisters, and a song tribute, "Candle in the Wind," sung by her good friend Elton John. There was also a moving and outspoken eulogy by her brother, Earl Spencer, that celebrated her independent spirit, saying "she needed no royal title to continue to generate her particular brand of magic." He also attacked those who had mistreated her, including the royal family and the press. "I don't think she ever understood why her genuinely good intentions were sneered at by the media, why there appeared to be a permanent quest . . . to bring her down," Spencer said. "My own, and only explanation is that genuine goodness is threatening to those at the opposite end of the moral spectrum." Following the funeral, Diana's body was laid to rest at Althorp, on a small island in an ornamental lake on the family estate. "She used to enjoy the quiet there," said Betty Andrew, a former housekeeper for the Spencer family. "It's a very peaceful place, among the trees and the birds. Very peaceful."

It's been difficult for many to explain how and why Diana touched so many people so deeply. In *Newsweek*, Michael Elliott offered this view. "She was beautiful, of course; she was young, and she was royal. In the shock of her death, the world struggled to reconcile the contradictory sources of her appeal: the Princess of Wales was both a pop icon and mother of kings, a very modern woman who owed her fame to the most archaic of institutions. Her secret was that she was all these things. Her death was followed by one of the most extraordinary outpourings of grief that the modern world has ever seen. In her own country, this woman of the most British stock imaginable became the focus of a display of raw emotion that mocked Britain's stereotypical image. Earl Spencer, her brother, in his eulogy at the funeral, wisely warned against sanctifying her memory; but as they laid their tributes before her home or threw them in the path of her cortege, the British had already made her their Lady of the Flowers."

Perhaps it was her brother who best summed up her appeal. In his funeral eulogy, Earl Spencer gave thanks for "the life of a woman I am so proud to be able to call my sister, the unique, the complex, the extraordinary and irreplaceable Diana, whose beauty, both internal and external, will never be extinguished from our minds."

FURTHER READING

Books

Davies, Nicholas. *Diana: A Princess and Her Troubled Marriage*, 1995
———. *Diana: The Lonely Princess*, 1996
Fairley, Josephine. *Crown Princess: A Biography of Diana*, 1992
Morton, Andrew. *Diana: Her New Life*, 1995
———. *Diana: Her True Story, In Her Own Words*, 1997
Seward, Ingrid. *Diana: An Intimate Portrait*, 1992

Periodicals

Current Biography Yearbook 1983

Independent, Sep. 1, 1997, p.12; Sep. 7, 1997, Features section

Life, Nov. 1997, p.61

New York Times, Aug. 31, 1997, Section 1, p.1; Sep. 1, 1997, p.A8; Sep. 3, 1997, p.A10; Sep. 4, 1997, p.A1; Sep. 5, 1997, p.A1; Sep. 6, 1997, Section 1, p.1; Sep.7, 1997, Section 1, p.1

New Yorker, Sep.15, 1997, p.50

Newsweek, Sep. 8, 1997, p.26; Sep. 15, 1997, p.24 (and other articles); Dec. 22, 1997, p.60

Newsweek, Fall 1997 (Commemorative Issue)

People, Sep. 15, 1997, p.56 (and other articles); Sep. 22, 1997, p.52 (and other articles); Oct. 13, 1997, p.96; Oct. 20, 1997, p.102

People, Fall 1997 (Special Tribute Issue)

Time, Sep. 8, 1997, p.30 (and other articles); Sep. 15, 1997, p.30 (and other articles)

Time for Kids, Sep. 12, 1997, p.4

Times of London, Sep. 1, 1997; Sep. 6, 1997; Sep. 7, 1997

TV Guide, Sep. 2, 1997, pp.16 and 20

WORLD WIDE WEB SITES

http://www.royal.gov.uk
http://www.princessdiana.com

Leonardo DiCaprio 1974-

American Actor
Star of the Hit Films *William Shakespeare's Romeo and Juliet* and *Titanic*

BIRTH

Leonardo Wilhelm DiCaprio was born in Hollywood, California, on November 11, 1974. His German-born mother, Irmelin, worked as a legal secretary and his father, George, was a performance artist and comic book distributor. The DiCaprios split up when their son was only one year old, but they remained good friends. Both stayed in Los Angeles so they could raise their young son together. Leonardo stayed primarily with his mother, but he saw his father frequently. Both parents eventually gave up their jobs to help manage his acting career. Leonardo has a stepbrother, Adam Farrar, who is now in his late 20s.

Leonardo was named after the famous Italian Renaissance painter Leonardo DaVinci. DiCaprio's mother was visiting a museum in Italy while she was pregnant. She was looking at a painting by DaVinci when she first felt her unborn baby kick. Thinking he might grow up to be a painter some day, she named him Leonardo.

YOUTH

Leonardo (whose close friends call him Leo) grew up surrounded by crime and drug addiction in a very rough section of Hollywood. It was clear to him at an early age that he would have to stay focused and come up with a plan for doing something better with his life. His parents went out of their way to create a good environment for their son. They read to him and took him to museums. With his mother, DiCaprio traveled to Germany several times to visit his grandparents.

DiCaprio displayed a gift for mimicry when he was very young. Every time his mother's friends came to the house to visit, he would do impressions of them as soon as they left. "My mom would laugh until she was red in the face," he remembers.

When he was five years old, DiCaprio appeared on his favorite television program, "Romper Room." He was so excited about being there that he was completely out of control. He kept running up and grabbing the camera and trying to pull his mother out of the audience to join him. His behavior was so disruptive that he was finally thrown off the set.

EDUCATION

DiCaprio's parents wanted to keep him away from some of the rougher kids in his Hollywood neighborhood, so Irmelin DiCaprio drove her son an hour each way to attend an elementary school in nearby Westwood. DiCaprio describes himself as "the nuttiest little kid" in school. He was always entertaining his classmates by doing somersaults, tap-dancing, break-dancing, and lip-synching.

In middle school one day, he created quite a stir with his impersonation of Charles Manson, a deeply disturbed man who was convicted of a series of high-profile murders in the 1960s. DiCaprio's performance was so convincing that it alarmed his teachers, and his father had to explain that it was only an imitation. By the time he was in ninth grade, his teachers started to recognize his talent. "You couldn't help but gravitate toward what he did," his drama teacher recalls. "When he did his monologue, it was so moving that he had the class in tears."

DiCaprio attended John Marshall High School in Los Angeles and the Center for Enriched Studies, but he admits that he was never much of a student. "I could never focus on things I didn't want to learn," he explains. "I just could not sit and do homework." He was getting regular work as an actor by the time he was in 11th grade and managed to finish high school with the help of a private tutor. At present, he has no plans to attend college.

FIRST JOBS

As a child, DiCaprio always enjoyed performing. But he didn't give much thought to acting until his stepbrother, Adam, appeared in a cereal commercial, from which he earned $50,000. At age 10, DiCaprio begged his father to take him to a talent agent, who rejected the young boy because he didn't like his haircut. Another agent suggested he change his name to Lenny Williams because his real name sounded "too ethnic." Finally, a friend of his mother's who had worked for a talent agency helped him find an agent. His parents drove him to more than 50 auditions before he landed a role in a commercial for Matchbox toy cars.

> By the time he was in ninth grade, his teachers started to recognize his talent. "You couldn't help but gravitate toward what he did," his drama teacher recalls. "When he did his monologue, it was so moving that he had the class in tears."

DiCaprio continued to do commercials for things like toys, cereal, and bubble gum, and he also started acting in educational films with titles like *How To Deal With a Parent Who Takes Drugs* and *Mickey's Safety Club.* In 1990, he landed a small part in the TV sitcom "Parenthood," based on the 1989 hit movie of the same name. But the show was canceled after only four months, leaving DiCaprio without a job. He finally accepted a role in *Critters 3* (1991), the third in a series of cult horror films. "It was one of the worst films of all time," DiCaprio confesses. Although it was a good learning experience, he was determined not to get involved in a similar project again.

The following year, DiCaprio won a role on the popular television series, "Growing Pains," which was already in its last season. He played Luke Brower, a homeless 15-year-old who is eventually adopted by the Seaver family. Although the show ended in 1992, DiCaprio attracted considerable attention and began appearing on the covers of teen magazines.

CAREER HIGHLIGHTS

This Boy's Life

DiCaprio was vacationing in Germany with his mother when he received the news that he had been chosen to play Toby in *This Boy's Life* (1993). Only 17, he was chosen from more than 400 young actors who auditioned for the part. *This Boy's Life* was based on the best-selling memoir by Tobias Wolff about growing up in the 1950s. In the movie, Toby and his recently divorced mother, Caroline (played by Ellen Barkin), drive across the country to the Pacific Northwest, where they hope to start a new life. But then Caroline meets and marries Dwight (played by Robert De Niro), who moves them to the grim, isolated town of Concrete, Washington. The movie portrays Toby's relationship with his physically and emotionally abusive stepfather, who mocks everything he says and criticizes his every action.

DiCaprio got the role of Toby, in part, because legendary actor Robert De Niro singled him out. De Niro thought that Leonardo lacked the mannerisms that many young actors use to mask their true emotions. Although DiCaprio was intimidated by De Niro's "tough guy" reputation, he discovered that the older actor was really very gentle and considerate. The script called for frequent physical fights between the two, and DiCaprio suffered a few bruises. But he emerged from the filming of *A Boy's Life* with a tremendous feeling of respect for De Niro and a strong determination to put television work behind him and concentrate on feature films. DiCaprio won rave notices for his performance, and director Michael Caton-Jones explains why. "He has this amazing ability to convey quite complex emotions," Caton-Jones said "All I wanted him to do was to be a kid. He did that magnificently."

What's Eating Gilbert Grape?

While *This Boy's Life* represented a breakthrough for DiCaprio, it was his role in *What's Eating Gilbert Grape?* that won him the respect and admiration of movie audiences across the country. The plot of this the offbeat 1993 comedy-drama revolves around a young man, Gilbert (played by Johnny Depp), who struggles to help his family survive, even though his 500-pound mother refuses to leave the house. DiCaprio portrays Gilbert's mentally impaired younger brother, Arnie, a boy whose brain can't keep up with his spirit. He prepared for the role by spending several days at a home for mentally disabled teenagers in Texas, then combining the behaviors he observed there with his own ideas about the character of Arnie.

DiCaprio almost didn't get the part, according to director Lasse Hallstrom, because he was too good-looking. But once he got into the role, it was clear that he could handle what the part required. He vomited, drooled, spit out his food, sobbed, twitched, and picked his nose — all while showing a spontaneous and

Claire Danes with DiCaprio in William Shakespeare's Romeo and Juliet

exuberant love of life. The result was an extraordinary and utterly real character. DiCaprio's powerful performance received both an Academy Award
nomination and a Golden Globe nomination for Best Supporting Actor.

In *This Boy's Life* and *Gilbert Grape*, DiCaprio began to show the talent for
which he is recognized today. Michael Caton-Jones, his director in *This Boy's
Life*, explained it like this after seeing *Gilbert Grape*. "He's going to be what we
call in England the thinking woman's crumpet. He'll do intelligent material
with depth, feel, and range, but he'll also have a lot of sex appeal. I saw his
performance in *Gilbert Grape*—that's what separates movie stars from everyday actors, the ability to take a flying moment of madness." After visiting him
on the set of a movie, Jesse Green explained his appeal in the *New York Times
Magazine*: "[When] rehearsal begins, it's DiCaprio you watch: his movements
are smallest, his stillness is deepest, his lines are tossed farthest away. His
acting is effortless and, in the best way, unschooled—which may be what
makes people behave oddly around him. It's as if he were a talisman, imbued
with dark magic. How else to explain his unnerving affinity for troubled characters? Plucked at 17 from the insipid "Growing Pains" to play the abused
stepson in *This Boy's Life*, he stole the movie from Robert De Niro. Then, as
the retarded brother in *What's Eating Gilbert Grape*, he transformed a grab bag
of schoolyard stereotypes into an achingly lyrical portrait of a misfit."

After his heartfelt portrayal in *Gilbert Grape*, DiCaprio went on to *The Quick and the Dead* (1995), a satiric western starring Sharon Stone, Gene Hackman, and Russell Crowe. DiCaprio played a Billy-the-Kid-style outlaw who is gunned down by his own father in a duel. The movie itself was not a box-office success, and it's not one of the films that he likes to talk about.

Controversial Roles

DiCaprio's next and most controversial role was in *The Basketball Diaries* (1995). This film was based on Jim Carroll's 1978 memoir, a cult classic about growing up in New York City as a teenage basketball star whose future as an athlete is destroyed when he becomes a heroin addict. "What Leo brings naturally to the role," the director Scott Kalvert said, "is a pure, angelic quality. He can do the horrible things this character does and people will still care about him." To prepare for his role as the young Jim Carroll, DiCaprio talked to drug counselors and studied videotapes of people coping with the agony of withdrawal from drugs. His graphic performance, which showed the depths of degradation of a drug addict, was so memorable that many people assumed it was based on personal experience. But DiCaprio declared that he had never taken drugs and that the movie's strong anti-drug message was one of the reasons he wanted to be in the film. And in fact, viewers found the film to be very powerful. Janet Maslin of the *New York Times* had this to say about his performance: "DiCaprio may harden into a practiced Hollywood actor someday, but for the moment he's a stunning natural performer who hides nothing, with the wrenching expressiveness of a latter-day James Dean."

DiCaprio also played a drug addict in *Total Eclipse* (1995), which was based on the life of the 19th-century French poet, Arthur Rimbaud. The film explores the love affair between Rimbaud and his mentor, the poet Paul Verlaine, who was ten years older. DiCaprio describes the role as "one of the most important of my career." *Total Eclipse* brought DiCaprio his first bad reviews. But he didn't regret making the film, and his strong performance as the French poet surprised even director Agnieszka Holland. "[He's] like a medium," she says. "He opens his body and his mind to receive messages coming from another person's life." Even though neither *Total Eclipse* nor *The Basketball Diaries* did particularly well at the box office, they gave DiCaprio a chance to develop his acting style and to prove he could tackle risky and controversial roles with ease.

William Shakespeare's Romeo and Juliet

DiCaprio's next big film was *William Shakespeare's Romeo and Juliet*. When award-winning Australian director Baz Luhrmann first approached DiCaprio about playing Romeo in an updated version of Shakespeare's play, the young actor was hesitant. "I didn't want to be leaping around in tights," he explains.

Luhrmann assured him that this would be a contemporary version of the romantic tragedy about true love gone awry when the son and daughter of two warring families fall in love. The characters would use Shakespeare's Elizabethan language but would live in a world of rock music and hip clothes and carry guns instead of swords. The action takes place not in Verona, Italy, but instead in Verona Beach, a fictional violent resort town that looks like Miami. The two families, the Capulets and the Montagues, are warring street gangs. With its quick-cut editing, designer costumes, violence, hip soundtrack, and speedy pacing, the film was described as Shakespeare for the MTV audience.

The contemporary spin on the story appealed to DiCaprio, but he still wanted to have a say in who was cast as Juliet. Luhrmann let him audition with most of the actresses who wanted the part, but he was unimpressed with their dreamy expressions and eyelash-batting approach to the role. Only Claire Danes—then best known as Angela Chase in the TV series, "My So-Called Life"—spoke her lines directly to him. "It was a little shocking, but it impressed me because most of the other girls auditioned looked off into the sky. Claire was right there, in front of my face, saying every line with power," DiCaprio recalls.

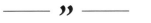

> "DiCaprio may harden into a practiced Hollywood actor someday, but for the moment he's a stunning natural performer who hides nothing, with the wrenching expressiveness of a latter-day James Dean."
>
> Janet Maslin, *New York Times*

DiCaprio and Danes (see the entry on Danes in *Biography Today*, September 1997) filmed *Romeo and Juliet* in Mexico City. He kept everyone on the set entertained between takes by doing cartwheels, dancing to hip-hop music, and impersonating Michael Jackson—much like the young boy who had amused his classmates with his imitations and break-dancing a decade earlier. The movie was a big hit, particularly with teen audiences. It eventually earned more than any other screen adaptation of a Shakespearean play since Franco Zeffirelli's 1968 version of the tragic love story.

After *Romeo and Juliet*, DiCaprio played another rebellious teenager in the family drama *Marvin's Room* (1996), with co-stars Meryl Streep, Diane Keaton, and Robert De Niro. DiCaprio appeared as the troubled son of Meryl Streep. He played a pyromaniac, someone who enjoys playing with fire. While DiCaprio was beginning to earn a reputation for sensitive portrayals of troubled young people, he didn't mind, at that point, being cast repeatedly in teenage roles. "People get into trouble forcing themselves into adulthood,"

Kate Winslet with DiCaprio in Titanic

he said at the time. "I'm going to do whatever teenage roles I can. After all, I'll never be able to play those roles again."

Titanic

Although DiCaprio had starred in a number of critically acclaimed films, none had prepared him for the unprecedented commercial success of his next venture: playing the romantic lead in James Cameron's *Titanic* (1997). The most expensive movie ever made, *Titanic* told the tragic story of the ocean liner that left Southampton, England, on April 10, 1912, on its way to New York City with 2,223 people aboard. The ship struck an iceberg in the North Atlantic during the early morning hours of April 15, 1922. Although it was considered unsinkable, it quickly sank to the bottom. More than 1,500 men, women, and children plunged to their death. At 3 hours, 14 minutes, the movie *Titanic* lasts just slightly longer than the 2 hours, 40 minutes it took for the real boat to sink.

DiCaprio and Winslet in the flooded first class reception area in Titanic

The story of the *Titanic* has become a legend, featured in movies, songs, and even a recent Broadway musical. "The tragedy of *Titanic* has assumed an almost mythic quality in our collective imagination," Cameron has said. "But the passage of time has robbed it of its human face and vitality. I hope that Rose and Jack's relationship will be a kind of an emotional lightening rod, if you will, allowing viewers to invest their minds and their hearts to make history come alive." And many critics and viewers alike felt that DiCaprio's performance accomplished exactly that. "[*Titanic*] is a spectacular achievement," Cathy Horyn wrote in *Vanity Fair*, "a film that is intimate and grand, turbulent and beautiful, but — above all, breathtakingly realistic. When DiCaprio's character, dressed in dazzling white-tie, spirits his wealthy new love to steerage for a rambunctious evening that ends in the backseat of a stored Rolls, he becomes a star of the first order and the exuberant heart of the picture."

In *Titanic*, DiCaprio plays the part of Jack Dawson, a young penniless artist who has just spent several years in Europe and who wins his passage back home in a poker game. He is traveling in steerage, the section of the ship with the cheapest tickets and the poorest passengers. On board, Jack meets and falls in love with Rose DeWitt Bukater (played by Kate Winslet), a first-class passenger who is returning home to Philadelphia with her mother and her wealthy fiancé to make final preparations for her wedding. The story explores the effect of class and money on these two young lovers. Told from the point of view of Rose, it also details her gradual transformation, with the help of her lover, from a dependent young woman tied to the conventions of her era to someone who is strong, independent, and free-spirited.

Preparing for and filming *Titanic* was quite an ordeal. The film makers spent five years doing research to ensure the historical accuracy of each detail—the layout and design of the ship, the carpeting and chandeliers, the furniture and china, the clothing and luggage, even the manners and behavior of the passengers and crew. Filming took place in Baja California, where a nearly life-size replica of the ship was built in a special 17-million-gallon tank at the water's edge. The replica was 775 feet long—only 10% smaller than the original ship. The camera operators sat on cranes suspended high about the set of the ship. There were many difficult sequences to shoot. For example, the First Class Dining Saloon and the Grand Staircase were built on a hydraulic platform at the bottom of a 30-foot deep tank. It was designed to be angled and flooded with 5-million gallons of filtered seawater. For the final stages of the disaster, the ship was separated into two pieces. At one point, right before the boat goes down for good, the bow of the ship descends into the water, sending the stern straight up in a vertical position. To recreate this, they built a deck on a special tilting platform—on a giant seesaw—at the edge of the tank. Here, DiCaprio describes one experience in filming these special effects. "I remember how they got one scene

Tim Rothman, president of production at 20th Century Fox, explained DiCaprio's on-screen appeal like this. "What you have in Leo is a gigantic star—and remember, he's a star worldwide—who's somehow able to open himself up on screen and let you in emotionally. You feel what his character in Titanic *feels. The same with Romeo. It's not just a question of good looks; there are plenty of good-looking guys out there. On the screen he's emotionally accessible. How many actors are like that?"*

ready in about two hours, and all of a sudden I'm being, like, towed up on the back of a poop deck with a harness around my waist. There's like, 200 extras ready to fall off and hit the cushioned girders. And then there's three cranes around us with huge spotlights. Kate and I just looked at each other, like, 'How did we get here?'" The visual effects shots were tremendous, giving audiences a vivid feeling of what it must have been like to have been trapped on the doomed ship.

DiCaprio had been hesitant about getting involved in a "big budget" movie that would rely heavily on special effects. He worried that the movie would be a disaster, and it took him three months to make up his mind to accept the role of Jack. Obviously, DiCaprio had nothing to worry about. The movie garnered four Golden Globe awards, including Best Picture, Best Director, Best Original Score, and Best Original Song. The movie also garnered 14 nominations for Academy Awards (Oscars). It went on to win eleven awards, including Best Picture and Director, plus nine additional awards for technical achievements in the areas of art direction, cinematography, costumes, sound effects, visual effects, editing, and music. With eleven Academy Awards, *Titanic* tied the record held by the 1959 movie *Ben Hur.*

DiCaprio didn't receive an Academy Award nomination for his performance in *Titanic.* But the film made him, at age 23, an international star. When *Titanic* premiered at the Tokyo Film Festival, guards were needed to protect him from the thousands of young female fans surrounding the theater. Many of them had stood in line for up to three nights, hoping to catch a glimpse of the young American actor. Since then, the movie has become a phenomenon. The love story between Jack and Rose has attracted legions of devoted fans who have seen the film several times each. And the special effects of the sinking ship keep them on the edge of their seats. By late March 1998, the movie had made over $1.2 billion worldwide. It has surpassed *Star Wars, ET: The Extra-Terrestrial,* and *Jurassic Park* to become the highest-grossing film ever. *Titanic* is now the biggest money-maker in movie history.

Current Projects

DiCaprio's most recent film is *The Man in the Iron Mask* (1998), based on the 19th-century French novel by Alexandre Dumas and featuring the Four Musketeers. He plays a dual role as King Louis XIV of France and his imprisoned twin brother. His co-stars in the film include several famous actors: Jeremy Irons, Gerard Depardieu, Gabriel Byrne, and John Malkovich. When the film open, *Titanic* was still the No. 1 film in the country, but *Man in the Iron Mask* shared the spot that first week, with each film grossing $17.5 million. The director, Randall Wallace, had this to say about DiCaprio's performance. "Most actors are like people. They're actually scared to play roles in which they portray openness and heroism, because they have an inherent and unusually unspoken fear that to attempt such a role would be to reveal their own inherent shallowness and cowardice. So actors hide behind quirkiness and cynicism. No one would accuse Leo of that. Cynicism is the last thing that he's about."

DiCaprio is also reported to be working on a film called *Bombshell,* based on the true story of a young physicist who is said to have leaked atomic secrets to the Soviet Union. There have been persistent rumors that DiCaprio will play

The Man in the Iron Mask

the legendary 1950s movie idol James Dean, to whom he has often been compared, but there is no indication that such a project is under way.

Yet DiCaprio consistently resists being called an idol. He is adamant that he wants to be seen as an actor, not a screen idol. Tim Rothman, president of production at 20th Century Fox, explained his on-screen appeal like this. "What you have in Leo is a gigantic star — and remember, he's a star world-wide — who's somehow able to open himself up on screen and let you in emotionally. You feel what his character in *Titanic* feels. The same with Romeo. It's not just a question of good looks; there are plenty of good-looking guys out there. On the screen he's emotionally accessible. How many actors are like that?"

HOME AND FAMILY

DiCaprio's name has been linked with a number of young models (Bridget Hall, Bijou Phillips, and Kristine Zang) and actresses (Alicia Silverstone, Liv Tyler, and Sara Gilbert). Still, he remains single and tries to keep his private life out of the press. He is very close to both of his parents and recently built his mother a new house in West Virginia. "My parents are so much a part of my life, they're like my legs," DiCaprio says. Mark Wahlberg (also known as

Marky Mark), who starred with DiCaprio in *The Basketball Diaries,* adds, "He has a lot of family support. They keep him sane." Since moving out of his mother's house in 1995, DiCaprio has lived in a Los Angeles bungalow with his pet bearded-dragon lizard.

CREDITS

"Parenthood," 1990 (TV series)
"Growing Pains," 1991 (TV series)
Critters 3, 1991
Poison Ivy, 1992
This Boy's Life, 1993
What's Eating Gilbert Grape? 1993
The Foot Shooting Party, 1994
The Quick and the Dead, 1995
The Basketball Diaries, 1995
Total Eclipse, 1995
William Shakespeare's Romeo and Juliet, 1996
Marvin's Room, 1996
Titanic, 1997
The Man in the Iron Mask, 1998

FURTHER READING

Books

Catalano, Grace. *Leonardo DiCaprio: Modern-Day Romeo,* 1997 (juvenile)

Periodicals

Current Biography Yearbook 1997
Entertainment Weekly, Mar. 24, 1995, p.6; Mar. 6, 1998, p.38
Harper's Bazaar, Nov. 1995, p.220
Interview, June 1994, p.58
Los Angeles Times, Dec. 14, 1997, Calendar section, p.6
Mademoiselle, Apr. 1995, p.98
New York Times, Mar. 16, 1998, p.B1
New York Times Magazine, Feb. 12, 1995, p.28
Newsweek, Apr. 5, 1993, p.56; Feb. 23, 1998, p.58
People, Dec. 9, 1996, p.119; Jan. 26, 1998, p.98
Premiere, Oct. 1996, p.89
Teen, Mar. 1997, p.34; Sep. 1997, p.64
US, Jan. 1994, p.84
Vanity Fair, Jan. 1998, p.70

ADDRESS

Addis Wechsler and Associates
955 S. Carrillo Drive, 3rd Floor
Los Angeles, CA 90048

WORLD WIDE WEB SITES

http://www.titanicmovie.com
http://www.leonardodicaprio.com

Walter E. Diemer 1904?-1998

American Accountant and Inventor
Creator of the First Bubble Gum

EARLY LIFE

Walter E. Diemer was born in about 1904 in Philadelphia, Pennsylvania, where he lived for most of his life. As a young man he went to work for the Fleer Company, which manufactured candy and chewing gum. He started working there as an accountant in about 1926, just a few years after his high school graduation. He continued with Fleer for about 45 years. He married as a young man, and he and his wife, Adelaide, had two children, a son and a daughter.

MAJOR ACCOMPLISHMENTS

Creating Bubble Gum

Chewing gum has been around in America since 1870. But nobody had created bubble gum until Walter Diemer came along. In 1928, the Fleer Company was not doing well financially. Employees had been told at the company Christmas party that business was so bad that they might not have jobs by the next Christmas. So everybody was looking for ways to cut costs and save money. One possible savings was in their use of pre-packaged ingredients.

At that time, the company made chewing gum by purchasing a pre-made gum base and mixing that with their own flavors and colors. The company president thought that he could save money by making the gum base more cheaply on his own. He set up a kettle in the lab next to Diemer's office and started experimenting with mixing and cooking different combinations of ingredients. One day, while working on a batch, he was called to the phone. At that time the company only had one phone — in the main office, which was two flights down from the lab. When the president got a call while he was working in the lab, they would page him over the intercom. As he left to take the phone, he asked Diemer to keep an eye on his mixture.

Over time, the president lost interest in his experiments. But Diemer kept at it. He had no background in chemistry, so he just kept cooking up different combinations of ingredients through trial and error. He would chew a wad from each batch to check on its texture and taste.

One day he noticed that a particular mixture was bubbling fiercely. When he tested it, he found that it was soft and pliable, and he could blow huge bubbles. And unlike some of his earlier attempts, it didn't stick to his face when it popped. "I had it!" Diemer later recalled. "Everybody tried some. We were blowing bubbles all over the office. Everyone said: 'What a great product!' and it really went to our heads. We were blowing bubbles and prancing all over the place!" But the next day, when they tried it again, it had hardened. "Wouldn't blow a bubble worth a darn," he said. Diemer thought it might have something to do with the temperature. So he went back to work, and four months later came up with another successful batch. For flavoring, he used a mix of wintergreen, peppermint, vanilla, and cinnamon — the primary flavor ingredients that are still used in bubble gum to this day.

In December 1928, Diemer was ready to mix the first batch of bubble gum. They dumped 300 pounds of ingredients into the mixer. "I was young, very self-conscious," he recalls, "and all the help was standing around looking skeptical. They just stared disapprovingly and I was certain they were all thinking, 'That crazy kid. That stuff he made is going to break the blades in our mixing machines.' Well, the machines started groaning, and the mix started popping and then . . . I realized I'd forgotten to put any coloring in the gum." He fixed that mistake the next day with the second batch. "Pink food coloring was the only one I had at hand. And that's the reason ever since, all over the world, that bubble gum has been predominantly pink."

———— " ————

"I was young, very self-conscious," he recalls, "and all the help was standing around looking skeptical. They just stared disapprovingly and I was certain they were all thinking, 'That crazy kid. That stuff he made is going to break the blades in our mixing machines.' Well, the machines started groaning, and the mix started popping and then . . . I realized I'd forgotten to put any coloring in the gum. . . . Pink food coloring was the only one I had at hand. And that's the reason ever since, all over the world, that bubble gum has been predominantly pink."

———— " ————

As soon as that batch was finished, they made their first test of the popularity of their new product. They cut the gum into pieces, wrapped it with a machine used to package salt water taffy, and sent 100 pieces of gum down to a nearby small grocery story. Called Dubble Bubble, the gum sold out in one afternoon. This good fortune surprised Diemer, and everybody else at Fleer. "I was conditioned to failure. Everything we had tried [at Fleer] didn't work." But the gum was a huge success. "We sold over a million and a half dollars worth that first year. People were knocking at our back door to get it. The biggest problem was getting the taffy wrapper machines to package the gum so we could keep up with demand." Even as the Great Depression got underway, people still wanted their penny bubble gum. Diemer started traveling around the East Coast, trying to find enough factories to keep up with demand. He had to teach the company salesmen how to blow bubbles so they could demonstrate the product as they traveled from store to store.

Diemer's invention has proven to be a great success. Fleer never patented the gum, and eventually other companies started to make their own versions. Bubble gum sales have grown consistently over the years, and today, bubble gum sales top $600 million each year. Here are some statistics to ponder the next time you're chewing gum.

The amount of bubble gum that Americans have chewed over the years would make a stick 113 million miles long—long enough to reach the moon and back 200 times. And every day, Americans expend enough energy chewing bubble gum to light a city of 10 million people.

Diemer stayed on with Fleer until his retirement in 1970. At that time he was a senior vice president and member of the Board of Directors of Fleer Corporation; he continued to serve on the Board of Director after retiring. He and his wife moved to Ocean City, New Jersey, and later relocated to a retirement village in Lancaster, Pennsylvania, where he became known for riding around the complex on a big tricycle and for entertaining children with big boxes of bubble gum. His own two children both died in 1986, and his wife Adelaide died just a few years later, in 1990. In 1996 he was remarried. At the age of 91, Diemer married 74-year-old Florence Freeman Kohler, an artist and fellow resident of the retirement village. Walter Diemer died of heart failure on January 8, 1998.

FURTHER READING

Books

Hendrickson, Robert. *The Great American Chewing Gum Book*, 1976

Periodicals

Lancaster (Pennsylvania) New Era, July 13, 1990, p.A10; Aug. 15, 1992, p.A1
Lancaster (Pennsylvania) Sunday News, July 15, 1990, p.G1
New York Times, Jan. 12, 1998, p.A17
Smithsonian, July 1990, p.74

Ruth Handler 1916-

American Businesswoman and Cofounder of
Mattel, Inc.
Creator of the Barbie Doll

BIRTH

Ruth Mosko Handler was born on November 4, 1916, in Denver,
Colorado. Her parents were Jacob and Ida Mosko. Jacob originally worked as a blacksmith shoeing horses, and he later set up
a business making custom truck bodies.

Jacob and Ida Mosko were immigrants from Warsaw, Poland. In
the early 1900s, the Russians occupied Warsaw, and Jacob was

drafted into the Russian army. In 1906 he was sent to Turkey, where he escaped from the army and came to the United States. In 1907 he arrived at Ellis Island in New York Harbor, where many immigrants started their life in the U.S. Like other immigrants with foreign-sounding names, his name was shortened there — from Moskowicz to Mosko. Because he was a blacksmith, the immigration people sent him to Denver to work on the railroad. But he went to work shoeing horses instead, and soon saved up enough money for Ida and their children to come to the States. In 1908, Ida crossed the Atlantic Ocean in steerage with their six children and traveled to Denver to join her husband. They had four more children in Denver, including Ruth, the last of their ten children, who was 20 years younger than her eldest sister. Her older siblings were Sarah, Reuben, Lillian, Louis, Doris, Max, Joe, Aaron, and Maurice.

Years later, some European cousins told Ruth that her father had left Europe not to escape the Russian army, as she believed, but instead to escape his gambling debts. Whatever his reason, the move probably saved all their lives. As a Jewish family living in Warsaw, they probably wouldn't have survived the Nazi invasion of Poland and the Holocaust, the Nazi's massive slaughter of Jews during World War II.

YOUTH

Ruth grew up in Denver. When she was just six months old, her mother, Ida, had to go into the hospital for gallbladder surgery. Ruth went to stay with her eldest sister, Sarah, and her husband, Louie Greenwald. When Ida came home from the hospital, she was weak and frail. Yet she had enormous amounts of housework to do to take care of her large family. So Ruth stayed on with Sarah and Louie for a while, and ended up staying with them for the next 19 years. She continued to see her parents frequently, but she says that "To me, they seemed more like loving, indulgent grandparents." That distance was increased because she found it difficult to communicate with them. They spoke Yiddish at home, which she didn't understand very well, and they had trouble understanding her English.

Ruth didn't feel deprived in any way by the circumstances of her home life; in fact, her life with Sarah and Louie was very happy. Unable to have children of their own, they doted on Ruth, showering her with love and attention. Ruth repaid their affection by helping out in the family's drugstore and soda fountain after school; later, after Sarah and Louie sold the drugstore, she helped out at their new business, a combination liquor store and luncheonette counter. Ruth loved to work; in fact, she preferred working to playing with other kids. She had a few friends, but mostly she was a loner. And despite her later success in creating the most popular doll of all time, she never enjoyed playing with dolls as a child. "I never had any interest in them," she says. "I

111

was a tomboy. I had a lot of brothers, and we played basketball and kick-the-can. But mostly I worked after school. I liked that. It was fun." Even at that time, Ruth always believed that it was normal—and even fun—for women to work outside the home.

EDUCATION

Ruth attended East High School in Denver, graduating in 1934. She followed that with classes at the University of Denver, where she studied business and planned to become a lawyer. She left school after her sophomore year.

MARRIAGE AND FAMILY

In 1932, when she was about 16, Ruth Mosko became involved with her future husband, Elliot Handler. They attended different high schools in Denver, but they met at a party given by a Jewish youth organization. Elliot was an art student who dreamed of becoming a professional artist. In high school he was already attending classes at the Denver Art Institute. Ruth and Elliot became very serious very quickly, which upset the Mosko family. They were sure that Elliot would be a starving artist and that, with him, Ruth would lead a life of miserable poverty. Ruth and Elliot dated on and off for the next several years, while she finished high school and started college. They would date for a bit, then break up to see other people, but they would always get back together again.

"The whole philosophy of Barbie," according to Handler, "was that through the doll, a girl could be anything she wanted to be."

At one point, when she was 19, Ruth decided to move to California. It was the summer after her sophomore year in college, and she decided to accompany a friend who was going to visit cousins in Los Angeles. There, she got a job as a stenographer at Paramount Pictures, a film studio in Hollywood. "I was visiting someone at the studio for lunch," she recalls, "and on impulse applied for a job. I was told they were virtually impossible to get, but I was hired the same day. I don't take no for an answer."

Ruth's family was delighted about her move to California, sure that this would finally break up her relationship with Elliot and hoping that she would meet someone new. Then Elliot showed up, planning to attend art school in Los Angeles. He got a job designing light fixtures, she continued working at Paramount, and they spent one carefree year together enjoying sunny LA before Sarah showed up. She convinced Ruth that she was in a dead-end situation, with no real hope for the future. Ruth quit her glamorous job, left Elliot, and moved back home to Denver. But that attitude didn't last. She wasn't home for long before Elliot wrote and asked her to marry him. They were married on June 26, 1938, and returned to California soon afterward. The Handlers later had two children—Barbara, born in 1941, and Ken, born in 1944—the namesakes for Barbie and Ken, the dolls that would earn their fortunes.

STARTING A BUSINESS

After moving back to California in 1938, Ruth returned to working at Paramount while Elliot continued to design light fixtures. He also studied industrial design at the Art Center School of Design. There, one class assignment was to design consumer uses for Lucite, a heavy-duty clear plastic that was new at that time. Inspired by the class, he began to create homemade decorative objects and furniture to fill their barren new apartment. He set up a shop, first in their garage and then in a Chinese laundry that they rented. He had the help of Harold "Matt" Matson, a friend from his job designing light fixtures. A skilled craftsman, Matson knew how to build or fix just about anything. He constructed the specialty oven that heated the Lucite plastic to soften it so that Elliot could shape it into a wooden mold. His designs turned out so well that he began making gift items, like bookends, trays, and candle holders.

Despite his artistic success, Elliot had no talent for talking to people or for salesmanship. So Ruth stepped in to help. In 1939, while on a lunch break from her job at Paramount, she took some samples of his work to an elegant, exclusive boutique in Beverly Hills. The owner was so impressed with their quality and originality that he ordered stock for his store. It was their very first sale. Next, she was able to secure an appointment with executives from Douglas Aircraft, then one of the biggest aircraft companies in Southern California. They were looking for unique, custom-made items to give to their customers as corporate holiday gifts. Elliot designed two pieces for them, bookends and a clock, and incorporated a model of a DC-3 airplane into each design. The Douglas executives were delighted with Elliot's clever and contemporary designs, and the Handlers' new business was on its way. From that point onward, their roles were clear: Elliot was the creative force, and Ruth was the business leader. Within just a few years, they were selling $2 million worth of gifts and jewelry.

At this point, Ruth was still employed at Paramount, although she was taking more and more days off to make sales calls for the new business. She ended up quitting her job during a difficult pregnancy with their first child, Barbara, who was born in 1941. For three years she was a full-time mother, staying home to take care of her daughter. But after their second child, Ken, was born in 1944, she decided that she was ready to go back to work—an unusual decision for a mother at that time.

CAREER HIGHLIGHTS

Forming the Mattel Company

The Mattel company was created in 1944, when Elliot and Harold "Matt" Matson decided to form a partnership. They combined their names to create the name of their new company, although Matson sold out his share of the company just three years later. But Ruth was involved with Mattel from the beginning. It was Ruth who suggested that the new company should make picture frames out of Lucite. Soon afterward, the U.S. government ordered that all plastic should be saved for the war effort, to help in constructing the materials needed for our armed forces to fight in World War II. So Mattel began making picture frames out of wood. Then they took the wood scraps and created doll house furniture. In 1945, their first full year, they sold $100,000 worth of doll house furniture and made a profit of $30,000, earning a 30% profit!

Suddenly, Mattel was a toy company. It proved to be a very lucky choice. The toy business in the U.S. was on the brink of tremendous growth, with the birth of the baby boom generation and the rise in disposable income that followed World War II. Mattel went on to manufacture plastic ukuleles, toy pianos, and music boxes, all of which were very successful and helped the company to grow. By 1951, Mattel employed 600 people and occupied a 60,000-square-foot building. By the following year, Mattel had sold more than 20 million music boxes. During this time, Handler was executive vice-president of Mattel. She held that position from 1948 to 1967, when she was named president. Later, she was also co-chairman of the Board of Directors. Ruth's responsibilities included the business areas—administration, finance, and marketing—while Elliot's responsibilities included product design and research and development.

In 1955, Handler had a brainstorm that would revolutionize the toy industry. Until that time, there wasn't much toy advertising on television. Like other toy manufacturers, Mattel only advertised on TV in a few big cities during the month of December, because at that time about 80% of toy purchases were made in the weeks leading up to Christmas. Also, ads at that time were directed at parents, not children. Handler decided to advertise Mattel's Burp Gun, an automatic cap gun, on the brand new Mickey Mouse show. And she decided to aim the commercials at children, rather than their parents. But the Disney Company, sponsors of the Mickey Mouse show, were requiring their advertisers to sign on for a full year—52 straight weeks of commercials. It was a risky decision for Mattel. The ad rates were so expensive that the company would have to see tremendous sales just to break even. But Handler's decision paid off. By advertising on a weekly show, she created year-round demand for their toys and tremendous brand recognition among their ultimate consumers—the kids themselves.

Ruth and Elliot Handler with Barbie, around 1961

Creating Barbie

In 1956, Handler saw the prototype for what would become Barbie. She and her family were on vacation in Europe and were out window shopping one day in Lucerne, Switzerland. Ruth and her daughter Barbara were transfixed by a doll they saw in a store window. Lilli was an 11-inch tall doll with the figure of an adult woman, with long tapered legs, a small waist, and breasts. Based on a character from a German comic strip, Lilli was considered a gag gift for men. But for Handler, she was the embodiment of an idea that she had been trying to sell to Elliot and the other Mattel toy designers for several years.

At that time, American toy dolls for children were baby dolls. Handler was eager for Mattel to enter the doll market, but she wanted to create a doll for young girls with an adult figure. She based that idea on watching her own daughter, Barbara, play with paper dolls with her friends. They always seemed to enjoy the paper dolls that looked like adults. They used them in pretend play to act out their own futures. Handler was convinced that a doll that looked like an adult woman would be as appealing to little girls as their adult paper dolls.

It took three years after Handler first saw the Lilli doll for Mattel to bring Barbie to market. First Handler had to convince her colleagues at Mattel that the company should make the doll, which she named after her daughter, Barbara. Then Handler and the Mattel designers had to figure out how to create the dolls out of soft plastic and find a manufacturer that could make them to Mattel's specifications. They eventually decided to work with a Japanese manufacturing company. They also hired a dress designer from Los Angeles, Charlotte Johnson, to create Barbie's wardrobe. They ran into many problems along the way. For example, they wanted to implant her hair into her head, rather than just gluing it onto the scalp, but it was difficult to find a machine that could sew doll hair onto such a small doll. They also had trouble with clothing fabrics because the patterns on the fabric were often too large for such small clothes.

In 1994, Handler offered this opinion of Barbie: "I feel proud of her. I think she is quite amazing. I'm humbled by the magnitude of the whole Barbie phenomenon. It's more than I could have imagined, that she would last 35 years and grow each year."

The original Barbie wore a black-and-white striped one piece bathing suit, high heels, and sunglasses. She had long hair tied back in a pony tail. Initially, she was available as a blond, brunette, or redhead, but the blondes quickly became the biggest sellers. Her face was intended to be pretty, but not gorgeous, so that girls could project their own personalities onto the doll and so that she wouldn't be too different from them. "The whole philosophy of Barbie," according to Handler, "was that through the doll, a girl could be anything she wanted to be." She had a whole wardrobe of outfits, too, suitable for the late 1950s. Some were for very glamorous events, for a beauty pageant, fashion show, or nightclub act. But she also had clothes for ordinary teenage activities, for a football game, a picnic, a school prom, a tennis game, or a regular job. All her clothes were beautifully made, with tiny details like darts, snaps, zippers, and buttons.

Although Handler is considered the creator of the Barbie doll, her name doesn't appear on any patents. "I didn't actually sculpt Barbie or sew her dresses," Handler says. "I set down the specifications and approved everything, but the physical work was done by others. I manage the process of creating the design, and then assign engineers and technicians to make them. . . . Very seldom is the boss named as the inventor. The boss has to know what the final product is to be. When you know the characteristics you're looking for, you get technicians to make it happen."

Introducing Barbie to the World

Handler was very excited to show Barbie at the 1959 Toy Show, a giant industry showcase. Manufacturers would come to New York to set up displays with all their new toys, and top buyers from stores all over the country would come to make decisions about which toys they would sell in their stores that year. A toy's success depended on convincing these store buyers that the toy would appeal to kids, that it would sell, and that they should stock it in their stores. Here's how the Mattel catalog announced their new doll: "New for '59, the BARBIE DOLL: A shapely teenage fashion model! Retail price $3.00. . . . An exciting all-new kind of doll (she's grown up!) with fashion apparel authentic in every detail! This is Barbie — one of Mattel's proudest achievements for '59. Girls of all ages will thrill to the fascination of her miniature wardrobe of fine-fabric fashions: tiny zippers that really zip . . . coats with luxurious linings . . . jeweled earrings and necklaces . . . and every girl can be the star. There's never been a doll like Barbie."

At the 1959 Toy Show, Barbie was a dud. Only about 20% of the buyers ordered Barbie for their stores. Most told Handler they thought that the doll wouldn't sell because mothers wouldn't buy a doll with breasts for their little girls. But they were wrong. In fact, Barbie was an immediate success. "There was no initial acceptance at the Toy Show," Handler says. "But the minute we got in on the [store] counter, it walked right off." The stores that had ordered Barbie couldn't keep the doll on their shelves, and soon stores all over the country were clamoring for more. That first year, more than 351,000 dolls were sold. Within the first eight years, sales revenues from Barbie and related items totaled $500 million.

Growth of the Company

Mattel thrived during the 1960s. The company made many types of toys for both girls and boys. Some of the most successful were the Chatty Cathy doll, a large doll with a pull string who could talk; Creepy Crawlers, squishy bugs and other gross things kids could make with Plastigoop and molds; Incredible Edibles, which used molds and a substance called Gobbledegook to make bugs and worms that you could eat; and See 'N Say, a pull-string educational toy for toddlers, where the child can use the pointer to pick an animal and then it makes the sound of that animal. One of Mattel's most successful products was Hot Wheels. Before that, other miniature cars were made as collectibles. Kids couldn't really play with them because their wheels didn't move. So Mattel made Hot Wheels, with moving axles and moving wheels, plus tracks for the cars to race on. Over the years, sales of Hot Wheels have been second only to sales of Barbie products at Mattel.

Barbie and related items were consistently the company's biggest sellers, and the line of products grew tremendously after its inception in 1959.

Barbie's boyfriend Ken, named after Handler's son, came out in 1961 in response to thousands of requests from young Barbie owners. The original Ken doll was more slender than the current version; he was remodeled in the late 1960s, with a stronger body, handsomer face, longer hair, and healthier skin tone. A best friend for Barbie, named Midge, came out in 1963, and then her boyfriend, Allan. Barbie's little sister, Skipper, came out in 1964, followed by two of her friends, Skooter and Ricky. Just a few of the other dolls from the late 1960s and early 1970s include Tutti and Todd, Barbie's younger sister and brother; a slimmer doll named Francie, Barbie's cousin, who wore the mod fashions then popular; Christie, Barbie's African-American friend; Twist 'n Turn Barbie, who could twist at the waist; Twiggy, a celebrity doll based on a British fashion model who was very popular during the late 1960s; Talking Barbie, who said things like "Help me fix my hair" and "I think I'll call Ken"; and Living Barbie, the most moveable doll that had ever been made. In 1967, when Mattel sponsored a Barbie trade-in promotion, over 1.25 million dolls were turned in—more dolls were traded in than actual cars that year. In addition to the dolls, the company created a whole Barbie lifestyle: cars, houses, furniture, and over 100 Barbie outfits each year. Malibu Barbie, for example, came out with dune buggies, surf boards, beach fashions, and other beach gear.

Medical and Legal Problems

After her great success with Mattel in the 1960s, Handler faced a host of personal and professional problems in the 1970s. Her life changed dramatically when she was diagnosed with breast cancer in 1970. She had a radical mastectomy that year, and later had a second one to remove the other breast. In a radical mastectomy, doctors remove the breast, underlying chest muscle, and lymph nodes from the adjoining armpit to make sure that all traces of the cancer are eliminated. It is a very painful procedure that is rarely recommended today. It left Handler with nerve damage and physical pain that she still suffers today. But the emotional scars that it left were as painful as the physical ones. After the surgery, she felt "unwomanized and disfigured," in her words. "I had lost my self-confidence because I had lost my self-esteem after the mastectomy. You can't be an executive if you can't lead with confidence. I couldn't stop crying, and I couldn't get rid of the hostility. I had always been able to manage my life very well. This I couldn't manage."

At the same time, Mattel was going through some financial and legal problems. The company experienced a series of setbacks in the early 1970s: they overproduced the Hot Wheels line so that they had to offer deep discounts just to move out their inventory; they had a fire in their Mexico plant; they had a strike by workers at their Hong Kong plant; and they diversified too much, spending too much money on mergers and acquisitions. Their sales

Angel Princess™ Barbie® Doll

were dropping, their profits were declining, their management force was bloated, and their spending was out of control. The company put out annual reports in 1971 and 1972 that overstated their profits for each year. Bankers and investors began to get skeptical. In 1973 the company finally admitted a loss, but it was too late. The *Wall Street Journal* offered this snide comment on the company's financial situation: "Have you heard about Mattel, Inc.'s latest talking doll? Wind it up and it forecasts a 100 percent increase in sales and profits. Then it falls flat on its face."

The Securities and Exchange Commission (SEC), a government agency that protects the interests of the public in connection with corporate stocks, started an investigation of Mattel. According to the official version of events, the SEC discovered that Handler and Seymour Rosenberg, an executive vice president, had been secretly selling off large quantities of their Mattel stock while at the same time reassuring the public that the company was fine. Ultimately, it determined that false statements about the company's finances were used to inflate the price of Mattel stock, which was used to acquire bank loans for the company. Then Handler and Rosenberg sold the stock for an undeserved profit.

In 1974, Mattel hired a special counsel to investigate its past financial statements. The special counsel's report confirmed that the company's public financial statements had been falsified. In November 1975, Mattel kicked out its two founders, Ruth and Elliot Handler, and required them to contribute $112,000 in court costs plus two million shares of company stock toward settling lawsuits that stockholders had filed against the company. In 1978, Ruth Handler and several top employees at Mattel were indicted by a federal grand jury and charged with 10 counts of conspiracy, fraud, and false reports to the SEC. They were accused of altering and hiding the company's real financial information from outside auditors by preparing false financial records. Although Handler vowed that she was innocent, she pleaded no contest to the charges in late 1978. She was sentenced to a 41-year prison term, which was suspended, was fined $57,000, and was required to devote 500 hours per year for five years to community service.

Young editors Kate Abbey-Lambertz (left) and
Catherine Ann Harris (right) interview Barbie

Handler offers a different version of events. After undergoing painful and debilitating surgery for breast cancer in 1970, she was not fully involved in the company's affairs during her recovery. She claims that she was unaware of the financial irregularities that caused the price of Mattel's stock to be inflated. She and Elliot were pushed out of power, and they were kept completely ignorant throughout the investigation of the company. She said that several key employees hadn't been interviewed by the special counsel, and those who had been interviewed had lied. In her words, "I was one of the last employees interviewed. It seems many of the [executives] already interviewed had pointed the finger at me and lied in order to save their own hides. And the people who could have absolved me of responsibility for the so-called irregularities simply weren't volunteering the information." She also argues that the investigators went after the wrong people, although she refuses to name names. According to Handler, she quit her job at Mattel.

At her court appearance where she pleaded no contest to the charges against her, Handler made a lengthy statement. It read, in part, "I am not admitting that I am guilty of any of the charges leveled against me. In fact, I steadfastly deny that I am guilty of any of the charges leveled against me. Nevertheless, I have found that over the last several years, during which I have had to endure seemingly endless investigations by batteries of lawyers and accountants, I have, little by little, lost my zeal to fight." She explained her desire to put the entire Mattel matter behind her to devote herself, instead, to a "new endeavor that I find greatly fulfilling."

Nearly Me

That new endeavor was a new company that Handler had already started up by the time of her trial. Ever since her mastectomy, she had had trouble finding breast prostheses, or artificial breasts, that looked natural and felt comfortable. Each prosthesis she had tried was heavy and shapeless. And each time she had tried to buy one, she had ended up feeling humiliated and embarrassed by the way she had been treated by the department store's sales staff. Salesclerks would throw it over the dressing room curtain and offer no help with fitting. Handler grew determined to change this. She found a designer who made custom prostheses, and then began working with him and a team of other designers to figure out how to produce quality prostheses in greater quantities.

They created a new company, Ruthton, that soon became Nearly Me. After developing a new type of prosthesis, Handler hired a team of female sales personnel, many of whom had also had mastectomies. She then set up a distribution system through department stores. Handler would set up a promotion at a large department store. Her staff would contact surgeons in the area, and then send handwritten invitations to their patients. She made sure to get a lot of coverage on TV and in newspapers to ensure that women would know about it. She and her sales staff usually found crowds waiting for them upon their arrival. They would fit each woman individually for her prosthesis. In this way, Handler made sure to sell quality products to her customers in a comfortable environment, thereby eliminating the miserable experience she had suffered.

In late 1991, Handler sold the company to Spenco Corporation, a division of Kimberly Clark. But she continues in a long-term public relations arrangement with the company, giving lectures at American Cancer events and other public forums.

In 1994, when Handler was in her late 70s, she renewed her connection to Mattel. That year, Mattel asked her to help celebrate the 35th anniversary of Barbie by attending a series of promotional events. She signed autographs at many big store events for people who waited for several hours to meet her. Three generations of women would come together: the grandmother, who bought one of the first Barbies for her daughter to play with; her daughter, the first generation to play with Barbie, now a mother in her own right; and her little girl, the proud owner of a Barbie today. Handler was astounded and moved by the deep and abiding affection of the generations of buyers who showed up to meet Barbie's mom.

The Barbie Phenomenon

Over the years, Barbie has become a phenomenon in her own right. Some of the statistics are mind-boggling. Somewhere in the world, two Barbie dolls are sold every second. The typical American girl between the ages of three and ten owns an average of ten Barbie dolls. Barbie is sold in 140 countries around the world. As of 1994, nearly one billion Barbie dolls (and family members) had been sold since the doll was created in 1959. Laid head to toe, they would circle the Earth more than seven and a half times. More than one billion pairs of shoes and Barbie outfits have been sold, using 125 million yards of fabric, which makes Mattel the world's largest women's clothing manufacturer. Barbie gets about 120 new outfits each year. Barbie has had more than 500 make overs since her debut, and Mattel confirms that Barbie had another make over in 1998. Of the 24 new dolls that are being introduced that year, six have a new face, and one has a new body. That doll, according to Mattel, is a teenage doll wearing baggy clothes, with a smaller bust and slimmer hips. Mattel also makes a line of collectible dolls to appeal to the many adults who collect old and new Barbies.

Part of what makes Barbie so amazing is the nature of the toy industry. Children's tastes in toys are very fickle, changing from year to year. The hottest selling toy one year might be the biggest dud the next. The toy industry has to anticipate demand. Toy companies have to decide in advance which

toys will be the biggest hit with kids and their parents to ensure that the factories make enough and that they ship enough to the stores. When the toy company guesses right, they have a big success. When they guess wrong, they have a flop. For Barbie, the amazing part is that she has been popular every single year since 1959, when the doll was first made.

But mere statistics can't begin to explain the effect that Barbie has had. What began as just a doll has turned into an icon of American culture. Mattel has changed Barbie every year, to kept her current and up-to-date. In the process, Barbie has come to reflect American culture and society's view of women. At first, in the 1960s, her jobs followed traditional stereotypes for women: nurse, fashion model, stewardess, candy striper (a hospital volunteer), and career girl. In the 1970s, as more women moved into the workplace, she was a surgeon and an Olympic athlete; in the 1980s she was an aerobics instructor, business executive, dress designer, TV news reporter, veterinarian, teacher, astronaut, rock star, and UNICEF ambassador; and in the 1990s, she has been in all four of the armed services, as well as a diplomat, music video star, presidential candidate, police officer, baseball player, pediatrician, scuba diver, artist, firefighter, engineer, and paleontologist. According to Jill Barad, the current Chief Operating Officer of Mattel, "I give a great deal of thought to maintaining the essence of Barbie. Fundamentally, she embodies everything little girls dream about, all the possibilities that are opening up for her. She has been absolutely right-on for every generation. That's why she's such a cultural icon."

———— " ————

The typical American girl between the ages of three and ten owns an average of ten Barbie dolls. Barbie is sold in 140 countries around the world. As of 1994, nearly one billion Barbie dolls (and family members) had been sold since the doll was created in 1959. Laid head to toe, they would circle the Earth more than seven and a half times. More than one billion pairs of shoes and Barbie outfits have been sold, using 125 million yards of fabric, which makes Mattel the world's largest women's clothing manufacturer. Barbie gets about 120 new outfits each year.

———— " ————

Some commentators have argued that toys say a lot about the culture that produces them. If so, that leaves many questions about the culture that produced Barbie. Her shape has been the subject of much controversy over the years. If her dimensions were projected into human size, her measurements would be about 39-20-33—a voluptuous bosom, tiny waist, and slim hips. Barbie's shape presents an idealized image of womanhood that is impossible to achieve, according to many critics. Barbie teaches young girls to strive for that idealized body image, even though most women don't—and can't—look like that. The prevalence of eating disorders in our culture, particularly anorexia nervosa and bulimia, makes this idealized body image frightening and potentially dangerous for young girls. By emphasizing her looks rather than her accomplishments, Barbie is also charged with implying that a woman's intelligence is less important than her sex appeal. Also, the emphasis on clothes and accessories has made her a symbol for consumerism, which worries many observers. For all these reasons, critics have challenged the idea that Barbie is an appropriate plaything for impressionable young children.

Yet Handler differs on these issues. "I'm sure you've heard some of the criticism that's been lobbed at Barbie in the last several years," she says. "Barbie cares only about clothes. Barbie's 'mind' is filled only with Saturday-night dates and/or wedding plans. My response is if that is so, it's because the little girl who is playing with her *chooses* to concentrate on those facets of a woman's life." In fact, Handler has only good things to say about Barbie. In 1994, 20 years after she left Mattel, Handler offered this opinion of Barbie: "I feel proud of her. I think she is quite amazing. I'm humbled by the magnitude of the whole Barbie phenomenon. It's more than I could have imagined, that she would last 35 years and grow each year."

WRITINGS

Dream Doll: The Ruth Handler Story, 1994 (with Jacqueline Shannon)

HONORS AND AWARDS

Outstanding Business Woman of the Year (National Association of Accountants): 1961, for exceptional contributions to the field of business
Growth Company of the Year Award (National Association of Investment Clubs): 1962
Outstanding Industrialists Honor Award (American Society of Tool and Manufacturing Engineers): 1965, with Elliot Handler
Woman of the Year in Business (*Los Angeles Times* Award): 1968
One of 75 Outstanding Women in America (*Ladies Home Journal*): 1971
Brotherhood Award (National Conference of Christians and Jews): 1972, with Elliot Handler
Dolls of the Years (DOTY) Lifetime Achievement Award (Dolls Reader and the International Doll Academy): 1987, with Elliot Handler
Volunteer Achievement Award (American Cancer Society): 1988
Toy Industry Hall of Fame (Toy Manufacturers of America) 1989, with Elliot Handler
Woman of Distinction Award (United Jewish Appeal): 1992
Junior Achievement National Business Hall of Fame: 1997

FURTHER READING

Books

Contemporary American Business Leaders: A Biographical Dictionary, 1990
Grolier Library of North American Biographies: Entrepreneurs and Inventors, Vol. 3, 1994
Handler, Elliot. *The Impossible Really Is Possible: The Story of Mattel*, 1968 (pamphlet)
Handler, Ruth, with Jacqueline Shannon. *Dream Doll: The Ruth Handler Story*, 1994
Jeffrey, Laura S. *Great American Businesswomen*, 1996

Lord, M.G. *Forever Barbie: The Unauthorized Biography of a Real Doll,* 1994
Vare, Ethlie Ann, and Greg Ptacek. *Mothers of Invention: From the Bra to the Bomb: Women and Their Unforgettable Ideas,* 1988
Vare, Ethlie Ann, and Greg Ptacek. *Women Inventors and Their Discoveries,* 1993

Periodicals

New York Times Book Review, Feb. 5, 1995, p.22
People, Mar. 6, 1989, p.186
Philadelphia Inquirer, Nov. 2, 1994, p.H1
USA Today, Mar. 9, 1994, p.D5
Washington Post, Dec. 8, 1994, p.D1

ADDRESS

Mattel, Inc.
333 Continental Boulevard
El Segundo, CA 90245-5012

WORLD WIDE WEB SITE

http://www.barbie.com

HANSON

Ike Hanson 1980-
Taylor Hanson 1983-
Zac Hanson 1985-

American Pop Music Group
Creators of the Hit Song, "MMMBop"

BIRTH

The three brothers who make up the pop group Hanson were born in Tulsa, Oklahoma. Clarke Isaac (Ike) Hanson was born on November 17, 1980; Jordan Taylor (Taylor or Tay) Hanson was born on March 14, 1983; and Zachary Walker (Zac) Hanson was born on October 22, 1985. Their parents, Walker and Diane Hanson, were high school sweethearts who both attended the University of Oklahoma and got married during their freshman year. Diane was a music major, Walker played the piano and guitar, and they both sang with a church group called The Horizons. After they graduated, Walker took a job with Helmerich & Payne, an international oil drilling and exploration company. Diane is a homemaker.

Ike, Taylor, and Zac are the eldest of six children. They have two sisters, Jessica and Avery, and a brother, Mackenzie.

YOUTH

The Hanson brothers grew up in a household full of music. Diane was always singing or listening to music, and Walker would often get out his guitar and play for his sons after dinner.

Walker eventually worked his way up to a position as manager of international administration for Helmerich & Payne, which meant that the family spent a year moving around the Caribbean and South America. With their three young sons, they lived in Ecuador, Venezuela, and Trinidad-Tobago. Being so far away from home taught the boys to focus on what they had, which was music and each other's companionship.

Because they couldn't listen to American music on the radio, the Hanson brothers sent away for the rock 'n roll and soul collections from Time-Life Records, which featured early rock stars from the late 1950s and 1960s. The boys often sang along to the records, and sometimes after dinner there would be family sing-alongs.

When the Hansons returned from their overseas stay, they settled in a rural section of West Tulsa. The boys began singing one night after dinner and discovered that they could harmonize. One of the first things they learned to sing in harmony was "Amen" at the dinner table. What started out as two-part harmony between Ike and Taylor became three-part harmony when Zac was old enough to join them.

EARLY MEMORIES

When Walker and Diane Hanson went out at night, they would leave explicit instructions about household chores that had to be done in their absence, such as washing the dishes. When they got home, however, it was clear that the dishes hadn't been touched. "Instead of doing our chores," Zac explains, "we usually spent the time writing a new song." While most parents would have been angry, the Hansons never were. "This better be good," they'd tell the boys and give them a chance to perform them what they had written.

EDUCATION

Diane and Walker Hanson have home schooled all their children. The Hanson parents have never publicly stated why they have chosen to home school their kids. It has required a big commitment from Diane Hanson, who buys their books and gives their exams on the dining room table. All the children are good students—they manage to maintain a B average—and the older ones feel that the amount of traveling they've done over the past several years has more than made up for the time they've missed in the classroom. While they tour, they still study and take their exams, which are reviewed by their mom.

It certainly made it easier to continue the children's learning while they lived out of the country. Many of the Hansons' friends in Tulsa were home-schooling their children as well, and the families would often get together and plan educational field trips.

In addition to their academic subjects, Diane thought that the boys should learn to play the piano. Ike took five years of classical piano lessons, and Taylor and Zac followed suit. Taylor turned out to be a natural at the keyboard.

——— " ———

When Walker and Diane Hanson went out at night, they would leave explicit instructions about household chores that had to be done in their absence, such as washing the dishes. When they got home, however, it was clear that the dishes hadn't been touched. "Instead of doing our chores," Zac explains, "we usually spent the time writing a new song."

——— " ———

CAREER HIGHLIGHTS

On Their Own

The trio got their start in show business in a rather unconventional way. At their father's office Christmas party in 1991—when Ike was 11, Taylor was 8, and Zac was only 6—they got up in front of everyone and began to harmonize to some old rock songs. The audience couldn't help snapping their fingers and tapping their feet. Their enthusiastic response made the Hanson boys eager to sing in public again.

In 1992, the Hansons performed in a competition at a local arts festival, singing a cappella (unaccompanied by musical instruments). They did versions of some of the classic rock 'n roll songs with which they were so familiar—such as "Splish Splash," "Rockin' Robin," "Johnny B. Goode," and "Summertime Blues." They were on stage for close to an hour, doing a 15-song set that in-

cluded six original compositions. Although they didn't win any prizes, the audience loved them. The Hanson brothers had begun to build up a local fan base.

Encouraged by the response they'd received from local audiences, the three Hanson brothers decided it was time to do more than just harmonize and snap their fingers. They added dancing to their act, worked on getting more involved with the audience, and occasionally sang to a pre-recorded backing track. As they got older, they became better at harmonizing and developed a more sophisticated stage presence.

If they really wanted to make it big, though, the Hansons knew they had to play their own instruments. Although all three boys had taken piano lessons, Taylor was the one who had picked it up the most easily. The family didn't own an electronic keyboard, so he borrowed one from a friend. Ike decided to follow in his father's footsteps and play the guitar. He found one in a pawn shop, and Zac found an old drum set in a friend's attic. As they improved on their instruments, the boys decided to get rid of the dance steps in their act and focus more on singing and playing.

The Hansons finally reached the point where they wanted to record their work. So in 1995 they hired some extra musicians, rented a local studio in Tulsa, and made *Boomerang*, a pure R&B (rhythm-and-blues) album. They sent it to every record company they could think of, but it was always rejected. Undiscouraged, they went on to record a second album, *MMMBop*, selling copies at their local gigs and continuing to send it out to record companies. Unlike their first album, *MMMBop* contained only songs that they'd written themselves and for which they played their own instruments. By this point they had changed their name to "Hanson" from "The Hanson Brothers" because it sounded too much like "The Handsome Brothers."

The Blue Rose Cafe was a well-known place in Tulsa to hear live music. The Hansons were invited to perform there, but they were too young to play in the bar. So they set their equipment up on a wooden deck outside, where three times as many people were able to hear them. The audience's response was overwhelming, and the brothers hoped that it would only be a matter of time before they were discovered.

"Our parents are completely supportive," Taylor explains, "and they say we can stop whenever we want. They're on our team; they're not like some record company person who likes you because you're making money for them."

Middle of Nowhere

In 1995 the Hansons brought their music to South by Southwest, an annual music conference in Austin, Texas, that brings together up-and-coming performers with agents, managers, and record label representatives. Although not officially booked to play there, they set up their equipment anyway and played on the street, hoping to attract attention. Christopher Sabec, a Los Angeles-based music attorney and manager who was in Austin to scout new talent, was having lunch when the boys came up to him and asked if they could sing for him. They performed a cappella, and Sabec was impressed. "Where are your parents?" he asked them afterward. "I need to talk to them right away."

Sabec became the boys' manager and sent their demo tape to dozens of record companies, only to get more rejections slips. Then Sabec played their tape for his girlfriend, who was an executive at Mercury Records. She passed it on to Steve Greenberg, the vice president for A & R (artists & repertoire). He was the person in charge of signing new talent. Greenberg assumed that their demo tape was a fake—that adults were playing the instruments and that the vocals had been manipulated electronically. But just to make sure, he flew out to Kansas to hear them play at a county fair. There were no adults in sight, and it was clear that Hanson was "the real thing."

In June 1996, Steve Greenberg offered Hanson a six-album recording contract with Mercury Records. The entire family moved to Los Angeles, where the boys spent seven months writing and recording *Middle of Nowhere.* It included a new version of "MMMBop," a song from their second independent album re-mixed by the Dust Brothers, one of the hottest production teams in pop music. When the single of "MMMBop" was released, it soared to Number 1 in just four weeks, and Hanson became famous. The album has since sold more than five million copies worldwide.

The basic message of the hit song "MMMBop" is the fleeting nature of human relationships. Even relationships based on love can be gone in an "MMMBop"—in other words, a split second. The song urges listeners to stay close to the people who really matter and to keep forming new relationships because they can never be sure which ones will last.

Why So Hot?

Hanson's bouncy, irresistible music has been described as a blend of folk-pop and Motown, an upbeat style of rhythm and blues associated with the city of Detroit and with certain black vocal groups since the 1950s. Hanson is tremendously popular with young teenage and pre-teen girls. It has been nearly a decade since the appearance of the last major teen-pop idols, New Kids on the Block. Like the Monkees and the Partridge Family before them, New Kids had been auditioned and selected for their looks and personality rather than just their musical ability. They were the highest-paid performers in the country back in 1991, but their popularity faded within a few years. Since then a new, larger generation of teenagers has come of age both in the U.S. and overseas—which might explain why "MMMBop" has hit Number 1 around the world. Unlike New Kids, Hanson started out together and intends to stay together. The trio is popular with parents as well, who see the three brothers as nice, wholesome kids with songs whose lyrics aren't obscene. As if to reinforce their squeaky-clean image, the "MMMBop" video shows the three brothers playing on the beach with surfboards and racing around on skateboards.

What Next?

Hanson has been interviewed by "MTV News," "VH-1," and MTV's "Week in Rock." They've appeared on "The Rosie O'Donnell Show," the "Today" show, "Late Night with David Letterman," and "Saturday Night Live."

They've recorded their first Christmas album, *Snowed In*, and have toured England, France, Germany, Taiwan, Korea, Japan, and Australia. When they recently appeared at a mall in Paramus, New Jersey, more than 6,000 screaming fans showed up. The question is, will Hanson still be on top ten years from now?

A great deal depends on how the boys' voices change as they mature and how gracefully they'll outgrow their innocent, boyish image. One thing in Hanson's favor is the fact that they write their own songs and play their own instruments. Even so, the band will have to create a unique identity for itself. It will have to be willing to experiment and to grow in a different direction.

MAJOR INFLUENCES

From the time they lived in South America and listened to the Time-Life records from the 50s and 60s, Hanson has been influenced by such early rock 'n roll stars as Chuck Berry, The Supremes, Otis Redding, The Beach Boys, and Aretha Franklin.

HOME AND FAMILY

The Hansons are an unusually tight-knit family who have always gotten along well with each other. Both Diane and Walker Hanson, who recently quit his job to oversee his sons' career, have often been accused of pushing their eldest three boys into a singing career. But the Hanson brothers are the first to admit that their parents have told them they can get out of the limelight at any time. "Our parents are completely supportive," Taylor explains, "and they say we can stop whenever we want. They're on our team; they're not like some record company person who likes you because you're making money for them."

The Hanson brothers and their parents have worked hard to protect the younger three Hansons from unwanted publicity. But some of the earliest songs the older boys wrote were about their siblings, including a lullaby called, "I'll Show You Mars." Mackenzie, the youngest Hanson brother, has already shown promise as a drummer.

A musical consultant and close friend of the family describes Hanson by saying, "They are the nicest kids I've ever met in my life. They come from an extremely centered, intelligent, spiritual family. They are polite and friendly, and it's easy to strike up a conversation with them." Even Steve Greenberg of Mercury Records admits, "Hanson's family is what keeps them sane."

HOBBIES AND OTHER INTERESTS

The Hanson brothers like to rollerblade and play speed hockey and basketball together. Hanging out at their local virtual-reality arcade is another favorite pastime. When they have some free time, Zac and Taylor both enjoy drawing.

RECORDINGS

Middle of Nowhere, 1997
Snowed In, 1997

TV CREDITS

"Meet Hanson," 1997

FURTHER READING

Books

Johns, Michael-Anne. *Hanson: An Unauthorized Biography,* 1997 (juvenile)
Matthews, Jill. *Hanson: MMMBop to the Top,* 1997

Periodicals

Entertainment Weekly, July 25, 1997, p.28
Los Angeles Times, May 13, 1997, Calendar section, p.1
New York Times. May 7, 1997, p.B12
People, July 7, 1997, p.89
Rolling Stone, Sep. 18, 1997, p.31
Seventeen, Aug. 1997, p.163; Dec. 1997, p.110
Times of London, May 25, 1997, Features section
USA Today, May 22, 1997, p.D6
YM, Sep. 1997, p.106

ADDRESS

P. O. Box 703136
Tulsa, OK 74170
e-mail hansonfans@hansonline.com

WORLD WIDE WEB SITE

http:// www.hansonline.com

Livan Hernandez 1975-

Cuban Baseball Pitcher with the Florida Marlins
Most Valuable Player of the 1997 World Series

BIRTH

Eisler Livan Hernandez was born on February 20, 1975, in Villa
Clara, Cuba. Villa Clara is located on Islas de la Juventud (Isle of
Youth), a small island off the Cuban mainland. His parents are
Arnoldo "El Duque" (The Duke) Hernandez, a baseball player
who played for Cuba's national team, and Miriam Carreras, who
worked as a typist in a government office. He also has an older
half-brother, Orlando, who is also a baseball player and who recently signed to play with the New York Yankees.

YOUTH AND EDUCATION

Livan Hernandez's childhood was a difficult one in many respects. Like many other Cuban children, he grew up in a poor neighborhood and received only limited schooling. "He ate whatever his mother put on the table, wore hand-me-downs without complaint, and occasionally savored luxuries such as candy bars and chewing gum," wrote *Miami Herald* columnist Michelle Kaufman. "His most prized possession was a baseball glove."

When Hernandez was nine years old, his alcoholic father permanently split up with his mother. Around the same time, Livan's brother Orlando left the family home to pursue his dream of playing professional baseball in Havana, Cuba's capital city. Livan and his mother were thus left to fend for themselves in Villa Clara.

Young Hernandez helped his mother buy food and clothing by working odd jobs. In his spare time, meanwhile, he spent countless hot afternoons playing stickball on the dusty streets of his neighborhood. Sometimes he and his friends did not even have a ball to play with, and instead they would play with a rolled up ball of tape. Even as a youngster, Livan attracted the notice of other players. Everyone knew who he was, since his father had been a top pitcher and his brother was then making a name for himself in Havana. But Livan also showed that he was a promising young player in his own right. Before long he had established himself as one of the top pitching prospects on Islas de la Juventud, and people began to wonder when he might move on to Havana to join his brother on the Cuban national team.

As a teenager, Hernandez rapidly rose through Cuba's junior leagues. At age 19 he was thrilled to learn that he had been promoted to the Cuban national team. He moved to Havana, where he stayed at his brother's two-bedroom apartment. Hernandez was nervous about playing on the national team. But Orlando, who by this time was firmly established as the team's ace pitcher, helped him to learn about opposing batters and work on his pitching form. "He taught me everything there is to know about pitching," said Livan.

CAREER HIGHLIGHTS

Cuban National Team

Baseball is the national pastime in Cuba. The sport is incredibly popular there, and ballplayers are heroes to the kids. The national team is made up from the best players in the Cuban baseball league. Cuban professional baseball players are considered fierce competitors, and the national team, which is supported by the government, has long been a powerhouse in international competitions. U.S. baseball scouts routinely attend these international games to check out the players.

Livan Hernandez quickly became a star pitcher on Cuba's national team. In 1992, he allowed only one hit and struck out 19 batters in 12 innings at the Junior World Championships, and a year later he went 2-0 with a great 1.59 ERA (earned-run average) during the 1993 Junior World Championships. But his monthly salary from the ballclub was only $5, which was not even enough for him to buy basic essentials. In fact, he was forced to sell hosiery in his free time so that he would have clothing and food. This really both-ered him, in large part because fans and fellow players kept telling him that he was talented enough to play in America's major leagues. Hernandez also heard about a few other Cuban baseball players who had defected to the United States and become millionaires.

But Hernandez knew that Cubans who tried to defect to the United States were taking a huge gamble. The governments of the two countries had been enemies ever since Cuba's premier, Fidel Castro, took control of the country in 1959. Castro had led a revolutionary movement that had toppled the previous government. When he took over, he quickly installed a government based on Communist philosophies. He eliminated private property, outlawed religion, and gave the central government great control over its citizens' lives. The government of the United States, however, thought that such a system was terribly wrong. America's unhappiness deepened when Castro's government established close

Hernandez found his first few months in America to be very bewildering. He did not speak English, and he was completely unfamiliar with American culture. "I got to this country blind. I did not know how this country works, or the customs or the foods. I knew nothing. I was scared and lonely. It was the most difficult decision of my life, but I did it for freedom and because I wanted to play in the best league in the world."

ties with the Soviet Union, a powerful Communist country that was regarded by the United States as its most fearsome enemy. By the early 1960s, the United States had severed all diplomatic and economic ties with Cuba, and they had convinced most other non-Communist countries to follow suit. Many countries would not purchase goods made in Cuba, which led to great economic hardships for the Cuban people. When the Soviet-led bloc of Communist nations collapsed in 1989, Cuba suddenly found that it was one of the few Communist governments left in the world. The disappearance of its Communist allies and trading partners further harmed Cuba's economy and brought even greater deprivation to the Cuban people. But the people of the country remained fearful of speaking out against Castro or trying to leave Cuba's shores. The Cuban government rarely allows people to leave the country, and those who have tried have been thrown in prison.

Nonetheless, as the months passed by in Havana, Hernandez thought more and more about how much better his life might be if he could defect and play baseball in the United States. He knew that American baseball players received huge salaries and that they were recognized wherever they went. In addition, he knew that people who lived in the United States had many more rights than people who lived in Cuba. But he was also aware that if the Cuban team's coaches or any government authorities learned that he was thinking about defecting to the U.S., the Cuban authorities might disqualify him from the national team and throw him in jail. He worried that his mother and family would suffer as well. He would have to be very careful.

Defecting from Cuba

During 1995 Hernandez attended several secret meetings with people who wanted to help him escape. He did not know these people very well, but their promises of freedom made him nearly crazy with the desire to defect. One day Hernandez was told that arrangements had been made to help him escape in September, when the Cuban team was scheduled to visit Monterrey, Mexico, for a baseball tournament. As the designated day of escape drew near, Hernandez thought about telling his mother and brother, but he decided that they might get in trouble with the Cuban government if they knew about his plans, so he did not inform his family about the defection attempt.

Once the Cuban team arrived in Monterrey, Hernandez decided that there was no turning back. Early one September morning, he dashed out of the quarters where he and his teammates had been staying and into a waiting car. In the driver's seat sat Joe Cubas, a local sports agent who had helped plan the escape. Once Hernandez was safely in the car, Cubas took off to deliver the star pitcher on the next leg of his journey to freedom. "Right at that moment, I felt I was free," remembered Hernandez. "It was the beginning of freedom."

Over the next 24 days, Hernandez bounced through three different countries. He ended up in the Dominican Republic, where he learned that the U.S. government had granted his request for asylum. The U.S. government has an immigration policy that lets in only a small percentage of the many people who would like to live in the U.S. But it will grant asylum, or safe refuge, to political refugees and others who have reason to fear for their lives if they return to their native countries. Because Livan could expect to be persecuted by the government of Cuba if he returned there, the U.S. offered him asylum. The government would forgo its usual immigration policies and allow him to enter.

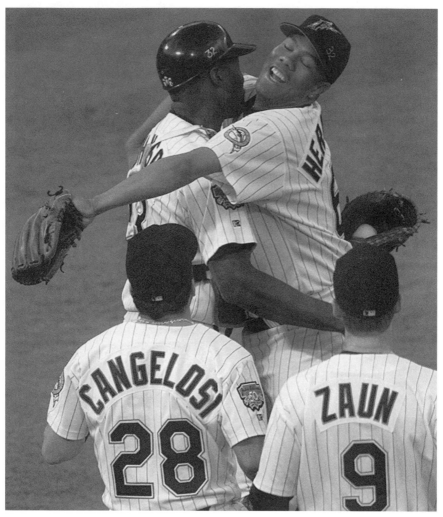

Hernandez after striking out 15 to lead the Marlins in a 2-1 win over the Braves
in Game Five of the 1997 National League Championship Series

By this time, all of America's Major League Baseball teams had learned of his dramatic escape, and representatives from many of the teams tried to convince him to throw his blazing fastball for their club. Hernandez had many choices, but he eventually decided to play for the Florida Marlins. His biggest reason for choosing the Marlins was the fact that the team played in Miami, which was home to hundreds of thousands of people of Cuban descent. He knew that Miami's Cuban community, which was very anti-Castro, would welcome him with open arms. In January 1996 he signed a four-year, $4.5-million contract with Florida.

Life in Miami

Despite the support he enjoyed in the Miami area, Hernandez found his first few months in America to be very bewildering. He did not speak English, and he was completely unfamiliar with American culture. "I got to this country blind," he said through an interpreter. "I did not know how this country works, or the customs or the foods. I knew nothing. I was scared and lonely. It was the most difficult decision of my life, but I did it for freedom and because I wanted to play in the best league in the world."

At first, though, it was difficult for him to adjust to his new surroundings. Hernandez's contract gave him far more money than he had ever had in his life. In addition, American stores had far nicer products than the ones back in his homeland, and he was dazzled by all the nice things that he could now afford. "Imagine if tomorrow you suddenly moved to Mars—that's about what this has been like for Livan," said his interpreter. "In Cuba, they had so little; a limited food allowance, and you can't buy any more than that. The first time Livan went into a supermarket in this country, he saw the meat counter and was shocked. He asked if all that meat was really for sale."

Within weeks of his arrival in the United States, Hernandez went on an extended spending spree. He bought a condominium and expensive cars, purchased lots of new clothes, and discovered American hamburgers. He also celebrated Christmas for the first time. "[Livan] didn't really know what Christmas was," remembered Juan Iglesias, his agent. "When he saw us wrapping presents one day, he asked us what we were doing. When we explained, he went out and bought $6,000 worth of presents for his friends."

At the same time, Hernandez prepared for his entrance into the world of American baseball. He was sent directly to the major league team, not to the minor league farm club, which is the route most players—even great ones—take to the majors. During his first few outings in spring training, he was terrific. After Hernandez pitched a total of seven scoreless innings against the Atlanta Braves and the Toronto Blue Jays, fans and reporters alike expressed great excitement about the team's new pitcher. Hernandez was happy with all the attention, but he also recognized that no pitcher is unbeatable. "I hope people understand that sometimes I will do good and other times I will not do good," he said. "When I'm not going good, I hope the people will still support me."

Minor League Ball

As spring training continued, though, Hernandez had a couple of rocky outings in which he gave up a lot of hits. The Marlins' coaches decided to assign him to their Class AAA team in Charlotte, North Carolina, so that he could get in more practice. Hernandez was a little disappointed, but he knew that

Class AAA was only one step below the Major Leagues. He figured that if he performed well, he would be added to the Florida Marlins roster within a matter of weeks.

But Hernandez pitched terribly in Charlotte. He was ripped in each of his first three starts, and although he performed better in subsequent games, he bore little resemblance to the overpowering pitcher that had dazzled Cuban batters. His coaches blamed the drop off in performance on the weight that he had gained over the previous few months. Looking back on that period of his life, Hernandez admitted that he ate too many pizzas, hamburgers, and bags of potato chips. He explained that in Cuba, "there isn't that much to eat. So when I got here, I ate different things I had never had before. Just to see what they were like." But he also worried a lot about his mother and brother, which sometimes made it hard for him to concentrate on baseball.

In May 1996 Hernandez was demoted to Florida's Double A team in Portland, Maine. The manager of the Portland Sea Dogs, Carlos Tosca, remembered that the young pitcher was not doing too well when he arrived. "He wasn't in very good shape, he was kind of afraid and not ready to handle his newfound freedom, wealth, and fame," Tosca said. "He was being bombarded with pressure from a lot of different areas, and that's an awfully big load for a lonely 20-year-old kid who can't even speak the language."

Soon after his arrival in Portland, however, Hernandez managed to turn his fortunes around. Encouraged by coaches and fellow players, he started an exercise regimen that melted away the pounds that he had accumulated. "They taught me how to be a professional," Hernandez said of his Portland coaches. He also made friends on the team, which did a lot to address the loneliness that had been making him so miserable. "He's a great guy," said one teammate. "There's a language barrier, but he's a lot of fun."

Within a matter of weeks, Hernandez had regained the 95 miles-per-hour fastball that had attracted the Marlins in the first place. He posted a 9-2 record at Portland in 1996, and in September of that year he was promoted to Florida's major-league roster for the last few weeks of the season. Florida already had a lot of pitchers, so Hernandez did not get many opportunities to take the mound. But near the end of the season he pitched three scoreless innings against the Atlanta Braves. This appearance made him confident that he had a good chance of making Florida's major league roster the following season.

Florida Marlins and Major League Status

Hernandez arrived at the Marlins' 1997 spring training camp in the best shape of his life. "I feel much better than last year, twice as good as last year. My arm feels better, my velocity has increased a lot, and my weight is down," he said. "We have more pitchers competing now, but I'll keep doing what I can do and worry about that later. I've learned how to prepare mentally, and that is very important."

As the Marlins completed spring training for the 1997 season, Hernandez was assigned to the minors once again. But Florida's coaches told him to stay in shape because they would probably promote him to the majors during the season. Sure enough, in June Hernandez was told to report to Miami to join the Marlins. The excited young pitcher packed his bags and hurried to Florida.

Hernandez made an immediate splash in the Major Leagues. He won his first nine decisions, a performance that helped the Marlins surge to the top of the league standings. He lost his final three decisions of the regular season to finish with a 9-3 mark, but observers pointed out that in two of those games he allowed only one earned run. As the regular season drew to a close, Hernandez tried to prepare himself for the upcoming playoffs. "I love playing with a full stadium and a championship on the line," he said. "That's what we all play for."

Many fans thought the Marlins had a very good chance of winning the championship that season. The team's owner had spent millions of dollars to attract good ballplayers, and the team was equipped with solid pitching and plenty of tough hitters. But their opponent in the National League Championship Series was the Atlanta Braves, a club that boasted baseball's top pitching staff, including four-time Cy Young Award winner Greg Maddux.

"Imagine if tomorrow you suddenly moved to Mars — that's about what this has been like for Livan,"
said his interpreter.
"In Cuba, they had so little; a limited food allowance, and you can't buy any more than that. The first time Livan went into a supermarket in this country, he saw the meat counter and was shocked. He asked if all that meat was really for sale."

Florida manager Jim Leyland originally left Hernandez out of the team's postseason pitching rotation. He was worried about how the young pitcher would respond to the pressure of the playoffs. But when one of the team's other pitchers suffered an injury, Hernandez took his spot. He quickly proved that Leyland did not have to worry—the young Cuban won two games in the series against Atlanta. The most memorable of these games was a magnificent showdown in game five against Maddux. Maddux was

Hernandez pitching in early innings of Game 5 of the 1997 World Series

terrific, but Hernandez was even better. The young Marlins pitcher struck out 15 batters to lead Florida to victory before a delirious crowd of 50,000 home-town fans. After he struck out the last batter, Hernandez started crying with happiness as his teammates rushed out of the dugout to embrace him.

After dispatching the Braves, the Marlins moved on to face the Cleveland Indians in the World Series. Leyland surprised some people when he announced that Hernandez would be the starting pitcher in game one, but the manager was not worried. "This guy is a tough kid, and he's got it all to-gether," he said. "I'm sure he's going to be nervous, like everybody else, but I think he'll be up to the challenge. He's obviously a pretty good choice, I would think. He had a great game in the NLCS [National League Cham-pionship Series], and I feel very comfortable with him pitching." As the se-ries opened, Hernandez proved that his manager's faith in him was well-founded. He won game one of the series with a gutsy performance in which he struck out five batters and gave up three earned runs in five and two-thirds innings.

Florida and Cleveland split the first four games of the series, so game five loomed as a pivotal contest. Hernandez was scheduled to pitch for the Marlins, and he knew that he would have to put together another good performance. Once again he came through. Florida won game five by an 8-7 score, as Hernandez pitched eight innings. He struggled at times — he walked eight batters and gave up five earned runs — but his performance was good enough for him to secure his second World Series victory, and his fourth of the postseason. The victory further cemented his popularity both in Miami and Cuba. Indeed, thousands of Cubans listened to the baseball playoffs on short-wave radios, and they cheered wildly for Hernandez, even though he was officially regarded as a traitor by the Cuban government.

Cleveland won game six, forcing the series to a deciding seventh game. As both teams prepared for game seven, Hernandez learned that his mother, who had been trying for weeks to get permission from the Cuban government to travel to America to see her son play, had finally been granted a six-month visa. She arrived in Miami a few hours before game seven began. Miriam and Livan had a tearful reunion at the stadium just minutes before the start of the final game of the World Series. "This is incredible," said baseball legend Joe Dimaggio, who was present for the reunion.

> *After the Marlins won the World Series, Hernandez shared his joy. "This is definitely the best day of my life. I'm very, very happy. I got to cry with my mother, talk to her a little bit, and then win a World Series. This is better than a dream."*

Florida won game seven in dramatic fashion. Down by a run in the bottom of the ninth inning, the Marlins squeezed out a run to send the contest into extra innings. Then, in the bottom of the eleventh inning, Florida's Edgar Renteria hit a two-out single to drive in the winning run for the Marlins. The Miami crowd exploded in celebration, and the Florida players mobbed one another out on the field. A short time later, Hernandez learned that he had been voted the World Series' most valuable player. "I love you Miami!" he said. "I felt good and was very happy that my mother could attend the game. I dedicate this victory and this trophy to her. Everything is for her. To those in Cuba who follow me, I want them to know that I love and support them. This victory is for Miami and all of Latin America as well. It belongs to all of you."

Hours later, Hernandez was still basking in the glow of Florida's victory. "This is definitely the best day of my life," he told a huge group of English-

and Spanish-speaking reporters. "I'm very, very happy. I got to cry with my mother, talk to her a little bit, and then win a World Series. This is better than a dream."

Off-Season Changes

Hernandez treasured the championship, but the months following Florida's World Series victory were turbulent ones for both the team and Hernandez himself. The Marlins' ownership had spent millions of dollars to fill the team's roster with stars. But after winning the World Series, the team traded many of their top players in order to save money. Baseball fans and sports reporters were furious about this tactic, which completely dismantled the team. In addition, many people said that the decision to trade away the players tarnished the 1997 championship and proved that Florida had basically bought the World Series for themselves.

Hernandez was not happy to hear about all the trades, but he was more concerned about making sure that his mother enjoyed herself in the U.S. He took her all around Florida, and bought her lots of clothes and jewelry. They visited nightclubs and Disney World. Hernandez moved into a new condominium so she could stay in his old one. He also gave her his BMW. He has said that her visa to stay in the U.S. would be extended for another six months, so that she could stay through the 1998 baseball season. When asked what would happen after that, Hernandez had this to say: "I would love for her to stay, but that's her decision."

Recently, Hernandez also received exciting news about his brother. He learned that Orlando and seven other Cubans had made a daring escape from Cuba by boat. On December 26, 1997, they set out to sail 90 miles across the ocean from Cuba to Florida. They were sailing in a leaky 20-foot boat built from scrap wood. Their only equipment was a compass made from household magnets, four oars, four cans of Spam, bread, water, and sugar. Their ordeal turned into a nightmare. The boat sank near a tiny deserted island belonging to the Bahamas. They spent four days on the beach huddled under the boat's sail trying to stay alive on seaweed, crabs, and raw conch. They were rescued by a low-flying U.S. Coast Guard helicopter. Livan Hernandez was thrilled to hear abut his brother's successful escape, which meant that he would finally have the opportunity to play in the Major Leagues. In January 1998, Orlando Hernandez was designated a free agent by Major League Baseball. In March, he signed a contract to play for the New York Yankees. His contract is worth $6.6 million over four years.

HOME AND FAMILY

Livan Hernandez lives in Miami in a condominium, several floors below the condo he recently gave to his mother. He is single. Hernandez loves salsa music and Mexican soap operas. He also spends a lot of time working with tutors who are helping him learn the English language.

HONORS AND AWARDS

National League Championship Series Most Valuable Player: 1997
World Series Most Valuable Player: 1997

FURTHER READING

Boston Globe, Oct. 12, 1997, p.A1
Maclean's, Nov. 3, 1997, p.41
New York Times, Oct. 18, 1997, p.B17; Oct. 19, 1997, p.1; Oct. 24, 1997, p.C3;
    Oct. 27, 1997, p.C4; Jan. 8, 1998, p.C8
Newsweek, Jan. 12, 1998, p.44
People Weekly, Dec. 29, 1997, p.136
Sporting News, Jan. 29, 1996, p.41; Feb. 19, 1996, p.23; Oct. 20, 1997, p.34;
    Oct. 27, 1997, p.25
Sports Illustrated, Mar. 25, 1996, p.72
Time, Mar. 11, 1996, p.77
Time for Kids, Nov. 7, 1997, p.8
Washington Post, Oct. 22, 1997, p.A20

ADDRESS

Florida Marlins
Pro Player Stadium
2269 NW 199th Street
Miami, FL 33056

WORLD WIDE WEB SITES

http://www.flamarlins.com
http://www.majorleaguebaseball.com/nl/fla/

Jewel 1974-

American Singer, Songwriter, and Poet
Creator of *Pieces of You*

BIRTH

The singer known today as Jewel was born Jewel Kilcher on May 23, 1974, in Payson, Utah. Her parents were Atz Kilcher and Nedra Carroll. At the time of Jewel's birth, her parents were attending school in Utah, but they returned to their home in Alaska just two months later. Jewel, the second of their three children, has two brothers.

Jewel grew up in a famous Alaskan family. Her grandparents on her father's side were Yule and Ruth (Weber) Kilcher, immigrants from Switzerland. Both Yule and Ruth had fled from Europe in the 1940s, during World War II, as they saw the Nazi destruction of Europe. Several friends planned to join them in Alaska, where they hoped to create a self-sufficient utopian community for artists. Their dream, in Yule's words, was to "create an artistic and spiritual community in the wilderness where we can engage in crafts and music in relationship with nature." But World War II intervened, and their friends never managed to leave Europe.

Yule and Ruth bought a small parcel of land on Kachemak Bay near the town of Homer (pop. 4,000). Kachemak Bay is on the Gulf of Alaska in the Pacific Ocean, on the peninsula that is just south of Anchorage. They moved there and became homesteaders. A way of encouraging pioneers to move west and settle the country, homesteading allowed people to take over wilderness land, clear it, build a home, create a farm, and live there for free. The Kilchers gradually took over more land, until their homestead grew to 800 acres. There they raised their family of eight children, including Atz Kilcher, Jewel's father. Years later, after he and Nedra Carroll were married, they raised their children, Jewel and her two brothers, on the Kilcher family homestead.

YOUTH

Jewel's early life has been described as an Alaskan version of *Little House on the Prairie*. Life as an Alaskan farm girl could be very difficult. She grew up in a log cabin with no electricity or running water. They had no phone, no TV, no radio. For water, according to Jewel, "We had a hose, and you hooked it up to the stream. But if there were worms because the stream flooded, there were worms in your faucet." They had baths just once a week, and they used an outhouse, summer and winter. Their house was only heated with a coal-burning stove — there was no central heating system. The land provided the family's food. They caught salmon, tended a vegetable garden, picked wild berries, and raised cows for slaughter. "Look, it was a lot of work," says Jewel. "We'd be canning salmon after school while other kids would be watching [the cartoon series] 'He-Man.' But I was also very proud of it, and it shaped me into a certain kind of person. You'd get up at five in the morning, and there would be frost on your eyelashes. I shared a room with my brothers. I'd cook breakfast, milk the cow, walk three miles to the road, and hitchhike to school. It was a very romantic and poetic existence."

Despite the hard work, Jewel clearly loved her childhood in Alaska. For their playground, she and her brothers had the ocean beach and the meadows filled with wild flowers, with glacier-topped mountains in the distance. They also spent time in the forest, learning how to identify edible mushrooms, how to make birch-sap syrup, and how to mix a salad from fireweed, dandelion shoots, and fiddlehead ferns. On Sundays the family would invite the neighbors from adjoining homesteads to a potluck, followed by a sauna and a dip in a homemade pool. Jewel spent hours riding her horse; she started riding at the age of two or three, and it remains one of her passions.

Early on, Jewel was exposed to different forms of the arts. "[My mother, Nedra], was an artist, so she instilled in us a lot of her attitudes about the creative process in general. We had the gift and the freedom and the liberation of that. My dad, Atz, has also always existed intuitively and instinctively as an artist. When we were young, he would take us out on winter days down to the edge of the canyon and we'd dig up sides of the cliff that would expose frozen willow roots that were tangled and curly like a woman's hair. They'd be frozen and crystallized in ice — beautiful images that we'd soak. We'd then weave the roots into baskets." Jewel also spent hours writing in her journal, preparing for the poetry workshop that her mother would hold for Jewel and her brothers on the first Monday of each month.

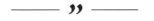

> "[Singing became] a very conscious study for me. That excited me and thrilled me. I spent most of my waking hours poring over tapes of my favorite singers, like Ella Fitzgerald. I'd learn one of my favorite songs of hers and practice it until I thought I could sound exactly like her—every thrill and trill and loop. Then I'd record myself and see how I differed, then try to correct the differences. . . . It taught me control over my voice."

Getting Involved with Music

There was always music in the Kilcher home. When Jewel was young, her father worked as a social worker, while her mother was a homemaker and artist. But both were also musicians. During the summers, they would sing six nights a week, doing dinner shows at hotels around Anchorage; during the winter, they did concerts on weekends. The kids would come along, and soon they were joining their parents on stage. They would show a film about the family's history and then sing and play various instruments—they even had homemade ones, like the homestead horn made from a hose and a funnel. "I'd sing with my parents, starting at about six years old, at hotels like the Hilton and Captain Cook Hotel," Jewel recalls. "Those days were filled with butterscotch Life Savers bought from hotel gift shops, waiting to go on, and talking with tourists from all over the world." Jewel developed her acclaimed talent for yodeling, as one resort owner recalls here. "I used to hire Atz, and he would cart Jewel along. She was always the show stopper. Their yodeling always brought the house down."

When Jewel was eight, her parents divorced, which was the beginning of a difficult time for her. Her mom moved out, and Jewel stayed with her dad on the family homestead. Atz Kilcher has been described as temperamental and mean. It's clear that Jewel loved performing with her father, whom she has called a charismatic entertainer. But it's also clear that she worked incredibly hard to earn his approval and goodwill—she has said that she'd practice as much as five hours a day. "We really had singing in common, so I sang my little

brains out. . . . He'd scream and curse, and I'd be crying, and I'd still sit there and practice." They often sang in bars, where even at a young age she learned how to perform for a live audience and even how to deal with drunks.

As Jewel grew up, music became an even more important part of her life. "[Singing became] a very conscious study for me. That excited me and thrilled me. I spent most of my waking hours poring over tapes of my favorite singers, like Ella Fitzgerald. I'd learn one of my favorite songs of hers and practice it until I thought I could sound exactly like her—every thrill and trill and loop. Then I'd record myself and see how I differed, then try to correct the differences. . . . It taught me control over my voice."

Jewel went through a tough time in her early adolescence. She was briefly adopted by a Native American Indian family, an informal process that doesn't seem to require the paperwork and bureaucracy that one would expect. "I went to a powwow and was adopted," Jewel once said. "I had these two uncles who were huge, huge Ottawa Indians. One said I was going to bring heart to the people." Tired of the cold and of living with her father, she then went to stay with relatives in Hawaii. When she returned to Alaska, she decided to live with her mother in Anchorage. At that time Nedra, a glass artist, was having some legal problems. "Investigators would come to my school," Jewel recalls, "and there would be things on me in the paper. We ended up having to hock our stuff and move." Nedra and Jewel moved to the small town of Seward, about 125 miles south of Anchorage.

EDUCATION

Jewel attended local schools through her sophomore year of high school, including the Steller Secondary School in Anchorage. There, she took a philosophy course that made a big impression on her. "I had a very rich life growing up, but that course taught me to think, really think. And that changed my writing. I started to write more critically and I became more articulate." Her teacher, Ken Ziegahn, agrees. "The class opened a whole new world for her," Ziegahn later said. "She developed some confidence in her own thinking. She took many of the human dilemmas we discussed in philosophy and turned them into situational dilemmas in her music lyrics."

—————— " ——————

"My first concern . . . was how I would exist in the business and remain true. I was looking for a producer who wouldn't produce me. I had met with a lot of them, and they all wanted to take me to the potential of what I could be in a couple of years naturally. I was looking for somebody who would let me at least be who I was, so I could be honest and recognizable to myself and my fans. I went with Ben Keith for those reasons."

—————— " ——————

For her last two years of high school, Jewel won a partial scholarship in vocal music to Interlochen Fine Arts Academy. Interlochen is a prestigious arts school located on a beautiful wooded campus in northern Michigan. She won a $6,000 scholarship, but she still needed an additional $11,000 to cover costs at the private boarding school. So she held a fund-raising concert and auction, asking local businesses to donate goods for an auction to raise money for her school expenses. She also got a job working at Interlochen, shoveling clay dust from the sculpting studios. "The things I had been taught at home, the discipline, the value of hard work, they all helped when I got to Interlochen," Jewel later said. "There were kids there who didn't even know how to shovel. I called my dad one day and said, 'I'm so sorry for all the [complaining].' Those are the words every parent wants to hear. But I really meant them."

For two years Jewel attended Interlochen, where she studied voice. "I wanted to study blues. They put me into opera, which I pursued but didn't take seriously." She also took classes in music, art, and dance, and she taught herself to play guitar and started writing songs. "My two years there were a turning point," she now says. "I saw a bigger world. I immersed myself in everything—drama, dance, sculpture, music." Jewel graduated from Interlochen in about 1992. She has said that she doesn't plan to attend college.

FIRST JOBS

After finishing school, Jewel traveled around for a bit before going to live with her mother, who had moved to San Diego, California. It was the beginning of another difficult time for Jewel. She held a variety of low-paying jobs, including waitressing, and got fired from most of them. "I worked

Jewel singing the National Anthem at the Super Bowl, January 1998

enough bad, crappy jobs where I thought, 'Wow, I could die (doing) this . . . and never have filled my life with passion.'" She was unhappy, and she knew she needed to make a change. "Even though I had been raised singing, I never thought I could make a living out of it. But it was the one thing that made me really happy, so I decided to go for it."

Jewel quit working and moved into her van to save money. As she told Oprah Winfrey, "That was really a blessing for me. I didn't have to live in my car; I could have tried paying rent somewhere and done that whole thing. But my mom, Nedra, really encouraged me to figure out what I wanted as a human, what I thought my purpose was here, why I existed, what my talents were, what gave me a sense of fulfillment so I wasn't just facing consciousness doing something I didn't like. . . . Living in my car was really like a spiritual time to reflect. . . . It was good." Her mother completely supported her decision; in fact, she even moved into her own van for a while as a form of encouragement, to help Jewel develop the courage to take such an unusual step. The two would often park next to each other, just like neighbors. As her mother recalls, "It was my suggestion that we move into our respective vans and cut out all this overhead. We would chose sites, park together, open our doors, and have tea."

Jewel holds her 1997 American Music Award for Favorite New Pop/Rock Artist

Jewel spent most of her time surfing and writing songs. She scrounged for enough to eat, lived mostly on carrots and peanut butter, used the bathrooms at the local Denny's restaurant, and relied on the kindness of friends to take showers. She struggled with medical problems, too: she had trouble with her kidneys, but didn't have enough money to pay for medical care. Soon, though, her choices started to pay off. She got a weekly gig at the Inner-change Coffeehouse in San Diego and started to build up a loyal fan base. Word of mouth spread about her shows, and each week her audience grew. First, an agent wanted to represent her. Then, limousines started pulling up in front of the coffeehouse, as executives from several different record companies came to listen to her. Soon they were in a bidding war, fighting for the chance to sign her to a contract. "I could hardly believe it when the first person asked if I wanted to make a record," Jewel recalls. "I asked if they were kidding, since I was only at this thing about four months." In 1994, when she was 19, Jewel signed with Atlantic Records.

CAREER HIGHLIGHTS

After signing with Atlantic, Jewel hooked up with producer Ben Keith, a long-time associate of Neil Young. "My first concern . . . was how I would exist in the business and remain true. I was looking for a producer who wouldn't produce me. I had met with a lot of them, and they all wanted to take me to the potential of what I could be in a couple of years naturally. I was looking for somebody who would let me at least be who I was, so I could be honest and recognizable to myself and my fans. I went with Ben Keith for those reasons." With his help, she recorded her first album, *Pieces of You* (1995), a collection of her own songs. Here, Jewel recalls her reaction to the record's release. "When my record came out, it was like a little fizzle," she recalled. "The moment I can really remember is when I sold 8,000 records in one week. I remember crying on my kitchen floor, just thanking God that I might not ever have to waitress or live in my car again."

Pieces of You

Pieces of You is a collection of 14 songs that Jewel wrote while still a teenager. Many listeners have commented on the emotionalism, idealism, naivete, and lack of sophistication of the lyrics and the unpolished, rough quality of the sound. Jewel herself admits that she made the record for her fans in San Diego, never expecting it to become a national hit. "It's really a time capsule," she explains. "When I recorded it, I thought, 'No one's gonna hear it. I'm just going to be honest and put it down on tape.' I didn't really clean up all the edges." She has even said that some of the songs are "dorky." A couple of the songs, in fact, were rerecorded before they were released as singles.

Despite such criticism of her recording, listeners routinely praise her powerful and evocative voice, which can range from ethereal to gutsy. *Time* magazine summed it up, calling her voice "an astonishingly versatile instrument ranging from soul-shattering yodels to the most eloquent of whispers to arch Cole Porter-ish recitative." Many people, including those at her record company, feel that Jewel is best enjoyed live. According to Atlantic executive Ron Shapiro, "The key to marketing her was to have her out there relentlessly. Even if you don't get the record, even if you don't think it's critically perfect, you can't deny what she does on stage. She has one of the most God-given voices I have ever heard an artist be given."

"To me creativity is one body; it just has different limbs — poetry, acting, music, whatever. I'm sure I'm not alone when I say that I need to do many different things to express myself fully."

After the release of *Pieces of You*, Jewel worked hard to earn the recognition and fan support that she has today. To take advantage of her appealing stage presence, she set out to do as many live shows as possible. She went out and toured mercilessly for the next two years to promote her music. Jewel worked seven days a week, often doing 40 shows in 30 days. "I'd do a high school show in the morning," she recalls. "Then I'd open for a gothic band, then a midnight show, drive three hours, sleep three hours. I was raised to work hard." She started out opening for other acts, moved up to headlining shows, and also moved up to bigger venues. It took a long time, but her hard work gradually paid off in multiple hit songs, millions of records sold, and a devoted group of fans. To date, *Pieces of You* has sold over eight million copies, testifying to Jewel's widespread popularity and appeal.

Other Creative Interests

Jewel, who has a wide range of creative interests, doesn't limit herself to just singing and writing songs. As she says, "[To] me creativity is one body; it just has different limbs — poetry, acting, music, whatever. I'm sure I'm not alone when I say that I need to do many different things to express myself fully." To that end, Jewel recently released some of her early poetry in a collection entitled *A Night without Armor: Poems* (1998). The collection has earned mixed reviews, with some critics deriding its lack of intellectual, emotional, and technical sophistication. Jewel herself says, "The poetry is very simple. I never wrote my poetry thinking people would hear it. I wrote it just out of my own need to understand what was going on in my life, and out of my own fascination with imagination, fairy tales, and that kind of thing. . . . Poetry for me is the most honest expression I can find—it's the most immediate expression. Sometimes with music, the lyric can become diluted or less significant next to the melody or the band or the ambience of a room. Whereas poetry, it's just the word and silence. I also need my poetry in a different way than I need music. Without writing every night, I don't do well. I need to write every night and every day. It's just how I process the world. I've always been the most frank, the most raw in my poetry writing. So it's very revealing in a much different way than my songs are."

In addition, Jewel is currently working on a movie. She plays a starring role in a drama about the Civil War, currently scheduled to be released in 1999. The movie is directed by Ang Lee, who made the critically acclaimed films *Sense and Sensibility* and *The Ice Storm*. Despite her inexperience as an actress Lee picked her for the film, in his words, because "Jewel is the perfect mixture of down-to-earth and ethereal." She has also been working on her next album, a follow-up to *Pieces of You*, which is due to be released in late 1998.

MARRIAGE AND FAMILY

Jewel, who is unmarried, lives in San Diego, California, when she is not on tour.

CREDITS

Recordings

Pieces of You, 1995

Writings

A Night without Armor: Poems, 1998

HONORS AND AWARDS

American Music Awards: 1997, Favorite New Pop/Rock Artist
MTV Music Video Awards: 1997, Best Female Video, for "You Were Meant for Me"

FURTHER READING

Books

West, Tracey. *Jewel: An Everyday Angel*, 1998

Periodicals

Alaska Magazine, Dec. 1989, p.22
Anchorage Daily News, Apr. 1, 1990, p.A1; Sep. 28, 1990, p.F1; Apr. 10, 1994,
    p.G1; Feb. 11, 1996, p.A1; Feb. 2, 1997, p.K5; July 24, 1997, p.D1
Details, July 1997, p.52
Interview, July 1997, p.88; June 1998, p.64
Los Angeles Times, Feb. 27, 1996, p.F1
People, May 6, 1996, p.22
Rolling Stone, June 13, 1996, p.22; May 15, 1997, p.36; Nov. 13, 1997, p.162
Seventeen, Oct. 1995, p.102
Time, July 21, 1997, p.66
Washington Post, Feb. 1, 1996, p.C3

Other

"The Oprah Winfrey Show," July 22, 1998

ADDRESS

Atlantic Records
9229 Sunset Blvd., Suite 900
Los Angeles, CA 90069

WORLD WIDE WEB SITES

http://www.jeweljk.com
http://www.atlantic-records.com/nonframes/home.html

Jimmy Johnson 1943-
American Professional Football Coach
Former Head Coach of the Super Bowl Champion
Dallas Cowboys
Head Coach of the Miami Dolphins

BIRTH

James William Johnson was born on July 16, 1943, in Port
Arthur, Texas. The second of three children born to Allene and
C.W. Johnson, he has an older brother, Wayne, and a younger
sister, Lynda. During Jimmy Johnson's early childhood, his fa-
ther worked as a mechanic at an oil refinery, but in 1949 C.W.
Johnson became the supervisor of a local dairy operation. At

this time, he moved his family into a nearby house that was owned by the company. It was in this house that Jimmy and his siblings grew up.

YOUTH

As a youngster, Johnson was known around the neighborhood as a bright, adventurous kid who loved to play football and other sports. Johnson himself recalled that he used to spend countless hours playing a particularly rough brand of football with neighborhood friends right outside his front door. A boulevard with a 10-yard wide grass median ran past the Johnson house, and "we'd play tackle football there — no helmets, no pads, with some local kids, the black kids," remembered Johnson. "I mean, we'd have some knock-down-drag-outs. I've got scars on my head because when you got knocked out-of-bounds, you'd go into the street."

Johnson also engaged in his share of mischief as he was growing up, though he apparently managed to hide most of his escapades from his parents. "Jimmy was a con artist," his brother Wayne once cheerfully said. "Probably still is." For the most part, though, family members and school friends remember him as a respectful son and good student.

EDUCATION

Johnson attended elementary school at a time when racial prejudice was vary common, especially in the south. Many public institutions were segregated, which means that people were separated by race. Johnson's school was segregated, so he did not have any African-American classmates. But many black children lived in his neighborhood, and he learned at an early age that bigotry against people simply because of the color of their skin was wrong. "Jimmy never thought there was any difference between him and the blacks," said his father. "And he didn't like it when anybody said anything about it, either."

By the time Johnson moved on to attend Thomas Jefferson High School in Port Arthur, all those hours of playing football with the neighborhood children had helped make him a very good player. He was a ferocious competitor, and his speed and strength enabled him to play both offensive lineman and linebacker. As a senior, he was regarded as one of the top high school players in the entire state of Texas, and he was a fixture on all-state teams. Johnson's athletic ability, along with his obvious intelligence and self-confidence, also made him one of the school's most popular students. One of his fellow students was Janis Joplin, who would go on to become a famous rock and roll singer before dying of a drug overdose in the late 1960s. Johnson recalled that he and Joplin once took a history class together, and that they spent much of the semester teasing each other.

In 1961 Johnson graduated from Thomas Jefferson. Many colleges approached him with football scholarship offers, but he eventually decided to attend the University of Arkansas. Despite weighing in at a little less than 200 pounds, Johnson played defensive nose-guard for the Arkansas Razorbacks football team. Each Saturday, he faced offensive linemen who were bigger and stronger than he was, but he still was one of the team's better performers. During his years at Arkansas, his teammates started calling him "Jimmy Jumpup," a reference to his ability to quickly jump to his feet even after being flattened by opposing linemen. Johnson enjoyed all four of his years at Arkansas, but the best year was 1964, his senior season. The team went undefeated and won the national championship. Johnson graduated from the University of Arkansas in 1965 with a bachelor's degree in psychology. He had done well in school, posting a 3.2 grade point average. He intended to continue his education and eventually secure a master's degree, but changed his mind and took a very different career path.

> *The Miami Hurricanes' loss to Penn State in the 1986 Fiesta Ball would haunt Johnson for years. "I don't know that I really committed myself totally to a job until after the disappointment of . . . having what I thought was the most talented football team in the history of college football in 1986 and not winning the national championship,"* he told **Sport** *magazine.*
>
> *"The next year we went undefeated and won the national championship with a less talented team. But that disappointment in '86 left a scar with me that I guess as long as I'm coaching football will drive me to cover all my bases. That one loss was the worst thing that ever happened to me in my coaching career."*

CHOOSING A CAREER

For most of his college career, Johnson had no inkling that he would go on to make a living in the world of football. During his senior season, however, several members of the coaching staff from Louisiana Tech University paid a visit to the Arkansas coaches, who often hosted coaching clinics for staffs from high schools and small colleges. As *Sports Illustrated* noted, "Johnson so thoroughly comprehended the [Razorbacks'] defensive scheme—the whole thing, not just the linemen's assignments—that the Arkansas coaches would send him to the chalkboard to lecture." His com-

Johnson celebrating with his team, the Dallas Cowboys,
after winning Super Bowl XXVIII

mand of Arkansas's defensive game plan—and his confident, well-spoken manner—bowled over the Louisiana Tech coaches. A year later, when their defensive line coach was forced to take the season off after suffering a heart attack, the Tech coaches remembered the bright senior from Arkansas. They asked Johnson, who had graduated by this time, to fill in for the coach during the 1965 season. Johnson leaped at the opportunity, thus sending him on the road to coaching stardom.

CAREER HIGHLIGHTS

Paying His Dues

Johnson spent one year at Louisiana Tech. After that, he knew that he wanted to try to make a career in coaching. As *People* observed, "Johnson had discovered his calling, and it soon became his obsession."

But the path was a bumpy one during the mid-1960s. While in college, he had married Lynda Kay Cooper, a fellow Arkansas student, and by this time the couple had a small son, Brent. The family's financial situation was tight. After an assistant coaching job at Florida State fell through, Johnson was forced to take an assistant coaching job at a high school in Mississippi.

In 1967 Johnson returned to the college ranks when he was asked to join the coaching staff at Wichita State University. "I knew right from the start that Jimmy was different," recalled Larry Lacewell, who hired Johnson. "He used to drive me nuts in meetings because he'd never take a note. Kept it all [in his mind]. Never forgot a detail." After a year at Wichita State, Johnson moved on to serve as the defensive coordinator at Iowa State University. In 1970 he moved again, joining the staff at Oklahoma University. The Oklahoma Sooners were one of college football's most powerful teams, and Johnson's performance there from 1970 to 1972 solidified his reputation as one of the country's brightest young assistant coaches.

In 1973 Arkansas Head Coach Frank Broyles asked Johnson to join his staff as defensive coordinator. Johnson was delighted with the opportunity to coach at his alma mater, and when Broyles announced that he was going to retire from coaching in 1976, Johnson was told that he was in line for the head coaching job. At the last second, though, Arkansas hired Lou Holtz to take over the program. Angry and disappointed about the broken promise, Johnson moved on once more. He landed at the University of Pittsburgh, where he worked as the Panthers' defensive coordinator until 1978. Johnson then received his first head coaching opportunity.

Oklahoma State Cowboys

At the conclusion of the 1978 college football season, Oklahoma State University had embarked on a search for a new head football coach. The football program at OSU was a troubled one at the time. The National Collegiate Athletic Association (NCAA) had imposed penalties on the program for illegal recruiting activities. In addition, OSU was a member of the Big Eight Conference, which also included the always-powerful Oklahoma and Nebraska teams. Those teams had been beating up on the Oklahoma State Cowboys for years, and the NCAA penalties that had been imposed on the program made it even less likely that OSU would be able to compete with those squads.

Still, when Oklahoma State asked Johnson if he would like to take over the reins of its football program, the ambitious coach immediately accepted. He knew that if he could put together a competitive team in the Big Eight, people all across the country would take notice. The penalties that the NCAA had imposed against the Cowboys limited the number of scholarships that Johnson could offer, but he was determined to succeed. He put together a patchwork squad of scholarship players and walk-ons (non-scholarship students), and in his first season at the helm, the Cowboys notched a surprising 7-4 record. Johnson was subsequently voted the conference's coach of the year.

The Cowboys posted only average records for the next three years, but in 1983 Oklahoma State put together its best season in years. The club nearly upset heavily favored Nebraska, and its 7-4 regular season record brought the team an invitation to play in the Bluebonnet Bowl, where the Cowboys defeated Baylor University.

Miami Hurricanes

Meanwhile, the University of Miami (in Florida) suddenly found itself without a head coach. Howard Schnellenberger had guided the Miami Hurricanes to the national championship in 1983, but in May 1984 he abruptly announced that he was leaving the university to coach in the United States Football League (USFL). Miami's athletic director, Sam Jankovich, asked Johnson who he thought might be a good replacement for Schnellenberger, and the OSU coach slyly responded, "I wouldn't mind living on the beach, Sam."

Intrigued by Johnson's ambition and confidence, Jankovich decided to hire the bright young coach, and in June 1984 the school announced that Johnson was their new head football coach. Johnson's first year with the Hurricanes, though, was a rocky one. "He walked into gale-force hostility from the media and the public, which resented Miami's hiring a country boy from a school that fell short of being a football power," reported *Sports Illustrated.* "And worse, he met resentment from Schnellenberger's old staff, which he was required to keep for one year." One year after winning the national championship under Schnellenberger, the Hurricanes limped to an 8-5 record. A couple of those losses stand among college football's most famous games of the last 20 years. In one game, the Hurricanes led Maryland 31-0 at the half, only to lose 42-40 after an amazing Maryland comeback. A week later, they lost 47-45 to Boston College in heartbreaking fashion. On the last play of the game, Boston College quarterback Doug Flutie threw a "Hail Mary" desperation bomb from midfield that was caught by one of his receivers for the winning touchdown.

After the 1984 season, Johnson's many critics fumed, convinced that Miami had made a huge mistake in hiring him. Johnson himself admitted that the season took a heavy toll on him. "I wouldn't ever want to go through that again," he said. But during the off-season he replaced the embittered holdovers from Schnellenberger's staff with his own coaches, and he quickly returned the Hurricanes to championship form.

From 1985 to 1988, the Miami Hurricanes posted an amazing 44-4 record, destroying most of their opponents with a combination of explosive offense and suffocating defense. During that time, Johnson came to be known not only for his football smarts, but for his ability to communicate with his players, many of whom were African-Americans from impoverished inner-city backgrounds. At the same time, the team was gaining notoriety in college football as some players were involved in incidents ranging from theft and assault to accepting illegal gifts from boosters. As Geoffrey Norman wrote in *Sport*, "Johnson, according to critics, did not take any of this seriously enough and did not do enough to prevent it. In fact, they said, he tended to encourage his players in their excesses either by his silence or sometimes by his endorsement."

At the end of the 1996 season, Johnson told Dolphins fans to be patient. "I came back for one reason," he said, "and that's to win. I didn't come back because I needed a job."

In 1985 the club finished with an impressive 10-2 record, and in 1986 the Hurricanes went unbeaten in the regular season. As the top-ranked Hurricanes prepared to play second ranked Penn State in the Fiesta Bowl that year, however, Johnson's team found that most of the country was rooting for Penn State. By kickoff time, Miami was "probably the most despised team in the country," remarked *Sport,* which pointed out that the Hurricanes had become "a team known as much for ugly behavior and felony arrests as for winning football games." As *Current Biography Yearbook 1994* noted, "Johnson's Hurricanes were notorious for their taunting of opponents after big plays, for strutting celebrations in the end zone, and for ruthlessly pounding hapless, weaker teams into submission. The intimidation tactics of the Miami players, who were wearing military fatigues when they deplaned in Tempe [the site of the Fiesta Bowl] stood in marked contrast to the unassailable comportment of Penn State coach Joe Paterno's polite, clean-cut athletes."

When Penn State went on to upset the Hurricanes 14-10, many reporters characterized the contest as a triumph of good over evil. After the game, Johnson—who usually defended his program and his players—apologized for the unruly behavior of some of his players prior to the contest. But years later, he continued to argue that Miami's bad press was, at least in part, due to the fact that most of his top players were black. "I think a lot of the resentment came that way," he said. "I don't know that there was racism involved in the resentment, but there was some ignorance involved—people who have had few dealings with other ethnic groups."

The loss to Penn State would haunt Johnson for years. "I don't know that I really committed myself totally to a job until after the disappointment of . . . having what I thought was the most talented football team in the history of college football in 1986 and not winning the national championship," he told *Sport*. "The next year we went undefeated and won the national championship with a less talented team. But that disappointment in '86 left a scar with me that I guess as long as I'm coaching football will drive me to cover all my bases. That one loss was the worst thing that ever happened to me in my coaching career."

But as Johnson indicated, Miami recovered from that disappointment to win the national championship in 1987, capping the season with a 20-14 Orange Bowl victory over Oklahoma. In 1988, only a one-point loss to Notre Dame during the regular season prevented the Hurricanes from posting back-to-back undefeated seasons. Under Johnson's guidance, Miami had become an established college football powerhouse. The fans that had initially been so angry when he had become head coach had long since changed their minds, and Johnson had become one of Florida's most popular public figures. Imagine their shock and dismay, then, when he suddenly announced that he was leaving the university to move to the professional leagues. He was the new head coach of the Dallas Cowboys.

Dallas Cowboys

The Dallas Cowboys had been one of the NFL's most successful teams since joining the league back in 1960. By the late 1980s the franchise had deteriorated into one of the league's worst, but the Cowboys were still one of the

NFL's marquee names. Early in 1989 businessman Jerry Jones, who had been one of Johnson's teammates back at the University of Arkansas, bought the Cowboys. Jones remembered how tough his old teammate had been, and he knew that he would need a tough person to push Dallas back to the top. Johnson happily accepted Jones's offer to coach the club, and in February 1989 the Cowboys announced that he was their new coach.

Once again, Johnson encountered a lot of hostility in his new position. To make way for Johnson, Jones had fired Tom Landry, a widely respected coach who had taken Dallas to two Super Bowl victories. Indeed, Landry had been the coach of the Cowboys for all 28 years of their existence, and many people felt that Jones's abrupt dismissal of Landry showed a lack of appreciation for all his years of hard work.

Johnson ignored the controversy and turned his attention to rebuilding the Cowboys. At first the task seemed overwhelming. The 1989 season was a disaster. Dallas went 1-15, and Cowboy fans grumbled that Johnson would never be able to duplicate his college success in the pros. But Jones remained certain that Johnson was the man for the job. "Jimmy was brought here because he'd been through adverse situations and jumped up and handled them. When we finished our first year together, I knew I'd made the right decision. I saw something during that 1-15 season that I couldn't have seen if we'd gone to the playoffs or walked into a honeymoon in Dallas."

Even as Dallas got trounced on the football field, Johnson made numerous trades to get the team back on track. The most famous of these was the one in which he traded Herschel Walker, one of Dallas's few stars, to the Minnesota Vikings for five players and seven draft choices. This trade, as well as Johnson's knack for signing underrated free agents from other clubs, gave the Cowboys a much-needed infusion of young talent. In 1990 Johnson guided the improved Cowboys to a 7-9 record. A year later, young stars like quarterback Troy Aikman, running back Emmitt Smith, and wide receiver Michael Irvin sparked Dallas to an 11-5 record and their first playoff appearance in five years.

The 1992 season marked the Cowboys' return to championship form. The team won the NFC East Division with an impressive 13-3 record and moved all the way through the NFC playoffs to a berth in Super Bowl XXVII. Dallas demolished the Buffalo Bills in the Super Bowl by a 52-17 score, thus completing Johnson's remarkable four-year transformation of the Cowboys from NFL doormat to NFL champion. The Dallas victory also marked the first time that a coach had led both a college team and an NFL team to the top of their respective leagues.

Johnson and the Cowboys repeated as Super Bowl champions the following year, posting a 12-4 regular season mark on their way to a rematch with the Bills. Once again the Cowboys romped, defeating Buffalo in Super Bowl

XXVIII by a 30-13 count. The victory made Dallas one of only five NFL teams to win back-to-back Super Bowls and established Johnson as one of the league's best coaches.

But growing tensions between Johnson and Cowboys owner Jerry Jones cast a shadow over the team following that second Super Bowl victory. Both Johnson and Jones enjoyed the spotlight, and it seemed that whenever one of them received the lion's share of attention from the media, the other grew resentful. In addition, Johnson had become tired of the owner's interference with football operations and his insinuations that he — and not Johnson — was the real reason that the Cowboys had returned to power. Their crumbling relationship became even worse after a clash at a restaurant in March 1994. Jones went over to Johnson's table to propose a toast to the Cowboys, only to be treated coolly by the coach and his friends. Jones was furious, but Johnson later pointed out that the people seated at the table included two people that Jones had recently fired.

In any event, attempts to patch up the relationship failed, and on March 29, 1994, Johnson resigned. "In the end . . . Johnson got what he wanted," wrote Peter King in *Sports Illustrated*. "An escape from the man he had grown to dread, a voiding of the last five years of his contract, and a $2 million [severance package] to boot. 'Jimmy orchestrated the thing brilliantly,' says quarterback Troy Aikman. 'He wanted out, he saw a crack, and he took it. He got a ton of money, and he got everyone to feel sorry for him.'"

Miami Dolphins

After spending the 1994 and 1995 seasons as a football analyst for the Fox Network, Johnson signed a contract to be the new head coach of the Miami Dolphins. Once again, Johnson was taking over for a very popular coach — longtime Miami coach Don Shula, in this case — but this time he received a fairly warm welcome. The Dolphins had not been a top contender for several years, and Miami fans were eager to see if Johnson would be able to work his magic with their team. In 1996 the Dolphins put together an 8-8 season that disappointed many of the team's followers. But Johnson pointed out that he had not won championships in his first seasons with the University of Miami or Dallas, either. He told Dolphins fans to be patient. "I came back for one reason," he said, "and that's to win. I didn't come back because I needed a job."

As 1997 drew to a close, the Dolphins were eliminated from the playoffs. This appears to be another building season for the Dolphins, and their dream of a Super Bowl will have to wait for another year.

MARRIAGE AND FAMILY

Johnson married Lynda Kay Cooper in 1963. The couple had two children, Brent (a lawyer) and Chad (a stockbroker) before divorcing in 1989. As Johnson himself admitted in his autobiography, *Turning the Thing Around,* he told his wife that he wanted a divorce in a pretty cold, unemotional fashion. But they managed to remain fairly friendly after the divorce. "We were growing apart, and our interests were in different areas," said Johnson. He is close to both of his sons, although Johnson concedes that he did not spend as much time with them as he should have when they were growing up. Johnson currently lives in Miami and spends much of his free time with his girlfriend, Rhonda Rookmaaker.

HOBBIES AND OTHER INTERESTS

Johnson's enthusiasm for Florida's climate and nightlife is well-known. "I think it's the people — you have a lot of different ethnic groups, I like that," he told *Sport.* "Plus, with the weather here, you have a resort-type atmosphere. I love warm weather and I don't like cold weather." He also likes boating, and he has a large boat on which he spends long hours during the off-season. He also collects exotic fish, and the rooms of his Florida home are dotted with large saltwater aquariums.

WRITINGS

Turning the Thing Around: Pulling America's Team Out of the Dumps — and Myself Out of the Doghouse, 1993 (with Ed Hinton)

HONORS AND AWARDS

Big Eight Conference Coach of the Year: 1978
College Coach of the Year (Walter Camp Foundation): 1986-87
NFL Coach of the Year (*College and Pro Football Newsweekly*): 1990
NFL Coach of the Year (United Press International): 1990
NFL Coach of the Year (Associated Press): 1990
NFL Coach of the Year (*Football Digest*): 1991
NFL Coach of the Year (ESPN): 1992, 1993
Victor Award (*Sport*): 1992, 1993

FURTHER READING

Books

Bayless, Skip. *The Boys,* 1993
Johnson, Jimmy, with Ed Hinton. *Turning the Thing Around: Pulling America's Team Out of the Dumps — and Myself Out of the Doghouse,* 1993

Lovitt, Chip. *Dallas Cowboys,* 1996 (juvenile)
Who's Who in America, 1997

Periodicals

Current Biography Yearbook 1994
Esquire, Sep. 1993, p.110
New Republic, Feb. 22, 1993, p.42
New York Times, Jan. 27, 1994, p.B17; Feb. 2, 1994, p.A14; Oct. 9, 1997, p.C2
Newsweek, Apr. 11, 1994, p.80
People, Sep. 16, 1996, p.15
Sport, Sep. 1988, p.60; July 1993, p.23; July 1996, p.37
Sporting News, Dec. 16, 1996, p.14
Sports Illustrated, Mar. 6, 1989, p.22; Mar. 20, 1989, p.26; Sep. 7, 1992, p.92;
    Apr. 11, 1994, p.36; Jan. 22, 1996, p.38; May 13, 1996, p.66

ADDRESS

Miami Dolphins
7500 W. 30th St.
Davie, FL 33329

WORLD WIDE WEB SITES

http://www.nfl.com
http://www.dolphinsendzone.com

Tara Lipinski 1982-

American Figure Skater
Youngest Gold Medalist in the History of Olympic
Figure Skating

BIRTH

Tara Kristen Lipinski was born on June 10, 1982, in Philadelphia, Pennsylvania. Her parents are Jack and Patricia Lipinski. Jack is an executive with an oil company, and Pat devotes herself to Tara's skating career. Tara is an only child and was named for the home of the heroine in the movie *Gone with the Wind*, her mother's favorite film.

EARLY YEARS

Tara spent her early years in Sewell, New Jersey. By her mother's account, she was always an active child. She started walking early, when she was only nine months old, and she was always full of energy. Her mom remembers that she would wake up each day and say, "Mommy, what are we going to do today?"

An often-told tale of Tara's early years involves her first "Olympics." When she was just two years old, she watched the Olympics on television. She didn't really care about the sports, what she loved to watch was the medal ceremony. She asked her mother for a piece of Tupperware, which she pretended was the medal stand. Then she had her mom give her plastic flowers and tie a ribbon around her neck. Even at two, Tara Lipinski liked the idea of being an Olympic champion.

STARTING TO SKATE

When Tara was just three years old, her parents took her to a roller skating rink for lessons. She loved it. For the next few years, she skated regularly, and when she was four, she started to compete. From a very young age, Tara Lipinski showed the determination and drive to win that has characterized all her endeavors. When she was six, her parents took her ice skating for the first time. She slipped and fell, but kept at it. Her parents were amazed. After only one hour on the ice, she was doing jumps.

In 1991, when Tara was nine, her father received a promotion and the family moved to Houston, Texas. They built a lovely home in the suburb of Sugar Land, and Tara and her mother looked around for a place for her to skate. In Houston, there isn't much opportunity for skaters. The only rink is in a shopping area called the Galleria. To get ice time, Tara had to get up at four in the morning. She started working with a new coach, Megan Faulkner, who recognized Tara's great potential and drive. Tara loved to skate, but if she were to continue to train at the highest level, she and her family were faced with a difficult decision.

A DECISION TO TRAIN SERIOUSLY

The top skaters in the U.S. train in a very few cities, and none of them are in Texas. The Lipinskis were convinced of Tara's ability, and her coach assured them that, with the right training, she could be a champion. But in order for her to train, the family would have to split up. After talking it over, the family decided that Jack Lipinski would stay in Texas and continue with his job. They would need the money to pay for Tara's training and to provide two homes. Tara and her mom would move to Delaware, where Tara would train at the University of Delaware Ice Skating Center. They would live apart and see each other only on weekends.

From the beginning, the sacrifice was hard on all the family. "Tara knows I'm sad being away from my husband," said Pat Lipinski after the move in 1993. "It's hard to do; it's lonely. But I'd give my daughter anything. She loves it. And we're seeing results. I can't just demand that she stop. For the rest of my life, I'd have to sit around and think, 'What if'." Tara's father felt the same way. "You have a child and you want to do everything for that child that you can possible do. Tara absolutely adores this. Whether she does anything more, if nothing else this has taught her that hard work pays off."

Yet there were tradeoffs. Tara didn't really have a regular childhood, with school and friends. Her schedule made it hard to make—and keep—friends. Her mother recalled, "The worst day of my life, I went through her book bag at the end of school and there was a note, blunt as anything, from one of her friends: 'Dear Tara, you have a choice to make, me or skating'. It rips your heart out," Pat Lipinski said.

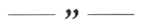

"When I stepped on the ice I had a feeling I knew what the Olympics were about," Lipinski said. "I had that feeling of pure joy, and I went out there and put it in my program."

EDUCATION

When Tara first started school, she attended public school in New Jersey and Texas. But when she and her mother made the move to Delaware, she began to study with a tutor, which she continues to do today. In Delaware, Tara worked with her tutor for several hours, then she would skate for several hours. Today, she lives and trains in Bloomfield Hills, Michigan, a wealthy suburb of Detroit. She studies with three different tutors for a total of four hours each day, then spends three hours skating. Even with the demands of her sport, Tara has always maintained straight A's.

CAREER HIGHLIGHTS

Once Tara and her mom moved to Delaware, her life truly revolved around skating. She started working with a new coach, Jeff DiGregorio. Within a year, she started to compete. Her first competition took place in Detroit, at the Novice Nationals in 1994, where she took second place. The summer of 1994, she skated in the Olympic Festival competition, where, at the age of 12, she won the gold medal. It was a stunning win, and it became the first of many "firsts" for Tara Lipinski—she was the youngest gold medalist in Olympic Festival history. In 1994, Tara also competed and placed first in the Southwestern Novice and Midwestern Novice competition. Next, she tried out for and won a place on the World Junior team. Now she would have her first try at international competition.

In 1995, Tara went to the World Junior Championships in Budapest, Hungary, where she placed fourth. Back home in the United States, she took part in the National Junior Championships in Anchorage, Alaska, and placed second. After that competition, she told the press that her goal was to "win the Olympics, whatever one, any Olympics."

By this time, Tara Lipinski was being recognized as a force to be reckoned with in the skating world. Although she is very small—just 4' 10" and 85 pounds—she is a strong, fast skater and a fierce competitor. Because of her small stature, she is able to do a number of difficult jumps with ease. She doesn't have the weight or the build of a mature female skater, so she can lift her body up easier, and spin faster, than bigger skaters. Competitive figure skating has changed over the years. Like women's gymnastics, it has become more focused on athleticism, especially jumping, than in the past. While she recognized that her athletic ability was her strength, Tara worked on her artistic ability to be as complete a skater as she could be. She began to study ballet one hour a day to develop a more elegant presence.

In 1995, Tara's mother made a coaching change. Pat Lipinski disagreed with Jeff DiGregorio on her daughter's training, and she and Tara began to look for another coach. They decided on Richard Callaghan of the Detroit Skating Club in Bloomfield Hills, Michigan. Callaghan is also the coach of men's figure skater Todd Eldredge, the 1996 and 1997 World Men's Champion. The Lipinskis also chose an agent for their daughter, Mike Burg of Edge Marketing.

In 1996, Tara competed as a senior for the first time in the National Championships, and she placed an amazing third. Just a few months later, Tara competed in her first World Championships as a senior. Figure skating competitions at this level include a "short program," skated in approximately two minutes and containing a series of required moves and jumps, and a "long program," which lasts four minutes and focuses more on artistry than on technical expertise. In the World Championships in 1996, Tara had a rough time in her short program and wound up in 23rd place. But the next day, in her long program, she skated beautifully, and managed to finish 15th overall.

National and World Champion

On February 16, 1997, Tara Lipinski made history again, when, at age 14, she became the youngest person to win the U.S. Nationals. She had won with a record seven triple jumps in her program, defeating the reigning champion Michelle Kwan. With this win, Tara came under more intense scrutiny in the press, which analyzed her size, her training, her parents' decisions to live apart, and her ability to take the pressure of the inevitable media onslaught. As her new agent announced that Tara now had her own web site, *New York Times* writer Jere Longman noted "the tropical storm of her celebrity had become a hurricane."

Lipinski at the 1998 Olympics

In March 1997, Lipinski won the World Championships in Lausanne, Switzerland. At age 14, she was again the youngest skater ever to win the Worlds. Once again she did seven triple jumps, including what has become her signature move, a triple loop-triple loop combination that she alone among all female skaters can do. Surprised by her victory, Tara said, "I never expected it, especially not this year, going into the Worlds. I just thought about my skating, but I knew what I had to do and I did it."

Lipinski set her sights on the 1998 Olympics, where she hoped that all the years of hard work and family sacrifice would lead to the realization of her dream—an Olympic gold medal.

As Lipinski moved to the top of her sport, her parents finally received some relief from the financial burden of paying for her training. While they have always said that the financial sacrifices have been worth it, the training of a top figure skating costs a lot of money. When Lipinski started, the total cost of her skating each year was about $40,000. As she moved to the top levels, the cost of her skating climbed to more than $58,000 per year, forcing her parents to remortgage their house to pay for her training, tutors, travel, and separate homes. By 1997, when it was clear that she was headed for the Olympics, she began to receive endorsements and fees from her skating that, for the first time, covered all of her expenses. She embarked on a year of training, performing, and media hype that would lead to Nagano, Japan.

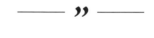

"What separates Tara from any other skater is she is a kid who can open up the kid's market to skating like no competitor ever before. We won't be trying to make her into an older woman. What she is is a darling little girl."

Getting Ready for the Olympics

In the summer of 1997, Lipinski took part in a skating tour, in part to earn money for her training and in part to give her more chances to perform. She also began to work on the artistic aspects of her skating, spending hours each day performing in front of a mirror. Meanwhile, the media began to promote the rivalry between Lipinski and Michelle Kwan, whom she had beaten twice in 1997, in the Nationals and in the Worlds. She seemed to take the pressure well, insisting that she loved the cameras and the competition. Her agent liked her marketing potential. "What separates Tara from any other skater is she is a kid who can open up the kid's market to skating like no competitor ever before. We won't be trying to make her into an older woman. What she is is a darling little girl."

Another figure skating sports agent, Michael Rosenberg, voiced another opinion about the marketing of Tara Lipinski. He said that "If we become a sport of little girls doing little jumps, instead of glamourous young women, we lose a significant portion of our appeal. But Tara Lipinski could be exceptional. Tara is smart, savvy, hardworking, tough. She has the same qualities Oksana Baiul had when she was 15."

Lipinski's coach, Richard Callaghan, worked with her on all aspects of her Olympic performance. She is a perfectionist, and if she misses a jump in practice, she will force herself to do it five times perfectly. When out of frustration, Tara would tell Callaghan, "I should quit; I'm no good," he would reply, "You're right, you should go back to roller skates." His attitude seemed to help her get a perspective on her skating.

In January 1998, Lipinski was competing again, this time at the U.S. Nationals, always considered an "Olympic warmup." Surprisingly, she fell in her short program, losing valuable points. Her rival Michelle Kwan skated to first place, with several perfect 6.0 scores for artistry. Lipinski placed second. The stage was set for the Winter Olympics, taking place in Nagano, Japan, in February.

1998 OLYMPICS

Tara Lipinski went to Nagano for the opening ceremonies of the Olympics, which took place almost two weeks before her event. She seemed to enjoy herself thoroughly, marching with the American team at the ceremonies, having her picture taken with the huge sumo wrestler Akebono, living in the Olympic Village with the other athletes, eating in the cafeteria. She met Wayne Gretzky, and one day, when she was sitting alone in the cafeteria, the U.S. Women's hockey team invited her to sit with them. "For most of the two weeks since she arrived in Japan, Lipinski generally has acted like a 15-year-old having the time of her life at the Olympics," observed Philip Hersch of the *Chicago Tribune.*"

Michelle Kwan, nursing an injury, did not take part in the opening ceremonies. When she did arrive in Japan, she stayed with her parents in a hotel rather than in the Village with the other athletes.

The media frenzy was on, and the television cameras were at the skating rink to film even the practices of the figure skaters. Tara worked that exposure in her favor, asking to review the films of her practices in her relentless pursuit of perfection.

When the figure skating competition finally began, Tara was considered the underdog, largely because of Kwan's recent win at the Nationals. She was happy with that status, claiming "I like being the underdog. I think it's good for me."

An Olympic Gold Medal

On the opening night of the competition, Tara skated beautifully, and with an exuberance that was infectious. In the words of *Sports Illustrated*'s E.M. Swift, she was "luminous—fast and light and joyful." When Kwan took the ice, she skated a program that was serene, lovely to look at, and technically flawless. At the end of the short program, Kwan was in first place, Lipinski in second. In the opinion of the media, the gold medal was "Kwan's to lose."

The second night of the competition, Kwan skated first among the top skaters. She seemed tentative and unsure of herself. Playing it safe, seemingly more afraid of losing than bent on winning, Kwan skated a beautiful long program. But it lacked something. In the words of Kwan's coach, Frank Carroll, Kwan "was going for accuracy and consistency. Her performance was very held in. It was

Tara Lipinski, front, Michelle Kwan, left, and Chen Lu, back

not the feeling of flying." When Kwan's marks were in, the judges had given her a number of 5.9s for presentation, but several 5.7s for technical performance. It left, in the words of *SI*'s Swift, "a sliver of room, which was all Lipinski needed."

"When I stepped on the ice I had a feeling I knew what the Olympics were about," Lipinski said. "I had that feeling of pure joy, and I went out there and put it in my program."

Then Lipinski took the ice—and the competition—by storm. She skated the program of her life, with the beauty, joy, and strength of a champion. According to Swift, "She soared and spun with abandon, filling the White Ring with her joy." She again landed all seven triple jumps, including the triple loop-triple loop. With every successful jump, Lipinski's smile grew wider and wider. She was having the time of her life. When she was finished, she raced across the ice in delight. When her marks were in, the judges had given her first place. Lipinski let out a whoop that filled the arena. She was the Olympic champion, and she loved it. Her win was another one for the record books — at 15, she was the youngest Olympic figure skating champion ever.

"It went by so quick," Lipinski said afterward. "I was happy, but a little sad, knowing I was going to have to get off. I couldn't think of anything wrong. I couldn't think of anything negative. Everything was perfect."

After the medal ceremony, and after the reality of what she'd accomplished set in, Lipinski said, "I'm so happy but also a little sad that the Olympics are slipping away." As she got ready to leave Nagano, she said, "I hate leaving. I'll miss the village and the cafeteria as much as the skating. I'll miss it, but I don't think I could do this again."

Right after the Olympics, Lipinski toured with the other Olympic stars, who skated in cities across the country as part of the Campbell's tour.

FUTURE PLANS

On March 9, 1998, Lipinski made an announcement that stunned some in the skating world. She announced that since the Olympics she had been suffering from fatigue and a glandular disorder, and she had decided she would not compete in the World Figure Skating Championships in late March. Lipinski also made a vague reference to the fact that her competitive skating career might be over. "We realized we wanted to be 100 percent and not hurting," she told reporters. "I think I've fulfilled everything I really, really wanted to. It's nice to leave it like this, with that kind of performance," she concluded, referring to her Olympic performance.

Then, on April 7, 1998, Lipinski announced that she was turning professional to spend more time with her family. She said that she wanted her family to be united, and not to live apart as they had during the years of her intensive training for the Olympics. "I don't want to be 22 and not know my dad," she said. "[My parents] gave up so much for me to get this gold medal. I could go back and try to get another one, but it would be greedy for me to have them live apart another four years." Because of her change in status, Lipinski will not be eligible to compete in the 2002 Olympics.

HOME AND FAMILY

At this point, Tara and her mom are still living in Bloomfield Hills, Michigan, where Tara continues to train. But now that she has turned professional, Lipinski plans to spend more time at her Texas home. Her dad lives in Sugar Land, Texas, with the five family dogs, Brandy, Camelot, Lancelot, Mischief, and Coco. In her spare time, Tara likes to cook and sew, and she loves to shop. She also collects stuffed frogs.

WRITINGS

Triumph on Ice, 1997 (with Emily Costello)

HONORS AND AWARDS

U.S. Olympic Festival: 1994, First
National Junior Championships: 1995, Second
World Junior Championships: 1995, Fourth; 1996, Fifth
National Championships: 1996, Third; 1997, First; 1998, Second
World Championships: 1996, Fifteenth; 1997, First
Olympic Figure Skating: 1998, Gold Medal

FURTHER READING

Books

Daly, Wendy. *Tara and Michelle: The Road to Gold*, 1997
Lipinski, Tara, with Emily Costello. *Triumph on Ice*, 1997
Lovitt, Chip. *Skating for the Gold: Michelle Kwan and Tara Lipinski*, 1977

Periodicals

Boston Globe, Feb. 17, 1997, p.F5; Mar. 21, 1997, p.D1
Chicago Tribune, Feb. 13, 1997, Sports, p.1; Feb. 17, 1997, Sports, p.8; Mar. 23,
    1997, Sports, p.3; Jan 4, 1998, Sports, p.1; Feb. 17, 1998, Sports, p.1
Houston Post, Feb. 6, 1994, p.B25; July 5, 1994, p.C1; Nov. 9, 1994, p.B1
New York Times, Oct. 11, 1994, p.B9; Feb. 8, 1995, p.B12; Feb. 17, 1997, p.A1;
    Mar. 23, 1997, p.A1; Oct. 21, 1997, p.C25; Feb. 19, 1998, p.C27; Feb. 21,
    1998, p.A1, p.B17
Newsweek, Mar. 17, 1997, p.64; Mar. 2, 1998, p.62
People, Mar. 3, 1997, p.56
Sports Illustrated, Feb. 24, 1997, p.28 Mar. 22, 1997, p.47; Mar. 2, 1998, p.48
Time, Mar. 2, 1998, p.66
USA Weekend, Feb. 6, 1998, p.6
Washington Post, Mar. 18, 1996, p.C1

ADDRESS

Edge Marketing
1808 East Boulevard
Charlotte, NC 28203

WORLD WIDE WEB SITE

http://www.taralipinski.com

Jody-Anne Maxwell 1986-

Jamaican Student
Winner of the 1998 National Spelling Bee
First Non-U.S. Winner

EARLY LIFE

Jody-Anne Maxwell was born in St. Andrew, Jamaica, on May 5, 1986. Her parents are Shirley and Lloyd Maxwell of Kingston, Jamaica. Shirley is a data processing specialist, and Lloyd is an accountant. Jody-Anne is one of five girls, with older sisters Karen, Karlene, and Janice, and younger sister Rachel.

Jody-Anne is an eighth grader at Ardenne High School in Kingston. She is a straight-A student and her favorite subject is math.

MAJOR ACCOMPLISHMENT

The National Spelling Bee

Jody-Anne participated in the 1998 National Spelling Bee, which is sponsored by the Scripps Howard media organization. Spellers can compete through the eighth grade. Each year, regional contests include more than nine million English-speaking students from anywhere in the world. This year's contestants came from the United States, Mexico, Guam, Puerto Rico, the Bahamas, and Jamaica. Over 200 winners of these regional contests go on to compete in the national championships. In all these events, each participant is given a word to spell. With a correct spelling, the student advances to the next round; with an incorrect spelling, the student is eliminated from the spelling bee. Participants are given lengthy lists of practice words that are used in the first few rounds of the spelling bee; after that, the words are unfamiliar and difficult.

Jody-Anne was part of only the second Jamaican team to participate in the National Spelling Bee. To prepare for the event, she and her two teammates, Bettina Mclean and Haydee Lindo, practiced looking up words and learning about the origins and meanings of all kinds of words. Their practice sessions were intense and went on for months.

At the start of this year's competition, Jody-Anne was one of 249 participants. In the first ten rounds, she spelled "alveolate," "whelp," "pampas," "tilak," "cerography," "allargando," "hyssop," "quixote," "parrhesia," and "daedal." She took her time with each word, taking advantage of the rules that allow a contestant to ask for definitions, alternate pronunciations, and origins of the words. Commentators noted Jody-Anne's impeccable enunciation, her deliberate responses, and her polite, reserved manner. Every request for a clarification included a "please" and "thank you, sir" to the moderator.

Finally, in Round 11, it was down to Jody-Anne and Prem Trivedi. Prem is a four-time veteran of the Spelling Bee who had placed second in last year's competition. He received the word "prairillon," meaning small prairie. He misspelled it. Jody-Anne was next. She got the word "chiaroscurist" (meaning an artist who works in vivid dark and light shades). She thought for a while, smiled, then asked the moderator to repeat it and put it in a sentence. Then she spelled it, perfectly.

The families and coach of the team cheered wildly and waved the Jamaican flag as Jody-Anne triumphed. The three Jamaican contestants, who call themselves the "three bees," hugged each other, and Jody-Anne shouted and waved her arms. She was the first non-U.S. resident to win the Bee in

Jody-Anne accepts the winning trophy from
Rich Boehne of the National Spelling Bee

its 71-year history. Jody-Anne revealed that although she looked calm on the outside, inside she was very nervous. "I had a lot of jitters, but I just tried to keep focused and calm," she said.

Jody-Anne won $10,000, an encyclopedia, and airline tickets. As soon as her victory was announced, she was asked to appear on television shows in New York and Washington, D.C., and she made a flurry of appearances. She told the press that it was "God and training" that had helped her to win the Bee. She offered to help next year's entrants from Jamaica. She also offered this advice to Spelling Bee hopefuls: "Trust God, work hard, and never lose sight of your goal." Her proud father, Lloyd Maxwell, claimed that Jody-Anne is "really a very organized, focused individual. Every evening she would go to her dictionary."

Jody-Anne has become a real celebrity in Jamaica. After one organization announced it would start a scholarship fund of $5,000, other groups pitched in and raised the figure to $50,000. Howard University in Washington, D.C., offered her a full college scholarship to study there. Unlike most participants, who are sponsored by their local newspapers, Jody-Anne and her teammates were sponsored by a stationery shop from Kingston, Phillips & Phillips Stationery Supplies. They took great pride in their champion, too, saying that Jody's victory "showed that Jamaica is not just a land of nice white beaches, not just the best all-inclusive hotels in the world. But it also has nice children with spunk, pizzazz, and excitement."

When she finishes high school, Jody-Anne would like to study to become a corporate lawyer. "I like to defend people and put forth their rights," she says.

In her spare time, Jody-Anne likes to play volleyball, read, and listen to music. She especially enjoys mystery novels and listening to classical music.

FURTHER READING

Houston Chronicle, May 29, 1998, p.A4
Memphis Commercial Appeal, May 29, 1998, p.A13
Miami Herald, May 29, 1998, p.A4
New York Times, May 30, p.A9
Seattle Times, May 29, 1998, p.A9
USA Today, May 29, 1998, p.A7
Washington Post, May 29, 1998, p.B1

ADDRESS

Scripps Howard National Spelling Bee
P.O. Box 5380
Cincinnati, OH 45201

WORLD WIDE WEB SITE

http://www.spellingbee.com

Dominique Moceanu 1981-

American Gymnast
Winner of a Team Gold Medal at the 1996
Olympic Games

BIRTH

Dominique Moceanu (pronounced moh-chee-AHN-new) was
born on September 30, 1981, in Hollywood, California. Earlier
that year, her mother, Camelia, had left her native Romania to
join her husband, Dimitry, who had come to the United States
in 1979. Dominique's father owned a series of car dealerships,
and her mother worked at a variety of jobs, including in a beauty salon. "Because my parents are Romanian, and because peo-

ple think I resemble a famous Romanian gymnast, Nadia Comaneci, many people assume that I am Romanian too," Moceanu noted in her autobiography, *Dominique Moceanu: An American Champion.* "But I feel very American. I've always lived in America, most of my friends are American, and I go to American schools." The Moceanu family also includes Dominique's younger sister, Christina.

YOUTH

Both of Moceanu's parents were gymnasts in Romania. When they married, they promised each other that their first child would be an athlete—preferably a gymnast. It was not long after Dominique's birth that her parents began watching for signs that she could fulfill their dreams. When she was only six months old, her father presented her with her first strength test: he strung a clothesline up in the kitchen, held Dominique up until she grabbed hold, and then slowly let her go. "They waited and waited for my grip to weaken, but I hung on," Moceanu explained. "I guess I was stubborn! As the minutes passed, my parents looked at each other with pride and excitement. . . . Later they told me that the clothesline actually broke before I would let go! And that was my first gymnastics test. I'm glad I passed it, and I'm glad my parents saw so much potential in me even back then."

When Dominique was just three years old, her father contacted Bela Karolyi, a world-famous gymnastics coach who had immigrated to the United States from Romania around the same time as the Moceanus. He settled in Houston and opened a gymnastics training camp there. Karolyi was the controversial coach of such famous gymnasts as Nadia Comaneci, Mary Lou Retton, and later Kerri Strug. He told Dimitry Moceanu that his daughter was still too young for formal training, so she was enrolled in a local gymnastics club instead. The family soon moved to Highland Park, Illinois, where young Dominique took her first gymnastics classes.

Two years later, the family moved to Tampa, Florida, where Moceanu continued her training at LaFleur's Gymnastics. Her parents viewed these years, between 1985 and 1991, as a kind of waiting period until Dominique was old enough to be trained by Karolyi. In the meantime, she enjoyed a relatively normal childhood, attending school and making friends. "In some ways I had a totally normal life, but I had already been bitten by the gymnastics bug," Moceanu admitted. "I loved gymnastics more than anything. I always have, for as long as I can remember."

Moceanu took part in her first gymnastics competition at the age of seven. Up until this time, she viewed the sport as a way to play and have fun; she didn't care how she ranked in comparison to other gymnasts. "Then I did my skills. And people applauded. They applauded for *me*," Moceanu recalled. "I think that's when I knew I was really hooked—there was no turning back. I liked being in the limelight. All of a sudden I wished I had done better. I resolved right then to compete again, and to do my absolute best, from then on."

Moceanu stuck to her resolution, taking practices and competitions much more seriously. But to her dismay, she did not do well at these early competitions. She made mistakes at every meet. "I had no patience for failure or mistakes," she stated. "Now I realize that there was no way I could be perfect when I was so young. And I also realize that if my mistakes hadn't bothered me so much then, I might not have gotten as far as I have today."

EDUCATION

Moceanu's early schooling was similar to that of other children. She was always a good student and usually achieved straight A's in school. As her gymnastics training progressed, however, she had to complete her education through alternate methods. As she started ninth grade in the fall of 1995—and trained many hours in preparation for the Olympics—Moceanu and her parents decided that she would take correspondence courses. Instead of attending classes, she watched videotapes of teachers at home every day. These videos covered a wide variety of subjects and even presented her with homework assignments. "But it's not as easy as it sounds," Moceanu admitted. "When I went to a real school, I had more friends, and took part in some nongymnastic activities. With video correspondence I need a lot more discipline."

"People applauded. They applauded for me," Moceanu recalled of her first competition. *"I think that's when I knew I was really hooked—there was no turning back. I liked being in the limelight. All of a sudden I wished I had done better. I resolved right then to compete again, and to do my absolute best, from then on."*

CAREER HIGHLIGHTS

In women's gymnastic competition, there are four different types of events—the balance beam, the uneven bars, the vault, and the floor exercise—as well as the all-around, which combines all four events. Moceanu's favorite and best events are the floor exercise and balance beam. At 4'5" tall and 70 pounds, she has a small, compact body—the "munchkin model" that is the preferred body type for world gymnastic champions.

Moceanu working out with her coach, Bela Karolyi

By the time she was ten years old, Moceanu was following the careers of the major gymnasts and their coaches, wishing she was among them. "Whenever they were on television, I was there, my nose glued to the screen," she noted. "These were athletes I looked up to and respected. They were the best. I wanted to be just like them." Many of these other gymnasts trained in Houston under Bela Karolyi, a coach Moceanu viewed as the best in the world and desperately wanted to meet. Expressing her desires aloud, Moceanu was surprised to hear her father behind her, speaking the words that changed her life: "We will go to Houston," she remembered him saying. "We will move there—all of us—so you can go to Karolyi's every day and train. That's what your mother and I have decided to do."

A few short weeks later, the family was on their way to Houston. "It's a good thing I was only ten years old—if I had been any older, I might have been scared to death at all the changes," Moceanu said. "A new state, new city, new house, new jobs for my parents—it was all happening because of me, only me. Just so that I, Dominique Moceanu, would have the chance to train under the world's most famous gymnastics coach." When Moceanu first entered Karolyi's Gymnastics in December 1991, she was both nervous and afraid, wondering whether she would be good enough to stay and train there. "When I first met Bela, I was totally intimidated by him," she recalled. "Not many people get to meet him, and I was so nervous about it that my stomach hurt. He's a big guy, with a big mustache. He dashes around so that it seems as if he's everywhere at once. I felt as if I came up only to his kneecaps!" One of the first things Moceanu had to do was to show her skills to Karolyi and his wife and fellow coach, Marta. She performed all the skills she knew, but she was so nervous that they looked sloppy and unfinished. It was clear that she had a lot to learn from her new coaches.

Both Marta and Bela Karolyi soon became major parts of Moceanu's training program. Her new routine consisted of working out at the gym every morning, attending private school from 11:00 to 3:00, back to the gym until 8:00, and then dinner, homework, maybe a little television, and bed.

After only seven months with the Karolyis, Moceanu's confidence was given a giant boost when she became the youngest person ever to make the Junior National Team. In 1994 she became the All-Around Junior Champion, winning gold medals for the vault and the floor exercise, and bronze medals for the uneven parallel bars and the balance beam. "I was so incredibly proud that day," she recalled. "I think those medals helped me feel that my parents' faith in me hadn't been misplaced. It made me much more confident. All along, I had hoped I could do it—now I really believed I could." This newfound confidence created a stronger bond between Moceanu and the Karolyis, and in this nurturing environment the young gymnast started to perform better than she ever had before. "She takes all her feelings outside. That's the American way," Bela Karolyi said of his rising star. "We need to see the human emotion on the floor, not just the stunts. Dominique's performances are very playful—she's like a little bird on a wire, all the time fluttering and chirping and always playing to the crowd."

In the early part of 1995 Moceanu moved her training sessions to the Karolyi ranch while a new gym was being built at the training center. The ranch—an hour outside of Houston—was where the Karolyis lived and was also where they held their summer training camps. While training at the ranch, Moceanu saw how hard Bela worked. "He has great strength of character—he always tries his best not to let things get to him," she explained. "He has enormous will, and he's tough. When he tells his gymnasts how hard we have to work, we don't doubt him. We see how hard he pushes himself."

Although it never appeared to bother Moceanu, Karolyi had been criticized in the past for putting too much pressure on his young athletes. In fact, Karolyi, other U.S. coaches, and the sport of gymnastics itself came under close scrutiny in the early 1990s. Critics claimed that girls who were too young to handle the stress were subjected to intense physical training that produced injuries, and to fitness regimes that stressed slimness to the point of causing eating disorders. But Moceanu always enjoyed her training sessions with Karolyi. "Everyone has good days and bad days, but Bela is always there to support us and help us in every way he can," she stated. She also ate a healthy diet to maintain her competitive weight.

While training for the 1995 U.S. National Championships, Moceanu participated in various other competitions. In the Reese's International Gymnastics Cup she came away with the gold medal for the uneven bars, the bronze medal for the balance beam, and fourth place for the floor exercise. At the American Classic Moceanu excelled in different disciplines, winning the gold medal for the vault, the silver medal for all-around, and bronze medals for the beam and floor exercise. Her best meet was the VISA Challenge, where she won her first all-around gold medal in the senior division; other medals included a gold for floor exercise, a silver for the uneven bars, and bronze medals for the beam and the vault. In addition, Moceanu's team won the gold medal in the team competition. "After that meet," she stated, "I wasn't sure I could ever do better. For just a moment I forgot Karolyi's Law: You can always do better."

Youngest U.S. National Champion

By the time Moceanu arrived at the U.S. National Championships in August 1995, both she and her coaches felt she was ready. Her complete attention was focused on the task at hand. The first part of the competition was the all-around, with each gymnast competing for herself. Moceanu excelled on each apparatus, from the vault to the uneven bars to the beam, and finishing with the floor exercise. In the end her total score was enough to make her, at 13, the youngest U.S. National Gymnastics Senior Champion ever. "There's no way to describe the excitement I felt at that moment, when I realized I had definitely won the gold," Moceanu explained. "Bela rushed over and swept me up into one of his huge bear hugs."

This accomplishment brought fame and fans to Moceanu, but it also brought pressure to work even harder and live up to her new title. "I felt two things: One, that I was suddenly under new pressure, the pressure to stay number one," she related afterward. "And two, that it was strange to find myself back at the gym, getting up early and doing my compulsories with the others." Bela Karolyi would not allow Moceanu to let up on her training, though, and she quickly got back into her daily routine, setting new goals for herself and working to achieve them.

But there were also new distractions in Moceanu's life after she won the U.S. National title: the media and a new legion of fans. Suddenly everyone wanted to interview the young champion, and it took her some time and practice to learn how to be a good interview subject. More exciting to Moceanu, though, were the fan letters she began receiving. "I realized that people from all over the country felt a special bond with me," she explained. "It was totally unexpected and amazing." Moceanu enjoyed the letters and tried to read and respond to all of them.

In the 1995 World Championships in Sabae, Japan, Moceanu brought home a silver medal for her performance on the balance beam and a bronze medal for her contribution in the team competition. This left her with one big goal looming—to become a member of the 1996 Olympic team. She even started keeping a countdown to this event immediately after the U.S. Nationals. During her intense preparation, Moceanu suffered her first major injury—a four-inch stress fracture in her right tibia (one of the bones connecting the knee and ankle). She was forced to take three weeks off and to petition for a spot on the Olympic team instead of participating in the trials. "If it is still hurting," she said during the trials, "we will see how tough I am and how much I want it."

> As former Olympic gold medal winner Bart Conner noted, "Dominique can really light it up. She's adorable and she knows it. Shannon Miller and some of the other champions, you know they've always wanted to be great gymnasts. With Dominique, you know she's always dreamed of being a star."

1996 Olympics

By the time the opening ceremonies for the 1996 Olympics were held in Atlanta, Georgia, Moceanu was ready to compete. She viewed the injury as merely a hurdle on the way to her life-long goal—an Olympic gold medal. "The only thing that would increase the thrill of participating in the 1996 Olympics would be to win a medal," she stated. "But no matter what the outcome, I will always remember who I am, and how hard I've worked to get this far, and all the people who have helped me in so many ways."

Thanks to her strong showing at the World Championships, Moceanu was considered among the favorites to win a medal in the floor exercise and balance beam. As a result, she became the center of a huge media onslaught. In addition to being photographed by the renowned photographer Annie Liebovitz for the cover of *Vanity Fair*, Moceanu was the subject of feature articles in both *Time* and *People* as well one of the stars in an Olympic advertisement by Kodak. None of this phased the young gymnast, though. "I'm just going to go out there and do my best," she stated. "I'm going to have fun and enjoy it."

In the team gymnastics competition, the United States surprised many people by narrowly defeating the Russians for the Olympic gold medal. The competition came down to the final event, when Moceanu's teammate Kerri Strug overcame a painful sprained ankle to land her final vault and clinch first place for the American team. Based on her team performances, Moceanu also qualified to compete in the individual all-around competition, as well as in the finals of the balance beam and the floor exercise. And when Strug was forced to withdraw from the finals of the vault because her injury, Moceanu also represented her country in the finals of this apparatus. Her performance in the individual events was a bit disappointing. Her best individual finish was fourth in the floor exercise, and she also placed sixth in the balance beam and ninth in the all-around.

Although Moceanu's failure to win an individual medal was disappointing, her energy and enthusiasm still captured the hearts of the American public. As former Olympic gold medal winner Bart Conner noted, "Dominique can really light it up. She's adorable and she knows it. Shannon Miller and some of the other champions, you know they've always wanted to be great gymnasts. With Dominique, you know she's always dreamed of being a star." Today, Moceanu continues to train and hopes to get another chance to earn an individual Olympic medal, although she no longer trains with Karolyi, who plans to retire from coaching.

FUTURE PLANS

Moceanu is already planning for her future. Realizing the importance of education, she hopes to attend college and study sports medicine. "When the time comes, I have another life, another career planned," she explained. "Right now, I'm still working on achieving my gymnastics goals. And that is helping to prepare me for what comes later."

HOME AND FAMILY

Moceanu lives with her family near Houston, Texas. Her home life combines her Romanian heritage and her American pride, through language and other family customs. She explained the benefits of this dual heritage in her autobiography: "I feel as if I have the best of both worlds: I enjoy the freedom of our American lifestyle (not to mention American clothes, music, and television), plus I have the added richness of a Romanian background, through both the language and my mother's fabulous Romanian cooking. It's a great combination."

Both of Moceanu's parents support and encourage her in everything she does. "They always showed me their love, and that helped me continue," she

The U.S. gymnastics team for 1996 Olympics, after winning the gold medal (from left): Amanda Borden, Dominique Dawes, Amy Chow, Jaycie Phelps, Dominique Moceanu, Kerri Strug, and Shannon Miller

stated. In addition, they counsel and coach Dominique in her career, drawing on their own backgrounds as gymnasts. Moceanu also enjoys a close relationship with her younger sister, Christina, who is also beginning to train as a gymnast. "She looks up to me and tries to copy everything that I do, which is partly really adorable and partly kind of annoying," Moceanu noted.

MAJOR INFLUENCES

Several other gymnasts have influenced Moceanu's career. The first gymnast she can remember watching on television was Kim Zmeskal, who won three U.S. Championships as well as a bronze medal as a member of the 1992 Olympic team. Moceanu also admired other members of this Olympic team—Kerri Strug and Betty Okino. "These three gymnasts are the ones I admire most, and they influenced me to pursue the same goals when I first joined Karolyi's Gymnastics," she stated.

Moceanu's other influences include two former Olympic champions to whom she has often been compared—Mary Lou Retton and Nadia Comaneci. Pointing out that Retton is an idol for many young American gymnasts, Moceanu admitted that "each time we meet it's a thrill for me all over again. She's very sweet and upbeat, and her smile fills the room."

193

Meeting Comaneci was also a great moment in Moceanu's life: "When Nadia found out I spoke Romanian, we became instant friends. Later I read more about her career and her tremendous struggles for freedom. She's an incredible inspiration to me."

HOBBIES AND OTHER INTERESTS

Outside of gymnastics, Moceanu enjoys swimming, reading, and listening to country music. One of her favorite things to do when she has spare time is to relax in her room and listen to music—it is her way of unwinding and helps her deal with the stressful times in her life. "I love being in my room at home," she noted. "That's where I keep all my souvenirs, all my collections." Among these valued possessions are a collection of small stuffed animals, souvenir spoons from the cities she has visited, and a collection of guardian angel pins (seven of which are attached to the gym bag that goes everywhere with her). And of course there are the medals, photos, trophies, and other mementos of Moceanu's gymnastics career, including a scrapbook compiled by her parents.

WRITINGS

Dominique Moceanu: An American Champion, 1996 (with Steve Woodward)

HONORS AND AWARDS

U.S. National Gymnastics Championships, Junior Division: 1992, silver medal (balance beam); 1994, 3 gold medals (all-around, floor exercise, vault), 2 bronze medals (balance beam, uneven bars)

Reese's International Gymnastics Cup: 1995, gold medal (uneven bars), bronze medal (balance beam)

American Classic: 1995, gold medal (vault), silver medal (all-around), 2 bronze medals (balance beam, floor exercise)

VISA Challenge, Senior Division: 1995, 3 gold medals (all-around, floor exercise, team competition), silver medal (uneven bars), 2 bronze medals (balance beam, vault)

U.S. National Gymnastics Championships, Senior Division: 1995, gold medal (all-around), silver medal (floor exercise), bronze medal (vault)

World Championships, Senior Division: 1995, silver medal (balance beam), bronze medal (team competition)

U.S. Gymnast of the Year: 1995

Olympic Gymnastics: 1996, gold medal (team competition)

FURTHER READING

Books

Layden, Joe. *Women in Sports: The Complete Book on the World's Greatest Female Athletes,* 1997

Moceanu, Dominique, with Steve Woodward. *Dominique Moceanu: An American Champion,* 1996

Periodicals

Cosmopolitan, June 1996, p.204
Entertainment Weekly, July 19, 1996, p.40; Aug. 2, 1996, p.48
Fitness, Dec. 1995, p.22
New York Times Magazine, June 23, 1996, p.28
Newsweek, Oct. 2, 1995, p.72; June 10, 1996, p.78; Sep. 30, 1996, p.67; Dec. 9, 1996, p.59
People, May 13, 1996, p.81; July 15, 1996, p.116
Publishers Weekly, Aug. 19, 1996, p.16
Sports Illustrated, May 8, 1995, p.54; June 10, 1996, p.30; July 22, 1996, p.86; Sep. 9, 1996, p.9
Sports Illustrated for Kids, May 1995, p.64; Dec. 1995, p.53; Jan. 1996, p.59; June 1996, p.70; July 1996, p.54; Jan. 1997, p.13; Mar. 1997, p.38
Time, Aug. 5, 1996, p.39; Summer 1996, p.64
Women's Sports and Fitness, Jan.-Feb. 1996, p.30

ADDRESS

Dominique Fan Club
P.O. Box 90908
Houston, TX 77290-0908

WORLD WIDE WEB SITES

http://www.usa-gymnastics.org
http://www.moceanugymnastics.com

Alexandra Nechita 1985-
Romanian-Born American Artist

BIRTH

Alexandra Nechita (ne-KEY-ta) was born in Vaslui, Romania, on August 27, 1985. Her father, Niki Nechita, escaped from Romania during its final years under communist rule, leaving his pregnant wife, Viorica, behind. After spending six months in Yugoslavia, Niki ended up in Hollywood, California, where he lived on white bread and soup made from catsup until he found a job. His wife and baby daughter, Alexandra, joined him there in 1987.

Niki and Viorica Nechita both worked at a factory that made prostheses (artificial limbs). Niki eventually worked his way up to a managerial position. They lived in Norwalk, a working-class suburb of Los Angeles. Alexandra has one younger brother, Maximillian, who was born in November 1994.

YOUTH

As a young child, Alexandra loved her coloring books and crayons. She spent hours and hours filling in the pages, until her parents began to worry that she was becoming too isolated. But when they took her coloring books away, Alexandra responded by drawing her own shapes and coloring them in. By the age of four, she was making her own coloring books from scrap computer paper that her mother brought home from work. By the time she was five, she was using pastels and water colors.

Many young children, of course, like to draw and paint. What set Alexandra apart was her attention span—she would draw for hours if her parents let her. The distorted creatures she drew were unusual as well. One, for example, had only a single eye and five hands. Her parents were concerned that these unusual drawings reflected the traumas she had endured during her early childhood as a Romanian refugee.

By the time she was seven, Alexandra was painting on canvas with acrylics and oils. Because her art supplies were getting so expensive, her parents allowed some of her work to be displayed at a public library so she could raise money to pay for her paints. At the age of eight, she sold her first painting there—a picture of a plant with the fingers turned into human faces—for $50. It was April Fools' Day in 1994, the same day that Alexandra Nechita became an American citizen and that her mother found out she was pregnant with Alexandra's brother, Maximillian.

At the end of third grade, the Nechitas enrolled Alexandra in art classes at the Barnsdall Junior Arts Center in Hollywood. Her teacher, Elmira Adamian, was the first to tell them that their daughter possessed an exceptional talent. Adamian advised them to take her out of art class so that nothing would influence the development of her style. Soon after, Alexandra's father quit his job at the prosthetics factory to become a lab technician in Beverly Hills. He chose the job for its location: during his lunch hours, he would visit art galleries there and try to get them interested in showing his daughter's work.

EDUCATION

Alexandra—whose friends call her Alex—attended the public elementary school in Norwalk. When her third grade teacher first saw her paintings tacked up all over her family's house, he was speechless with amazement. Her classmates, however, often made fun of her because she didn't draw the way they

Summer in Europe

did. In the beginning, Alexandra was hurt by their teasing remarks. But as she got older, she grew more comfortable with the idea of being "different."

Alexandra is currently a seventh grader at a middle school in Norwalk, where her favorite subjects are history, literature, and math.

CAREER HIGHLIGHTS

After the success of her first exhibit at the library, Alexandra began to show her paintings at bookstores and coffee houses. It was at one of these shows that a client of Ben Valenty, president of International Art Publishers in La Jolla, discovered Nechita's work. Valenty came to look at her paintings for himself. His first response was, "There's no way a nine-year-old did these paintings." He asked Alexandra if he could come to her studio—a converted family room in the Nechitas' modest Norwalk home—and watch her paint. At the end of an hour, he realized that he was in the company of a prodigy. He signed her up as one of his clients and began to promote her work.

Although Valenty has been criticized for exploiting Alexandra's talent, there's no denying that her decision to sign with International Art Publishers changed her life. Two weeks later, Valenty mounted an exhibit of 35 of her paintings at his gallery in Costa Mesa. More than 600 people showed up, and the entire show sold out in 19 minutes—at $8,000 to $12,000 a painting. Valenty also arranged for Alexandra to appear on the "Today" show and on "CBS Sunday Morning," which brought her more exposure and increased the demand for her work.

"Finally I've found somebody who paints similar to my style," she told her mother on seeing Picasso's work.

Valenty's reputation is not exactly untarnished: he was recently banned from the telemarketing business for selling vastly over-priced movie posters from the 1920s and 30s to unsuspecting consumers over the phone. He has also been criticized for taking almost 70 percent of Alexandra's earnings (50 percent is the standard fee) and for promoting her so aggressively. But he has helped to make her the most famous young artist in America—and a millionaire who can now afford to send both herself and her younger brother to college some day.

The 'Pint-Sized Picasso'

Alexandra's paintings are large—she often has to stand on a stool to reach the top of the canvas—and full of vibrant colors. She paints oversized flowers and human figures with elongated facial features and twisted bodies put together in strange ways. These images have triggered comparisons with a number of modern masters, including Joan Miró, Henri Matisse, Marc Chagall, and Vasili Kandinsky. One of her paintings, *Blueberry Man*, is her interpretation of what a person would look like if he or she ate blueberries all day. Another, *The Conductor*, is Alexandra's idea of what a conductor looks like while leading an orchestra.

The artist to whom Nechita has been compared most often is Pablo Picasso. Picasso is usually associated with Cubism, a style of painting and sculpture popular during the early 20th century that reduced natural forms like the human body to a series of geometric shapes. Alexandra has even been accused of imitating Picasso's style, although she says she was eight years old and had sold a number of paintings before she ever saw any of Picasso's work in a museum. Her response was to feel reassured: "Finally I've found somebody who paints similar to my style," she told her mother.

Picasso started out painting in a more traditional style and then, after many years of experimentation, abandoned realism and started producing his abstract, cubist works. Many art experts feel that it's impossible to take Alexandra's work seriously, because she started out as an abstract artist at such a young age, without first learning the basics of drawing and painting. But others, like William Emboden, an art researcher affiliated with the Los Angeles County Museum of Art, thinks that her talent is for real. "Alexandra has assimilated all the tenets of 20th century art—cubism, futurism, every 'ism' that has permeated this century. However, there is no copying, no artifice," he comments. "She is an incredible genius; there is no other explanation." Alexandra's painting inspired by the 1995 bombing of the Alfred P. Murrah Federal Building in Oklahoma City has been compared to Picasso's "Guernica," a painting that commemorates the Spanish Civil War.

Artist to the Stars

Nechita has had a great success with sales of her work. A growing number of celebrities—including talk show host Oprah Winfrey, rock star Melissa Etheridge, former Chrysler executive Lee Iacocca, clothing designer Calvin Klein, and comedians Whoopi Goldberg and Ellen DeGeneres—have bought Nechita's oil paintings, for which they have paid as much as $125,000. Her paintings also hang in the art collections of Queen Elizabeth II and the Emperor of Japan.

Nechita was chosen as the "official artist" of the 1996 Grammy Awards, and she was also asked to create a painting for Polaroid's 50th anniversary. She has appeared on the "Rosie O'Donnell Show," the "NBC Nightly News with Tom Brokaw," and "Late Night with David Letterman." To launch the publication of her coffee-table book, *Outside the Lines*, Alexandra appeared in *People* magazine and on the "Today" show. In the spring of 1996 she toured seven European countries, where she received the kind of media coverage that is usually reserved for heads of state. Television producers have already expressed an interest in making a TV movie about her life, and publishers want to print her autobiography. She has done more than 600 interviews in a single year.

Buckets of Detangler

Everybody's main fear is that all this attention will go to her head, ruining both her character and her career. But she laughs off such worries. "I just concentrate on what I am doing," she says. "It doesn't change me in any way."

What Lies Ahead?

People are buying Alexandra's paintings faster than she can produce them, even though she paints for two or three hours after school every day and all day on weekends. She is beginning to experiment with etching and sculpture, and is interested in trying ceramics. Although she has not yet had any formal art education, she thinks that she'd like to take classes at a school of visual arts some day.

Alexandra's mother makes sure that her daughter reads all the reviews of her work, even the negative ones. "I do not want her to grow up thinking the whole world adores her work," Viorica Nechita says. "She is an artist. She needs to understand some will not approve."

MAJOR INFLUENCES

Alexandra says that she has been inspired by the sculptor Henry Moore as well as by the painters Picasso, Matisse, Miro, Kandinsky, and the French cubist Georges Braque. "Paintings inspire me by their shapes, but mostly by their colors," she says. "Color is the number one thing that supports a painting; it's the life of the painting, the beauty and the richness."

"Paintings inspire me by their shapes, but mostly by their colors. Color is the number one thing that supports a painting; it's the life of the painting, the beauty and the richness."

But Alexandra's real hero is her father. "He went through so much to bring me and my mom to America," she says. "He risked his whole life for us." Not surprisingly, several of her paintings deal with the themes of freedom and democracy.

FAVORITE BOOKS AND MUSIC

Alexandra enjoys the music of Hanson, Color Me Badd, the Fugees, and Alanis Morissette. When she paints, Alexandra enjoys classical music, especially Vivaldi. She has a collection of more than 170 CDs—mostly Beethoven, Bach, and Mozart.

Although she doesn't have much time for reading, Alexandra prefers Disney stories and the *Goosebump* books.

HOME AND FAMILY

Thanks to their daughter's financial success as an artist, the Nechitas have been able to move out of their gang-ridden neighborhood east of Los Angeles recently and into a new house in a safer area. Some of the money she earns goes to pay for her art supplies; the rest goes into a trust fund for herself and her brother. Even though she is a millionaire, Alexandra must live on a $5 weekly allowance from her parents and wash the dinner dishes on Wednesday nights.

Niki and Viorica Nechita recently quit their jobs so they could travel with their daughter and help manage her career. When she's not giving interviews, appearing on television, or painting in her studio, Alexandra's favorite activity is playing with her three-year-old brother, Max.

HOBBIES AND OTHER INTERESTS

Like most 12-year-olds, Alexandra likes to rollerblade and watch television. She has always loved swimming, and tries to set aside an hour every day in the summer to splash around and enjoy the sun.

WRITINGS

Outside the Lines: Paintings by Alexandra Nechita, 1996

FURTHER READING

Books

Nechita, Alexandra. *Outside the Lines: Paintings by Alexandra Nechita,* 1996

Periodicals

Boston Globe, June 9, 1997, p.A1
Girls' Life, Aug.-Sep. 1996, p.14
Los Angeles Times, Apr. 26, 1996, Life & Style section, p.3; May 6, 1996, p.E1
Newsweek, June 3, 1996, p.70
People, June 10, 1996, p.133
Times of London, Dec. 3, 1995, Home News section
USA Today, June 27, 1996, p.D1
U.S. Kids, Dec. 1996, p.28
Weekly Reader, Sep. 12, 1997, p.7

ADDRESS

Alexandra Nechita Enterprises
P. O. Box 9129
Whittier, CA 90608

WORLD WIDE WEB SITE

http://www.ecfineart.com/alexandr.html

Brad Pitt 1964-

American Actor
Star of *A River Runs through It, Interview with the Vampire, Legends of the Fall,* and *Seven Years in Tibet*

BIRTH

William Bradley Pitt was born on December 18, 1964, in Shaw-nee, Oklahoma. He was the oldest of three children born to Bill Pitt, who managed a trucking company, and Jane Pitt, who was a high school guidance counselor. Brad's brother, Douglas, was born two years later, and his sister, Julie, came five years later. When Brad was very young, his family moved to Springfield, Missouri.

YOUTH

Pitt was raised as part of a close-knit, middle-class family. His mother was very religious and made sure that the whole family attended South Haven Baptist Church in Springfield every Sunday. His father worked long hours but still made time for the children, often taking them to drive-in movies or on camping trips to the nearby Ozark Mountains. Bill Pitt instilled his values in the children in a straightforward, no-nonsense manner. "He only says what's needed," Brad recalled. "Everybody would be going on and on, and he'd just drop in a word of wisdom, shooting straight through the conversation. He's good that way." Brad still remembers one time when his father gave him particularly good advice. Brad was playing in a tennis tournament and behaving very badly, screaming and throwing his racquet. His father walked out onto the court between games and asked him if he was having fun. "I got all huffy and said no. He looked at me and said, 'Then don't do it,' and then walked away," Brad related. "Boy, that put me in my place."

Pitt was very creative as a boy. He enjoyed drawing and sometimes carried a sketchbook around with him, and he also took guitar lessons. But one of his favorite childhood pastimes was going to the movies. "*Planet of the Apes* was my favorite," he recalled. "I remember going to an Ape-athon: all five *Planet of the Apes* movies, all day long. My mom packed me a lunch. My peanut-butter-and-jelly sandwich got smashed against the seat back. I had some Hot Tamales. It was a great day." Another movie that made an impact on him was *Butch Cassidy and the Sundance Kid,* a wild-west adventure starring Robert Redford and Paul Newman. Despite this early love of movies, however, Pitt never really thought about becoming an actor. "It's not a reasonable possibility growing up in Missouri," he explained. "It's something that you read about, but not something you'd think about doing."

EDUCATION

Pitt was an outgoing and popular student during the time he attended the public schools in Springfield. "I was a good kid overall," he noted. "I played sports, was active in school activities, and got good grades." At Kickapoo High School, he participated in choir, student government, sports, and school plays. He graduated from Kickapoo High in 1983.

Pitt then attended the University of Missouri at Columbia. He majored in journalism and planned to become an art director at an advertising agency. While at Missouri, Pitt joined the Sigma Chi fraternity. "It was incredible to get away from home, living with a bunch of guys," he stated. "We had this idea of *Animal House,* and there was definitely that aspect. It was a highlight, without a doubt. Then — like everything — you grow out of it." When some fellow students put together a "Girls of Mizzou" pin-up calendar and it sold well, Pitt came up with the idea of doing a male version. With Pitt himself featured prominently in the pictures, that calendar quickly sold out as well.

Toward the end of his college days, Pitt was involved in a serious car accident that may have helped change the direction he had planned for his life. "I got hit by an 18-wheeler. Not much left of the car. Took the roof with it," he recalled. "No one was even hurt. It was just kind of like once we had a roof and now we don't." Before long, he decided to put aside his idea of becoming an art director and instead go to California to try and make it as an actor. "You keep finding things out in little increments," he explained. "Each one of those little increments led me to saying, You know what? I don't want to do this. I want to go over there and see what that's all about."

Pitt left Missouri in 1987—just two credits short of graduation—and drove to Los Angeles in a beat-up Datsun he called "Runaround Sue." He had just $325 in his pocket and no contacts in the film industry. "It was such a relief," he said of his decision. "I was coming to the end of college and the end of my degree and the beginning of my chosen occupation. I knew I didn't want to do it. I remember being so excited as I passed each state line." He told his family and friends that he was going to take classes at the Art Center College of Design in Pasadena so they would not worry about him.

"I remember going to an Ape-athon: all five **Planet of the Apes** *movies, all day long. My mom packed me a lunch. My peanut-butter-and-jelly sandwich got smashed against the seat back. I had some Hot Tamales. It was a great day."*

CAREER HIGHLIGHTS

First Jobs

Upon arriving in California, Pitt moved into a cramped apartment with seven other struggling young actors. Each one of them had a corner of a room for his mattress and possessions, and they all shared an answering machine to field calls from agents. Pitt then took on a series of unusual jobs to help make ends meet, including delivering refrigerators, making sales calls for a telemarketer, dressing up as a giant chicken to attract customers to a restaurant called El Pollo Loco, and driving a limousine for a strip-o-gram company. This last job helped him find an acting coach. One of the strippers that he drove around introduced him to Roy London, a well-known acting coach who had worked with famous stars like Michelle Pfeiffer and Sharon Stone. A similar bit of good luck helped Pitt land an agent. "I was in an acting class," he related. "A girl in the class needed a scene partner for an audition for an agent. So I was the scene partner for the audition, and I ended up getting signed."

A River Runs through It

After appearing as an extra in several films, Pitt landed a small part on the hit television show "Dallas" as the boyfriend of one of the younger characters. Since it was his first speaking role, he was not sure what he was supposed to do on the set. "I was like, 'But-but-but, Wait a sec. I just got here from Missouri, see?'" he recalled. This part soon led to other work on television. Pitt spent a week on the daytime soap opera "Another World," then had small parts in the sitcoms "Growing Pains" and "Head of the Class," and in the dramas "21 Jump Street" and "thirtysomething." Finally, in 1989, he made his film debut in a teen slasher movie called *Cutting Class,* which he later described as "awful."

In 1990, Pitt was cast as one of the leads in "Glory Days," a television series about four male friends and how their lives progress after high school. However, the show proved unsuccessful and was dropped after six episodes. He also appeared in the movie *Across the Tracks* with Rick Schroeder. The two young actors played brothers who were very different and very competitive with one another. Although the movie was not a success at the box office, it did show that Pitt could handle a dramatic role. A short time later, Pitt underwent a complete image change for the TV movie *Too Young to Die?* (1990), which was based on the true story of the first minor to be sentenced to the death penalty. He played a slimy, low-life drug addict who abused a teenaged runaway, played by Juliette Lewis, convincing her to become a prostitute and to murder her ex-boyfriend. He became romantically involved with Lewis during the making of that film and ended up living with her for several years.

The Big Break

Pitt's big break came in 1991, when actor William Baldwin dropped out of the female buddy picture *Thelma and Louise,* which starred Geena Davis and Susan Sarandon. Pitt stepped in to play the role of JD, a charming drifter who seduces Thelma (played by Davis) and then steals her money. Even though he was only on screen for 14 minutes, Pitt became an instant heartthrob because of his steamy love scene with Davis. It also helped that *Thelma and Louise* was one of the most talked-about films of the year. "I figured it would be a role like JD—something I'm good at, a Southern guy—that would make the break," Pitt noted. "It basically opened the door for some kind of respect, working with all those great people."

Suddenly Pitt had his choice of many coveted movie roles, but he tried to take a variety of different parts in order to keep from being typecast. His first starring role came in *Johnny Suede* (1991), a low-budget art film about a would-be rock star with a ridiculous pompadour hairdo. Although the film received praise from critics, it did poorly at the box office. Next he played a police detective in the 1992 movie *Cool World,* which combined live action with animation. Since he spent most of the movie interacting with animated characters that were drawn in later, Pitt found making *Cool World* to be a difficult experience. Whether the scene involved fighting or kissing another character, he had to perform the actions alone on a sound stage. "That'll humble you real quick," he said of the experience. "It just became a dance." Unfortunately, the movie turned out to be a flop at the box office.

"The book and the script for **A River Runs through It** *were so beautiful. I don't know how you could leave that film with your heart not ripped apart. I think for anyone who places any kind of importance on family and who maybe has a brother, I don't see how it can't hit you."*

A River Runs through It

Another important step in Pitt's career came in 1992, when he was chosen to star in *A River Runs through It.* This movie was directed by Robert Redford, who had been a hero to Pitt ever since his boyhood days of watching movies. In fact, Pitt wanted to be in the film so much that, after deciding that his first audition went badly, he sent the director a videotape of himself performing two scenes from the script, in costume. He also taught himself to fly-fish by practicing on rooftops in Los Angeles. "I'd hook myself in the back of my head all the time," he recalled. "One time, they had to dig the barb out with pliers."

Based on an autobiographical novel by Norman Maclean, *A River Runs through It* tells the story of two very different brothers growing up in Montana in the 1930s. Pitt played the younger brother, Paul, a reckless golden boy whose life begins to go downhill due to excessive drinking and gambling. Craig Sheffer played the concerned older brother, Norman, who has trouble understanding Paul and is powerless to prevent his downfall. "The book and the script for *A River Runs through It* were so beautiful. I don't know how you could leave that film with your heart not ripped apart," Pitt stated. "I think for anyone who places any kind of importance on family and who maybe has a brother, I don't see how it can't hit you." Pitt earned good reviews for his performance—he was even compared to a young Robert Redford—and the movie proved popular at the box office as well.

For his next role, Pitt chose a character that would stretch his abilities as an actor. He grew a beard and wore his hair long and greasy in order to play a sociopathic serial killer named Early Grayce in the 1993 movie *Kalifornia.* "He doesn't have any redeeming features that I can think of off-hand," he said of his character. "But I like him." The movie co-starred his then-girlfriend Juliette Lewis, although they broke up shortly after filming was completed. Just for fun, Pitt took a cameo role as the pot-smoking hippie roommate of the main character in *True Romance* later that year.

The Rise to Superstardom

Pitt's popularity exploded in 1994, after he starred in two big movies. First, he played Tristan Ludlow—the wild middle brother in a family of three brothers—in the epic movie *Legends of the Fall.* He wanted the part as soon as he read the script. "This story was one of the only ones where I've ever said, 'I'm the guy for this one.' I've always felt there was someone else who could do a little better. But not on this one: this story I felt like I knew from the beginning to the end," he noted. "I like the wildness in [Tristan], I like the love in him, and I like the hate in him. His whole journey makes sense to me." The movie was shot in the rugged Canadian Rockies with Aidan Quinn as the older brother, Henry Thomas as the younger brother, Anthony Hopkins as the father, and Julia Ormond as the woman they all fight over. Unfortunately, Pitt was less than pleased with the finished product, because he felt that many important scenes were lost in the editing process. "By taking out as much as they did, the movie becomes too mushy," he stated. "If I'd known where it was going to end up, I'd have fought against the cheese." Critics agreed with Pitt's assessment of the film, although it still proved popular with audiences.

Immediately after completing *Legends of the Fall,* Pitt played the reluctant vampire Louis in *Interview with the Vampire.* Based on a best-selling novel by Anne Rice, the movie also starred Tom Cruise as the vampire Lestat. Unfortunately, the filming of *Interview with the Vampire* experienced problems from the start. First, Rice publicly expressed her unhappiness with the casting choices. Then, sadness descended on the set after River Phoenix, who was supposed to play the interviewer, died of a drug overdose during filming and had to be replaced by Christian Slater. There were also rumors that Pitt and Cruise did not get along, although Pitt claims that the main problem was that he did not like having to portray such a morose character for five months.

Legends of the Fall

"When I read the book, I thought it was great, and I think the movie is great. It's just that, for me, making the movie wasn't so great," he noted. "It messed with my day. Somewhere in the third or fourth week, you respond to things a little differently, like your character would respond. I don't like it. I can't wait to get my own clothes back on." Still, the film proved popular with fans and was a hit at the box office.

Pitt appeared in another big film in 1995. He played a naive young detective in the dark, gritty, psychological thriller *Seven,* which co-starred Morgan Freeman as his partner and Gwyneth Paltrow as his wife. The story involves the two detectives tracking a serial killer who commits murders based on the Bible's seven deadly sins. Pitt ended up doing some of his own stunts for the film and actually breaking his arm during a chase scene. Some of the scenes that had been shot earlier then had to be reshot to accommodate the cast on his arm. *Seven* proved to be an important film for Pitt both professionally and personally, as he entered into a serious romantic relationship with Paltrow after filming was completed.

The Perils of Fame

Pitt and Paltrow immediately became the new hot Hollywood couple, and as a result the media would not leave them alone. In April 1995, when the pair went on vacation to St. Bart's in the Virgin Islands, a photographer took pictures of them sunbathing nude on their private hotel balcony. The pictures ended up appearing in European tabloids and on the Internet. Later, Pitt successfully sued to keep them from being published in magazines in the United States. For Pitt, these public pictures of an intimate moment were an unwarranted attack on his privacy. "Enough's enough," he stated. "I don't feel that when our forefathers made the laws they thought of 600-millimeter lenses. People say, 'He's famous, he has no right to privacy.' I didn't read that anywhere in the Bill of Rights." Pitt and Paltrow stayed together for over two years and were engaged for a while, but they eventually broke up.

For his next film, Pitt accepted a role as a mentally ill animal-rights activist in the 1995 futuristic thriller *Twelve Monkeys,* which was directed by Terry Gilliam and starred Bruce Willis. He realized that this part contrasted with his pretty-boy image. "It was something that I normally wouldn't have been chosen for. And I understand that. People don't know what you're capable of until you prove it," he admitted. In order to prepare for the role, Pitt spent two weeks attending group therapy sessions for people suffering from manic depression and checked into a psychiatric ward for a day. He also wore brown contact lenses to cover his blue eyes and adopted all kinds of strange mannerisms and nervous twitches for the role. But the gamble paid off: he was so convincing that he earned a Golden Globe award and an Academy Award nomination as best supporting actor.

Pitt starred in another epic drama in 1997, when he took the role of Heinrich Harrer in *Seven Years in Tibet.* Based on Harrer's best-selling memoir of his experiences, the film follows the Austrian mountaineer as he escapes from a British prison camp in India and makes his way to Tibet. There, he ends up tutoring the young Dalai Lama, the spiritual leader of the Buddhist religion (see entry on the Dalai Lama in this issue); Harrer also undergoes a spiritual awakening. To prepare for this role, Pitt had to practice mountain climbing in Austria and Italy, even though he was afraid of heights. Shortly before the movie came out, it became the subject of some controversy when it was revealed that Harrer had been a member of the Nazi party, the group led by Adolf Hitler that killed millions of Jews during the Holocaust. "Would I have taken the part if I'd known the truth?" Pitt asked. "Probably not, because I'd have looked at the story and the man in a whole different way. But the film is still about a journey in life and faith and one of which I am proud."

Pitt's next challenge involved playing an Irish Republican Army (IRA) terrorist in *The Devil's Own*, which also came out in 1997. The IRA is a group of radical Irish Catholics that has tried to force England to abandon its rule over Northern Ireland, which they believe should be an independent Catholic state. The IRA is a very controversial group because they often use violence, including terrorist acts against civilians. In the movie, Pitt's character flees to the United States, where he ends up staying at the home of an unsuspecting Irish-American police officer played by Harrison Ford. The two men form a close bond before Ford's character realizes that he has been harboring a fugitive. Shortly before the filming started, Pitt was upset to find that the script had changed dramatically from the first version he had read. In fact, much of the movie was

"[You] want to get to where you have the pick of films you want to do. You want people to be entertained. You want your work to be respected. To accomplish all that, all this comes with it."

filmed without a final script in place, which Pitt called "the most irresponsible bit of filmmaking—if you can even call it that—that I've ever seen." He even tried to break his contract to appear in the film but stayed on when he was threatened with a lawsuit. When *The Devil's Own* finally came out, however, Pitt claimed that he liked the finished product. Unfortunately, the movie was poorly received by critics and did not fare well at the box office.

As of 1998, Pitt remains a huge star who is in great demand in Hollywood. Although he has his choice of roles, he still enjoys playing a wide variety of characters in order to keep his career interesting. "I've been watching some of the bigger guys, and it seems to me that they're picking films that fill some sort of format that they think people will want or that the studio thinks would be good for their career," he stated. "I want to avoid that trap and keep doing movies that mean something to me." He seems to be growing more comfort-

Pitt as Heinrich Harrer in Seven Years in Tibet

able with all the attention that comes with being one of the hottest young actors in show business. "How seriously can you take it? I have a sister and she had Andy Gibb's poster on her wall when she was 12 and it was sweet and cute and that's what it is," he noted. "See, the thing is, you want to get to where you have the pick of films you want to do. You want people to be entertained. You want your work to be respected. To accomplish all that, all this comes with it."

HOME AND FAMILY

Pitt lives in Los Angeles in a turn-of-the-century mansion situated on several acres with a pool, a pond, and lots of trees. He shares his home with three large dogs—Purty, Todd Potter, and Saudi—and 40 chameleons and iguanas that live in cages outdoors. Pitt also owns 600 acres of land in the Ozark Mountains near his family home in Missouri, where he hopes to one day build a house big enough to host family reunions. He remains very close to his family, and refers to his parents as "the biggest guides in my life."

Although Pitt has never married, he has dated many of female co-stars and been engaged twice — to actresses Juliette Lewis and Gwyneth Paltrow. "I am not anti-marriage," he explained. "My parents have been married for 35 years and I want it to be for life. I want to be a husband and a father. I will one day wear the ring, the suit, and kiss the bride."

HOBBIES AND OTHER INTERESTS

In his spare time, Pitt enjoys studying architecture and design, reading classic novels, playing guitar, and collecting antiques and handcrafted furniture. To escape from the fan and media attention that follows him everywhere, he buys bicycles and leaves them in various cities so that he can ride off on his own the next time he is there. "I have bicycles locked up all over the world," he admitted. "When I leave a place, I find a good hiding place and lock it up. I figure when I go back, maybe it'll be there. I have bikes in Amsterdam, Canada, Oregon, New York, and Vegas — I have all the keys on my key chain."

SELECTED CREDITS

On Television

"Another World," 1987
"Dallas," 1987
"Head of the Class," 1987
"21 Jump Street," 1988
A Stoning in Fulham County, 1988
"Growing Pains," 1989
"thirtysomething," 1989
"Glory Days," 1990
The Image, 1990
Too Young to Die?, 1990

On Film

Cutting Class, 1989
Happy Together, 1989
Across the Tracks, 1990
Thelma and Louise, 1991
Johnny Suede, 1991
Cool World, 1992
A River Runs through It, 1992

Kalifornia, 1993
True Romance, 1993
Legends of the Fall, 1994
Interview with the Vampire, 1994
The Favor, 1994
Seven, 1995
Twelve Monkeys, 1995
Sleepers, 1996
Seven Years in Tibet, 1997
The Devil's Own, 1997

HONORS AND AWARDS

MTV Movie Award for Best Male Performance: 1995, for *Interview with the Vampire*
Golden Globe Award for Best Supporting Actor: 1996, for *Twelve Monkeys*

FURTHER READING

Books

Dempsey, Amy. *Superstars of Film: Brad Pitt,* 1998 (juvenile)
Guzzetti, Paula. *Brad Pitt: An Unauthorized Biography,* 1998 (juvenile)
Robb, Brian J. *Brad Pitt: The Rise to Stardom,* 1996
Sietz, Matt Zoller. *Brad Pitt,* 1996
Who's Who in America, 1998

Periodicals

Chicago Tribune, Aug. 23, 1992, p.6
Current Biography Yearbook 1996
Detroit Free Press, Jan. 16, 1995, p.E2
Entertainment Weekly, Nov. 6, 1992, p.30; Apr. 11, 1997, p.32
Houston Chronicle, Sep. 23, 1995, p.4
New York Times, July 7, 1991, p.B11
Newsweek, Feb. 3, 1997, p.48
People, Jan. 30, 1995, p.56; Jan. 15, 1996, p.64; Jan. 13, 1997, p.108; June 30, 1997, p.80
Philadelphia Inquirer, Nov. 4, 1992, p.C1; Jan. 17, 1995, p.E1
Premiere, Oct. 1994, p.56; Nov. 1997, p.86

Rolling Stone, May 14, 1992, p.54; Dec. 1, 1994, p.92; Apr. 3, 1997, p.38
San Francisco Chronicle, Aug. 16, 1992, p.33
Toronto Star, Oct. 3, 1997, p.C1
USA Today, Oct. 22, 1992, p.D1; Dec. 27, 1995, p.D1
Vanity Fair, Feb. 1995, p.70

ADDRESS

Creative Artists Agency
9830 Wilshire Blvd.
Beverly Hills, CA 90212-1804

LeAnn Rimes 1982-

American Country Music Singer
First Country Singer to Win a Grammy Award for
"Best New Artist"

BIRTH

LeAnn Rimes was born on August 28, 1982, in Jackson, Mississippi. Her parents, Wilbur and Belinda Rimes, were married when they were only 17 years old. They settled in the small town of Flowood, Mississippi, about 10 miles south of Jackson. Wilbur Rimes sold seismic equipment for an oil company, and Belinda worked as a receptionist.

The Rimeses were told a few years after they were married that they could never have children. After 12 years, they had almost given up hope. Then Belinda started praying. Six weeks later, she was pregnant with LeAnn.

YOUTH

LeAnn spent the first six years of her life in Flowood. Her mother loved to sing, and at the age of 18 months, LeAnn started singing along with her. Her parents always said that as a toddler, she sang more clearly than she talked. Wilbur Rimes made tapes of his daughter singing popular songs like "You Are My Sunshine" and "Getting to Know You" while he accompanied her on his guitar.

LeAnn started taking tap lessons when she was two to develop the coordination needed to correct a walking problem. Her dance teacher heard her singing one day and encouraged the Rimeses to enter her in some local talent contests. LeAnn entered her first song-and-dance competition when she was only five. Her parents were worried because they knew that she would be competing with children twice her age. She sang "Getting to Know You" from the Broadway show *The King and I* and won the contest. The first place trophy she brought home was taller than she was. Wilbur Rimes went out hunting that day because he couldn't bear to see his daughter lose the competition. When LeAnn walked in the door with the huge trophy, he burst into tears of joy.

That contest changed her life forever. LeAnn told her parents that she wanted a career in show business. Her father knew that she'd never get anywhere if they stayed in Mississippi. So he requested a job transfer to the Dallas area, which was a regional center for country music. He sold his guns, his hunting dogs, and his truck to raise the money to move the family to Texas. Only six weeks after their daughter's triumph at the talent show, the Rimes family moved into a two-bedroom apartment in Garland, about 15 miles north of Dallas, so LeAnn could pursue her dream.

LeAnn began appearing on "Opry stages" in the Dallas-Fort Worth area every weekend. "Opry stages" are performance halls where local musicians play country music. "Opry" refers to the "Grand Ole Opry," the performance hall in Nashville that has served as the premiere site for country music for decades. Even though she was only six, LeAnn showed a remarkable dedication to performing in front of live audiences. "She'd be sleeping in the car as we drove to the next Opry, and then she'd get up on the stage and sing 'Crazy,' and then get right back in the car and go to sleep," her mother recalls. "Crazy" was a song written by Willie Nelson that had been popularized in the late 1950s by the famous country singer Patsy Cline. It was LeAnn's favorite song, even though she was far too young to have experienced the heartbreak that was the song's theme. "Dad would explain that it was a sad song, and I would sing it that way," LeAnn says. Like Cline, the first female country singer to "cross over" and have hit songs on the pop charts, LeAnn sang with the emotional intensity of a mature woman.

By the time she was eight, LeAnn was a regular on the *Johnnie High Country Music Revue*, a local talent showcase in Arlington, Texas. She also went on *Star Search*, a weekly television program that gave young actors, dancers, comedians, and singers a chance to show off their talents. LeAnn auditioned for the lead role in *Annie II* the sequel to the successful Broadway musical based on the comic strip *Little Orphan Annie*, but she was rejected because of her youth and southern accent. To console her, her parents bought her a dog she named "Sandy," after Annie's dog in the show.

> LeAnn began appearing on "Opry stages" in the Dallas-Fort Worth area every weekend. Even though she was only six, she showed a remarkable dedication to performing in front of live audiences. "She'd be sleeping in the car as we drove to the next Opry, and then she'd get up on the stage and sing 'Crazy,' and then get right back in the car and go to sleep," her mother recalls.

Soon LeAnn was being invited to sing "The Star-Spangled Banner" a cappella (unaccompanied) at Dallas Cowboys football games, the Walt Garrison Rodeo, and the National Cutting Horse Championships in Fort Worth. Her parents spent so much time driving her to her various performances that they decided to quit their jobs and devote themselves to managing her career. "I knew what I wanted and worked at it," LeAnn emphasizes. "My parents didn't push me. They supported me."

EDUCATION

LeAnn enjoyed elementary school. But when she got to junior high school she was already known as a regional star, and some of her classmates started harassing her. She decided to drop out of school at the end of sixth grade and start working with a tutor. Since she had maintained a straight-A average throughout her years in public school and had very high test scores, she was able to skip seventh and eighth grade.

Currently, LeAnn is learning how to balance her career with her education. She spends three hours with a tutor each day and one hour doing homework. She then spends the rest of her time working with her father on her music. Now that her career has taken off and she is frequently on tour, her tutor travels with her. She has discovered that the best time to study is right after a concert while her adrenaline is still flowing—even though it's often after midnight when she sits down to do her homework. Even though she is still a high school student, her lessons are sent to Texas Tech University for grading, and she takes her exams at a college in Dallas. Not surprisingly, her favorite subject these days is music.

CAREER HIGHLIGHTS

First Album

LeAnn got her first big break when she was only 11 years old. In 1993, an attorney named Lyle Walker heard her sing at *Johnnie High's Country Music Revue*. He couldn't believe he was listening to a pre-teenager. "She had the most amazing voice I'd ever heard," Walker said, "a once-in-a-lifetime talent. I told her that what she needed was an album." Walker owned the studio in Clovis, New Mexico, where rock legend Buddy Holly had recorded his earliest hits. He invited LeAnn and her father to come to Clovis, offered to put up the money needed to record an album in exchange for a share of the profits, and eventually became LeAnn's co-manager.

All That, the album LeAnn recorded under an independent label when she was 11, created quite a stir in Nashville, Tennessee, the heart of the country music recording industry. The executives of several major record labels started competing with each other to sign her up for her next album. By this time, country music was starting to gain popularity among pop music fans, and sales of country albums were at an all-time high. What record companies wanted was to get more teenagers interested in listening to country music by signing young, good-looking singers like LeAnn. But her father didn't want her to rush into anything, and it was two years before she signed her first contract with a major recording studio, Curb Records.

Blue

LeAnn's first CD for Curb Records, *Blue*, came out in July 1996. It featured a song, also called "Blue," that had been written for Patsy Cline back in 1958 by a Dallas-Fort Worth disc jockey named Bill Mack. Cline died in a plane crash before she had a chance to record the song, and it lay forgotten in Mack's desk drawer for almost 35 years. When Mack heard LeAnn sing the national anthem at a Dallas Cowboys game, he said, "The hair stood up on my arms." He knew that he'd found the singer he'd been looking for. LeAnn loved the song the minute she heard it, but her father told her it was much too old for her. She finally won him over by adding something that made the song uniquely her own: a yodeling effect, or what Bill Mack describes as a "soul break."

The *Blue* album also included a duet between Rimes and the legendary country music star Eddy Arnold, who was 78 at the time. But it was LeAnn's haunting rendition of "Blue," with its 1950s-era traditional and twangy country sound, that transformed the 13-year-old into a star. The song had just as much appeal for young country music fans, who weren't familiar with its more traditional country sound, as it did for older listeners, who were reminded of singers like Patsy Cline and Brenda Lee. Within three weeks of its release, requests for the song were pouring into radio stations. Two months later, when the album *Blue* was released, it propelled LeAnn Rimes to Number 3 on the *Billboard* pop chart and Number 1 on the country chart, making her the youngest country singer ever to have a debut album hit the top spot during its first week.

LeAnn embarked on her first full-time concert tour in the summer of 1996. Country music tours are different from rock tours in that the performers make as many appearances at small county fairs and amusement parks as they do at big concerts. Although she didn't really like being on the road all the time, she enjoyed seeing different parts of the country and getting on stage to perform for her fans. Traveling on a luxuriously-equipped tour bus meant that she has her parents, her co-manager, her tutor, her sound man, and the six members of her band with her wherever she went. Rimes also toured Australia, where *Blue* had gone triple platinum (a record "goes platinum" if it sells at least two million singles or one million LPs) in the spring of 1997.

After *Blue*

Rimes's next album, *The Early Years/Unchained Melody*, also debuted in the Number 1 spot on the *Billboard* country chart when it was released in February 1997. It featured seven songs from her independent album, recorded when she was 11, and three more songs that she recorded at age 12 — including "Share My Love," a song that she'd written when she was only nine. This was followed by an album of newly recorded material called *You Light Up My Life*, featuring the pop hit by the same name originally recorded by Debbie Boone 20 years earlier. Described as a collection of "inspirational" songs, it features LeAnn's versions of "God Bless America," "Amazing Grace," and "The Star-Spangled Banner" as well as Simon & Garfunkel's "Bridge Over Troubled Waters" and Bette Midler's "The Rose." Her next album, for which she has selected material from more than 30 songs made available to her by acclaimed songwriters, is scheduled for release in the spring of 1998.

Rimes has recently gone on to new challenges. She appeared in "LeAnn Rimes In Concert" on the Disney Channel and co hosted the TNN/Music City News Country Music Awards. She starred in her first TV movie, "Holiday in Your Heart," in December 1997. Rimes played a young and upcoming singer about to make her debut at the Grand Old Opry. Just then, she learns that her grandmother is sick. She is forced to choose between her dedication to her career and her love for her family. Rimes also participated in the CBS special, *Opryland Country Christmas*, recorded at Nashville's famous Grand Old Opry.

LeAnn's life hasn't always been easy. She continues to be criticized for singing about experiences that someone her age can't possibly understand. "Like an actress interpreting a script, I'm an interpreter of a song," she often explains to those who say she hasn't got the maturity to sing about sex, romance, and broken hearts. At one point there was a rumor circulating that she was actually much older than 13. She finally had to show her birth certificate on national television to put the rumors to rest. People have also criticized her parents for pushing her too hard, but LeAnn is always quick to point out that everything she has done from the very beginning has been her own idea. "They've always looked out for me, to be there to tell me what's right and wrong," she says. "But this is something I've wanted all my life."

FUTURE PLANS

Although she hopes to be singing for at least the next 20 or 30 years, LeAnn has thought about becoming an actress. College is also an option. "I've always wanted to help children, and I've thought about studying speech pathology," she adds. One time she sang at the bedside of a seven-year-old fan who was in a coma following a car accident, because the family hoped that hearing LeAnn's voice might waken the girl from her long sleep.

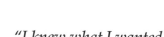

LeAnn Rimes has often been compared to Tanya Tucker and Brenda Lee, two country singers who were also 13 when they became stars. Brenda Lee, who had her first country hit in 1957, "One Step at a Time," went on to become one of the biggest stars of the 50s and 60s. Tanya Tucker, whose "Delta Dawn" hit the Top Ten in 1972, is still

"I knew what I wanted and worked at it. My parents didn't push me. They supported me."

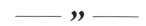

turning out hit records, although she has suffered drug problems. Belinda Rimes, LeAnn's mother, is worried about the impact that fame at such an early age may have on her daughter. Wilbur Rimes says, "We want her to grow up and be a stable human being, and I hope we can take her through this and make that happen."

MAJOR INFLUENCES

LeAnn started listening to music at a very young age. She would listen to her parents' Broadway show records and imitate every song she heard. Her earliest influences were Barbara Streisand and Judy Garland. Then she discovered country music and Patsy Cline, who has had a major impact on her singing style and choice of material. She is also a big fan of Reba McEntire and Wynnona Judd.

Wilbur Rimes, LeAnn's father, has played an important role in her life and career as well. "He is my producer and my manager and has helped me out through everything," she says. Her father still chooses most of the songs she sings, although she won't sing a song that she doesn't love.

FAVORITE MOVIES AND MUSIC

LeAnn's favorite movie is *The Bodyguard* with Whitney Houston. Her favorite song is "Fade to Blue," written by Lang Scott, the husband of country music artist Linda Davis.

HOME AND FAMILY

LeAnn and her parents lived for years in a tiny two-bedroom apartment in Garland, Texas. Her success eventually bought them a new four-bedroom house in which she has her own sitting room and a 13 x 13 foot closet — big enough to be a room in itself! Despite their devotion to their daughter and her career, Wilbur and Belinda Rimes announced in September 1997 that they were getting a divorce. Since both of her parents have always traveled everywhere with LeAnn, it's unclear how they will continue to handle their daughter's career.

LeAnn has never led the life of a typical teenager, but she doesn't feel she has missed out on anything. She dated briefly in sixth grade, but since then, she hasn't been in one place long enough to meet anyone who might want to ask her out. The members of her band, who are like family to LeAnn, often joke that they're not going to let her date until she's 40.

HOBBIES AND OTHER INTERESTS

LeAnn, who claims that her "worst habit" is shopping, loves to shop for clothes, makeup, jewelry, and hats. When she isn't on tour, she likes to call up her friends in Texas and go out to a movie or shop for CDs. Sometimes she goes rollerblading or bowling with them. She also enjoys riding cutting horses, which are extremely nimble horses trained to separate a cow from its herd.

TV CREDITS

"LeAnn Rimes in Concert," 1997
"Holiday in Your Heart," 1997

HONORS AND AWARDS

American Music Award for Best New Country Artist: 1997
Grammy Award for Best Female Country Vocal Performance: 1997
Grammy Award for Best New Artist: 1997
Horizon Award (Country Music Association): 1997
TNN/Music City News Country Award for "Female Star of Tomorrow": 1997
Top New Female Vocalist (Academy of Country Music): 1997

FURTHER READING

Books

Catalano, Grace. *LeAnn Rimes: Teen Country Queen,* 1997 (juvenile)
————. *Dream Come True: The LeAnn Rimes Story,* 1997 (juvenile)

Periodicals

Chicago Tribune, Feb. 23, 1997, p.13
Country Weekly, June 17, 1997, p.28
Esquire, May 1997, p.40
People, Sep. 2, 1996, p.75
Times of London, Aug. 16, 1996
TV Guide, Sep. 28, 1996, p.43
USA Today, June 11, 1996, p.D1; Mar. 14, 1997, p.D4
USA Weekend, Sep. 27-29, 1996, p.4
Washington Post, June 22, 1996, p.D1

ADDRESS

LeAnn Rimes Entertainment
Twin Sixties Towers, Suite 816
6060 North Central Expressway
Dallas, TX 75206

WORLD WIDE WEB SITE

http://www.curb.com

Emily Rosa 1987-

American Student
Conducted Scientific Study of "Therapeutic Touch"
Medical Treatment

EARLY LIFE

Emily Rosa was born on February 6, 1987. She is the only daughter of Linda Rosa, a nurse. She lives with her mother and stepfather, Larry Sarner, a mathematician and inventor. They live in Loveland, Colorado, a rural town located north of Denver.

Even as a young child, Emily was very curious about the world around her. She learned to read in kindergarten, and by the end of first grade she was so bored that her parents decided to educate her at home. They felt that by home-schooling Emily, they could teach her one-on-one and provide her with a more challenging and stimulating environment. After one year of being taught by her stepfather, Rosa returned to school. But she was so far ahead of the other third graders that she was moved up into the fourth grade after only two weeks. After completing fourth grade, she returned to home school and her mother assumed the teaching duties.

——— " ———

"I like learning at home. Your teacher gets to focus on one student instead of 30. They can help you individually. We get to do interesting projects. I'm learning Spanish and have taken some Greek, Japanese, and I'm doing oil-painting this year."

——— " ———

"I like learning at home," said Rosa. "Your teacher gets to focus on one student instead of 30. They can help you individually. We get to do interesting projects. I'm learning Spanish and have taken some Greek, Japanese, and I'm doing oil-painting this year." She does admit, though, that she sometimes misses having other children around during the day.

MAJOR ACCOMPLISHMENT

Emily Rosa became famous because of an experiment she did on a medical treatment called Therapeutic Touch, or TT. Therapeutic Touch is a technique in which practitioners attempt to heal sick people by passing their hands over the patient's body without actually touching the patient. People who use this alternative medical treatment believe that by passing their hands over the patient's body, they can manipulate what they call the "human energy field" that emanates from every person. This alternative healing method is used by an estimated 43,000 medical professionals around the United States, and it is studied in more than 80 hospitals nationwide. But Therapeutic Touch is not universally accepted by all members of the medical profession. Many doctors believe that it does not have any true healing powers, and some critics contend that sick people waste thousands of hard-earned dollars on such treatments. In fact, both of Emily's parents are members of organizations that criticize the technique as a useless exercise that does not really help anyone recover from any kind of medical condition.

One night in 1996, Rosa was home trying to figure out what sort of experiment to do for an upcoming fourth grade science fair. Glancing into the next

Linda and Emily Rosa

room, she noticed that her mother was watching a videotape. "I had heard of TT before because my mom is a nurse, and she questioned it," confirmed Emily, who walked over to the couch to watch the videotape with her mother. "[The videotape] interested me because I wondered if it was really true that they could detect a human energy field. I decided to find out for myself. I thought that if TT were true, practitioners should be able to detect energy fields they couldn't see. I just had to figure out how to test that."

Devising a Test of Therapeutic Touch

Rosa soon came up with a simple, inexpensive plan for her science fair experiment. She took out advertisements to reach TT practitioners, 21 of whom eventually agreed to take part in her study. She then tested each therapist's ability to detect her "human energy field" by seating herself on the opposite side of a screen from each participant and flipping a coin. The coin flip determined whether Emily would put her hand over the healer's left or right hand. The healer was then asked to say where Emily had put her hand. Emily's test was based on the theory that if the therapist could detect her energy field, he or she should be able to detect where Emily's hand was.

Over the next several weeks, Emily conducted 10 to 20 tests on each of the TT volunteers. On many occasions she conducted the test right in the home or office of the volunteer. By the time her study was complete, she had conducted a total of 280 tests. In those tests, the therapists correctly identified the location of Emily's hand 123 times. That total gave the volunteers only a 44 percent success rate, which was even lower than the 50-percent success rate that would be expected from random guessing.

Emily did most of the experiment herself, although she admits that her parents helped her out once in a while. "I tried to do as much on my own as I could, but when I came to a problem, my parents helped," she said. "They always encourage and praise me and tell me to go for it!"

Results Published in Scientific Journal

After reviewing the project results, Linda Rosa and Larry Sarner were convinced that their daughter had put together a test that proved that TT did not really work. Working with their daughter and Dr. Stephen Barrett, they put together an article describing the experiment and its results and sent it off to the *Journal of the American Medical Association (JAMA)*. The magazine is one of the most prestigious medical journals in the entire world, so Emily was terribly excited when *JAMA*'s editors contacted the Rosas to tell them that they were interested in publishing the results of her study.

The article describing Emily's project was published in the *Journal of the American Medical Association* on April 1, 1998. The article triggered an immediate reaction from doctors, nurses, and the popular media. Many people marveled that the study had been devised by a girl who was only nine years old at the time. But *JAMA* editor Dr. George D. Lundberg said that her young age did not matter. "Age is irrelevant," he said. "It's the quality of the science that matters. Mozart did some of his best work when he was five and Shirley Temple got an Oscar when she was six."

In the weeks following the paper's publication, Emily was hailed as the youngest person ever to publish a paper in a major scientific journal. She made guest appearances on a number of national television shows, including "CBS This Morning" and the "Today Show," and she was interviewed by CNN. Rosa's study also received front-page coverage in some of America's best-known newspapers, including the *New York Times*, the *Denver Post,* and the *Los Angeles Times.*

Debate over the Test Results

The response to Emily's test varied widely. Many members of the medical community came forward to cheer her work. Some doctors, nurses, and researchers had always been skeptical about whether Therapeutic Touch really worked, and they pointed to her project as proof that the alternative treatment did not help people. Indeed, Emily's study prompted some medical professionals around the country to question whether it was appropriate to teach TT in nursing schools.

But Emily's test was not universally praised. Many practitioners of Therapeutic Touch criticized the test as biased and flawed. One TT practitioner told the *Boulder Daily Camera* that "for at least 10 years, [Emily's] parents have been trying to debunk Therapeutic Touch. They are invested in the outcome. They definitely want Therapeutic Touch out of nursing school. And a nine-year-old child is obviously influenced by her parents." Others complained that Emily did not place her hand close enough to the screen when conducting the test, or that she misunderstood the way in which TT works. TT practitioner Damaris Jarboux, for instance, argued that Therapeutic Touch "works through the principles of compassion and connection with the [patient]. It is difficult to prove that Therapeutic Touch is curative because, alone, it is not. All energy healing is self healing. . . . Most practitioners feel that [Emily] was probably withdrawing her field, though not consciously. She is just a little girl." Finally, some people who believe that they have been cured of physical ailments through TT spoke out on behalf of the alternative treatment.

The debate over the merits of Emily's test and Therapeutic Touch treatments is not likely to end any time soon. Many supporters of TT continue to say that the girl brought too many biases to her test for its results to be taken seriously. Critics of TT, meanwhile, say that Emily's project provided proof that the practice does not work. Emily reacted calmly to the whole controversy, telling reporters that she hoped to test other kinds of alternative medical treatments as she gets older.

FUTURE PLANS

"I probably want to be a veterinarian when I grow up," said Emily, who cares for two dogs, two birds, a cat, and a tarantula. She is also interested in exploring a career as an astronaut. In the meantime, her interests are pretty similar to those of other girls her age. She is a big fan of the Spice Girls and *Xena: Warrior Princess,* and enjoys playing with her pets and neighborhood children.

FURTHER READING

Periodicals

Boulder Daily Camera, May 12, 1998, p.10
Chicago Tribune, May 17, 1998, p.3
Denver Post, Apr. 1, 1998, p.A1
Journal of the American Medical Association, Apr. 1, 1998, p.1005

Los Angeles Times, Apr. 1, 1998, p.A1
New York Times, Apr. 1, 1998, p.A1
New York Times Magazine, June 28, 1998, p.34
People, Apr. 27, 1998, p.93
Plain Dealer (Cleveland), Apr. 2, 1998, p.B1
Washington Post, Apr. 7, 1998, p.Z9

ADDRESS

Rural Route #2
P.O. Box 1568
Crandon, WI 54520

David Satcher 1941-

American Doctor, Scientist, and Public Health
Administrator
U.S. Surgeon General

BIRTH

David Satcher was born on March 2, 1941, in Anniston,
Alabama. His father, Wilmer Satcher, was a foundry worker and
farmer, while his mother, Anna Satcher, was a homemaker.
David Satcher grew up in a big family. His parents had nine children, but one baby died in childbirth and another baby lived for
less than a week. His parents also took in a relative's child to live
with them, so that David grew up in a family of eight children.

Like his brothers and sisters, he was born at home, on the family's 40-acre farm.

YOUTH

Satcher grew up as a poor black in the deep South during the 1940s and 1950s, a time when segregation and discrimination against African-Americans were widespread and routine. Yet he went on to accomplish so much, both academically and professionally — earning a medical degree and a doctoral degree in science; founding and directing several different medical programs, both large and small, in hospitals and in church basements; teaching at several colleges, and even serving as a college president; heading up the Centers for Disease Control and Prevention; and becoming the Surgeon General, the nation's top doctor. Satcher traces the roots of this success to the influence of his parents and his community during his early years.

Satcher's parents were deeply religious Baptists who were involved in their church community. His father, in fact, taught himself to read by memorizing Biblical passages at church and then picking them out of the family Bible. Neither of his parents had much formal education — both left school before finishing the elementary level — although they strongly supported their children's education. With such a big family, they didn't have much money while David was growing up. But for Satcher, these problems did not pose a severe hardship. "I may have come from a poor family economically, but they were not poor in spirit," he once said. "We had a rich environment from the spirit of my parents, both of whom had a vision for their children. They didn't keep us out of school working in the fields. They made it clear that school came first, and that teachers were heroes."

The kids did help out on the family's 40-acre farm, though. On school days, they rose while it was still dark to finish their chores before leaving for school. On weekends and in the summer they spent hours in the fields where, according to one of David's brothers, they would quiz each other on vocabulary words. "We'd take rest breaks in the fields and pull out copies of *Reader's Digest*, calling out words to each other, to see who could get them," says Robert, David's older brother who is now a chemist. "David was very competitive and he kind of embarrassed me because he would beat me." When he got older, David also worked part-time in the foundry where his father was employed for 55 years.

EARLY MEMORIES

Satcher's earliest memory came from a life-threatening experience when he was just two years old. In 1943 he contracted whooping cough (also called pertussis). This is a highly contagious disease that starts out like a cold. But the cough eventually becomes much more severe, with lengthy attacks of violent coughing. It can become very serious, even deadly. Whooping cough was a major cause of death for young children before a vaccine was developed in 1923. Twenty years later, when young Satcher was sick, vaccines like that simply weren't available to poor black families living in the deep South; in fact, the Satcher family really didn't have much access to medical care at all.

Although he was only two at the time, Satcher clearly remembers lying on his back, painfully gasping to catch his breath between coughing fits. None of the white doctors in the area would help him because he was black. Fortunately, there was one African-American doctor nearby. He came to the house, examined David, and gave advice to his mother, Anna Satcher, on how to keep his fever down and how to keep his lungs clear. But young David had also contracted pneumonia, and his chances weren't good. According to his older sister, Lottie Washington, "I remember the doctor telling my mother that he wouldn't live until the next day." Yet Anna Satcher was determined that her son wouldn't die. Despite all medical expectations, she nursed him back to health.

"I may have come from a poor family economically, but they were not poor in spirit," Satcher said. "We had a rich environment from the spirit of my parents, both of whom had a vision for their children. They didn't keep us out of school working in the fields. They made it clear that school came first, and that teachers were heroes."

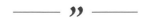

As he was growing up, Anna Satcher told young David the story of his illness and his recovery over and over, until it became a part of family lore. By the time he was eight years old, Satcher had decided to become a doctor. He was undeterred by such obstacles as his family's modest financial circumstances and his parents' lack of education. "In a way," journalist Anne Rochell wrote in the *Atlanta Constitution*, "the decision [to become a doctor] was the beginning of a long and eloquent thank-you to all the people who told him he had the power to rise above the poverty, racism, and lack of medical care he faced growing up."

Another part of that early experience sticks with Satcher to this day. When he was desperately ill, the neighbors gathered on the front porch of their home, coming to comfort the family of a sick child. "They came to be supportive," Satcher says. "They didn't have any medical expertise. They were there because a family was about to lose a child." The importance of that strong sense of community deeply touched him. To this day, he has strong views on the role of community in combating such social problems as teen pregnancy, violence, gangs, and guns.

EDUCATION

When Satcher was growing up, schools in the South were still segregated. White children attended one set of schools, while black children attended others. Their schools, like other services for African-Americans, were always dilapidated, with old rundown buildings, inadequate textbooks, outdated equipment, and poorly paid teachers. In Satcher's school district, there was only one bus for all the black students in the county, so the bus took hours driving back and forth all over the county picking up all the students. Riding the school bus for hours each day, Satcher would pass two schools for white kids before they arrived at the segregated school for blacks. He would encounter such outright discrimination throughout much of his school career.

But Satcher didn't let these obstacles stand in the way of his education. He was an excellent student, in part because he studied throughout those long rides on the bus. In high school, he was so good at chemistry that he would sometimes teach the class when his teachers were out sick. In his senior year he was named valedictorian, the student with the highest grade-point average in his graduating class. He was one of only three students from his class to go on to college.

Satcher earned a full scholarship to Morehouse College, a traditionally all-black school in Atlanta, Georgia. But when he received the acceptance letter, Satcher was afraid that he wasn't a good enough student. "I was so scared, I spent the whole summer studying to make sure that when I got to Morehouse I could survive." Despite his fears, Satcher didn't have anything to worry about. When he took the standard placement tests during his first week at Morehouse, he placed ninth out of 240 students. He did so well, in fact, that he was placed in a special program for advanced students.

College Years

Morehouse College proved to be an excellent choice for Satcher, one that helped him to thrive both academically and emotionally. "From day one the attitude at Morehouse was 'You are somebody. We expect great things of you,'" he once recalled. That message was emphasized by Benjamin E. Mays, the president of the college, who became a mentor to Satcher. "He'd always say, 'Satcher, you must aim for the ceiling and not the floor.'"

At Morehouse, Satcher first started confronting the issue of racism and becoming active in the civil rights movement. "Before that it was just the way things were," he said. "My parents taught us self-respect, but they also adapted to the environment in which we lived. The movement in Atlanta was the chance to act." He became involved in the Student Nonviolent Coordinating Committee (SNCC, pronounced snick), ultimately becoming the head of its

Satcher with President Bill Clinton and Vice President Al Gore

Atlanta chapter. This group, which was founded by students, became one of the major organizers of civil-rights activities in the South.

With SNCC, Satcher got involved in sit-ins, a tactic used to integrate all-white restaurants, movie theaters, bus stations, and the like. During a sit-in, black people would sit at a segregated or "white" lunch counter, for example, and refuse to move until they were served. Those involved in sit-ins and other civil rights protests believed that people should use nonviolent actions to disobey and challenge racist laws. They believed that it was right to break a racist law in order to change the law, and they were willing to go to jail for their beliefs. Satcher was arrested and sent to jail several times for his civil rights activities, sometimes for days. In that time of hostility in the South, it took great courage to participate in such confrontations, and serving time in jail was considered a badge of honor. Satcher didn't let his protest experiences distract him from his school work, though — he would take his books along and study in jail. During his senior year at Morehouse, he was elected class president, won the J.J. Starks Student Leadership Award, and was elected Phi Betta Kappa. Satcher graduated magna cum laude with a B.S. degree in 1963.

With an excellent record from his undergraduate years, Satcher was determined to attend medical school. Yet he was rejected by his first choice, Duke University in North Carolina, because of his race. Instead, he attended Case Western Reserve University in Cleveland, Ohio. He was one of only two black students in its medical school. At Case Western, he fought against unequal and discriminatory practices in patient care, for which he was almost expelled. He also faced discrimination as a black doctor in a primarily white environment. Here, Satcher describes one of those experiences. "As a medical student in Cleveland, during my first rotation as a student in the [hospital] ward, one of my patients was a white man from Mississippi. When his family found out I was black, they got him out of the hospital. I wasn't fazed," he recalled with a smile. "There were some advantages to having grown up in Alabama."

During his medical training, Satcher was also enrolled in a doctoral program in cytogenics, a branch of cell biology that links the study of genetics with the study of cell structure. As part of his doctoral research, he did a lengthy study of the effects of radiation on chromosomes to understand the relationship between radiation dosage and chromosome damage. To fund the study he received a three-year research grant from the university and then an additional grant from the National Cancer Institute, a great accomplishment for a student. When he earned his M.D. and his Ph.D. in 1970 with election to Alpha Omega Alpha Honor Medical Society, Satcher became the first African-American at Case Western Reserve University to earn both degrees concurrently.

Satcher also got married during this time. He had met his wife, Callie Frances Herndon, while he was attending Morehouse and she was a student at Spelman College. They were married in 1967, while he was in medical school at Case Western, and soon began a family that grew to include four children over the next ten years.

CAREER HIGHLIGHTS

For over 25 years, Satcher has had a varied and distinctive career as a practicing doctor, a scientific researcher, and an administrator of public health and medical programs. In all these roles, he has also been an effective advocate for good medical care for all people, particularly those with the greatest need. As Sheryl Gay Stolberg explained in the *New York Times*, "Dr. Satcher's medical career has been marked by the twin themes of race and poverty." That view was echoed by Dr. Mark Rivo, a friend and public health administrator who has worked with Satcher on health reform. "One of the most impressive things about Dave is that he always keeps his sights on the needs of the most vulnerable members of our society, particularly minorities, the poor, women, and children. Every policy decision he makes factors that into it — it's not just a rhetorical position for him," Rivo said. "One thing is real clear, he is in his element when he's out in the community. He's one of those people who has the ability to carry himself in a way that triggers respect and admiration — whether he's at a meeting of medical school deans or hospital execs, or out in public housing. He connects with people."

Early Jobs

Satcher's first job as a doctor was at Strong Memorial Hospital, the teaching hospital affiliated with the University of Rochester School of Medicine in Rochester, New York. He worked there as a medical intern and resident from 1970 to 1972. He also worked as a doctor at a neighborhood health center and later at a health center for migrant workers. In addition, he served as a consultant on sickle-cell anemia to a local medical program. Sickle-cell is an inherited disease of the blood that primarily affects those of African descent. Outbreaks of the disease, which can include fever, jaundice, and abdominal and joint pain, can be excruciating. There is no cure for the disease, which is often fatal. In 1972, Satcher made a film about sickle-cell anemia.

Dr. Mark Rivo, a friend and public health administrator who has worked with Satcher on health reform, said, "One of the most impressive things about Dave is that he always keeps his sights on the needs of the most vulnerable members of our society, particularly minorities, the poor, women, and children. Every policy decision he makes factors that into it —it's not just a rhetorical position for him."

That same year, Satcher moved to southern California. From 1972 to 1979, he concurrently held a variety of positions in patient care, teaching, and administration. From 1972 to 1975 he worked at the Martin Luther King Jr. Medical Center in Watts, an economically depressed section of Los Angeles that is predominantly African-American. The King Medical Center was opened in response to a promise made to the residents of Watts after the deadly 1965 riots. There, he was director of the Community Hypertension Outreach program, a clinic affiliated with the Charles R. Drew Medical School, which treated patients with high blood pressure. In 1973 Satcher joined the staff of the King-Drew Sickle-Cell Research Center, which offered programs in community education, early diagnosis, screening, counseling, and treatment of sickle-cell disease. He served as its associate director from 1973 to 1974 and as its director from 1974 to 1979. At the same time, he also served on the faculty of the Drew Medical School. From 1974 to 1975 he was an assistant professor and interim chair of the Department of Community Medicine at Drew; from 1976 to 1979 he was a professor and chair of the Department of Family Medicine there; and from 1977 to 1979 he was the interim dean of the medical school at Drew. In addition, he was also affiliated with the University of

California at Los Angeles (UCLA) School of Public Health. He taught epidemiology there from 1974 to 1979, creating an innovative program whereby medical students would study two years at UCLA and then two years at Drew, where they would provide free care to Watts residents. And on top of all that, he still made time to establish a free medical clinic in Watts in the basement of a Baptist church where he was a member; he served as the clinic director from 1975 to 1979.

In 1979 Satcher left the Los Angeles area for a deeply compelling reason. His first wife, Callie, had recently died from cancer, and he wanted to take their four children to live closer to their families in the south. So he returned to his alma mater, Morehouse College in Atlanta, Georgia. There he joined the School of Medicine, where he served as the chair of the Department of Community Medicine and Family Practice from 1979 to 1982. During that time he was also remarried, to the poet Nola Smith.

— " —

"[If] you look at the major cause of death today it's not smallpox or polio or even infectious diseases. Violence is the leading cause of lost life in this country today. If it's not a public health problem, why are all those people dying from it?"

— " —

Meharry Medical College

In July 1982, Satcher was named president of Meharry Medical College, the only independent black four-year medical school in the country. Located in Nashville, Tennessee, Meharry has great historical significance for many African-Americans. It was established in 1876, at a time when very few medical schools admitted blacks. In fact, African-Americans could attend few of the country's white medical schools before 1960. Even in 1980, after over a decade of more open enrollments, almost half of the black doctors and dentists in the country had graduated from Meharry — including the doctor who had treated Satcher years before, when he was so sick as a child. The school's mission is to educate primary-care doctors, to encourage them to practice in under-served communities, and to focus especially on prevention. And 80% of Meharry graduates practice medicine in inner-city or rural communities, areas that have traditionally lacked adequate medical coverage. Satcher was particularly interested in Meharry's mission of serving the poor. "I didn't want to be a college president," he explains. "But after I visited Meharry and learned that this institution had sent more of its graduates to serve in inner-city communities than any other medical school in the country, I thought I could make a difference."

When Satcher joined the administration in 1982, Meharry was facing a host of problems—heavy debt load, declining enrollment, the departure of key faculty and administrators, the loss of accreditation in many of its programs, and the lack of patients in its teaching hospital. Satcher set about improving the school's reputation by recruiting new faculty members, securing tens of millions of dollars in federal loans and donations from alumni, and ensuring the survival of the hospital. To that end, he proposed a merger between Meharry Hubbard Hospital, which had too many empty beds, and the Nashville public hospital, Metropolitan General, which operated in an aging and deteriorating building. Satcher proposed that the public hospital should be merged with Meharry Hubbard and that patient care should be provided by the staff at Meharry.

This proposal—that a city-controlled hospital run by whites and serving primarily white patients should be merged with a black hospital and run by black doctors and administrators—turned out to be very controversial. During the four years that Satcher fought for the merger, "The proposal walked a political tightrope in which race—specifically, fears about entrusting medical care to black doctors and administrators—was the constant subtext," Peter Applebome wrote in the *New York Times*. "Race is not the only issue involved here, but it is the central issue," Satcher said. "The merger strikes at the heart of what integration means in the 1990s, an issue that America is still having so much trouble with. Integration is not just blacks going to white institutions. It means a redistribution of resources." The plan "evoked a community debate that spanned several years and resulted in a coalition of support which cut across all racial, ethnic, and economic lines," explained Satcher, who ultimately commanded the respect and admiration of all these segments of the city. According to Nashville mayor Phil Bredeson, who worked to support the merger, "He provided moral leadership to the community." In July 1993 Meharry took over full clinical responsibility for Nashville General. Satcher's plan went forward, saving Meharry from an uncertain and unstable future. Since that time, many have credited Satcher with saving the college.

The Centers for Disease Control and Prevention

In 1993, Satcher was named director of the Centers for Disease Control and Prevention (CDC). This federal agency, located in Atlanta, Georgia, is the top U.S. organization for tracking and preventing disease. It works closely with local, state, and federal agencies, as well as international groups, to protect the public health. The mission of the CDC is "To promote health and quality of life by preventing and controlling disease, injury, and disability." With a budget of $2 billion, the CDC employs approximately 6,900 people in the U.S. and around the world, including over 4,500 employees in the Atlanta area.

Historically, the CDC was known as an epidemiological agency created to battle infectious diseases. It started out fighting malaria in 1946, and since then has gone on to fight smallpox, polio, tuberculosis, whooping cough, and, recently, Legionnaires' disease and AIDS. It's now considered the premier epidemiological organization in the world, tracking infectious diseases world-wide and developing prevention strategies. But today it does even more, in its centers devoted to such health issues as chronic disease prevention; genetics and disease prevention; environmental health; health statistics; HIV (Human Immunodeficiency Virus, which causes AIDS), STDs (sexually transmitted diseases), and TB (tuberculosis) prevention; infectious diseases; injury prevention and control; occupational safety and health; global health; and immunizations.

In recent years, and particularly under the direction of Satcher, the CDC has taken an all-encompassing view of public health. He continued to support the agency's traditional approach by working to increase immunization rates for young children, improving the nation's system for responding to emerging infectious diseases, and creating an early warning system to detect and prevent illnesses carried in food. He also placed a greater emphasis on preventing disease, by encouraging a healthy lifestyle with physical activity and a well-balanced diet. Yet the CDC has also widened its scope to tackle chronic diseases (like heart disease and cancer), injury prevention and control (like car accidents and domestic violence), occupational safety (like accidents on the job), environmental hazards (like pollution and toxic dump sites), and social problems (like violence, drug abuse, and teen sexual activity). The CDC has placed an increasing emphasis on the needs of African-Americans and the poor, earning Satcher a national reputation as an expert on the medically underserved. "He understands the disadvantaged populations very well and that's critical," says Dr. Harold Freeman, who serves on CDC's Director's Advisory Committee. "He understands the disparities related to race and health care and has been on the cutting edge of trying to improve conditions for black Americans."

The CDC's approach to some issues has been very controversial. The CDC has taken a public health approach to some of the most divisive social issues of our time. Smoking is one example. Of the two million deaths each year in the U.S., about 20% — or 420,000 — are related to smoking. These are preventable deaths from cancer, respiratory disease, and heart disease that the CDC wants to address, yet its critics feel that it shouldn't intervene in the sale of tobacco. Violence, another example, is the leading cause of death for black males in this country. Yet when the CDC began to do research into violence prevention programs, critics said that the agency had stepped out of its role as a public health agency and entered areas that are the responsibility of the criminal justice system and social services agencies. Some felt that the CDC was promoting a political campaign against gun ownership. But Satcher dis-

Satcher testifying before the U.S. House of Representatives, May 1998

agreed. "Our position is that violence is, in fact, a criminal-justice problem. It is, in fact, a social problem. But it's still a public-health problem. And we believe we can apply the public-health approach to violence." For Satcher, the CDC had a clear role to play. "[If] you look at the major cause of death today it's not smallpox or polio or even infectious diseases," he said. "Violence is the leading cause of lost life in this country today. If it's not a public health problem, why are all those people dying from it?" Another example is the agency's response to AIDS. The CDC has been at the center of a national debate over different approaches to giving out information on AIDS. Some people feel that education for young people should stress abstinence, without providing other strategies for avoiding AIDS. Those at the CDC also stress abstinence, but they believe in emphasizing the deadly consequences of unprotected sex and explaining how people can protect themselves from AIDS. Ultimately, Satcher feels strongly that only science should dictate public health policy. "In the process of promoting health," he says, "we're not going to let differences in politics, religion, and culture get in the way. We can't afford that."

The U.S. Surgeon General

In November 1997, Satcher was nominated to become the U.S. Surgeon General. The Surgeon General, whose term in office is five years, is the top public health official in the country. Often called America's top doctor and the nation's family doctor, the Surgeon General leads the Public Health Service Commissioned Corps, which includes 6,000 medical professionals who respond to public health emergencies. The Surgeon General is also the nation's spokesperson on matters relating to public health, charged with interpreting scientific information on health matters and presenting it to the American public. Past Surgeon Generals, for example, raised the alarm about venereal diseases, smoking, secondhand smoke, television violence, and HIV and AIDS. At the same time, Satcher was also named Assistant Secretary for Health in the Department of Health and Human Services. This position has less public prestige than that of the Surgeon General. But the Assistant Secretary for Health has a policy-making role, giving him more say in the government's approach to public health and medical issues.

> "I want to be the Surgeon General who reaches our citizens with cutting-edge technology and plain, old-fashioned straight talk. As the Assistant Secretary for Health and the Surgeon General, I want to take the best science in the world and place it firmly within the grasp of all Americans." True to his past, Satcher is determined to reach all Americans. "Whether talking about smoking or poor diets, I want to send messages of good health to our cities and suburbs, our barrios and reservations, and even our prisons."

Satcher's nomination came after the position of Surgeon General had been vacant for almost three years. Its previous holder, Dr. Joycelyn Elders, was ousted by the White House in December 1994 because of her controversial statements on drugs and sexuality. Then President Bill Clinton nominated Dr. Henry W. Foster, Jr. But his nomination was blocked by the U.S. Senate, which by law must confirm the president's nominee, because some people objected to the fact that he had performed abortions earlier in his career as an obstetrician/gynecologist. The Surgeon General's post remained vacant for some time, until President Clinton nominated Satcher. There was some controversy during Satcher's confirmation process about his views on abortion, because he believes that late-term abortions should be allowed when required to save the life of the mother. Yet he ultimately won confirmation by the Senate. Satcher was sworn in as Surgeon General on February 13, 1998. At the time he called it "an American dream come true," saying "It is a privilege to have this opportunity to give back to America what it has given me."

Satcher has certain goals that he hopes to accomplish as Surgeon General. He plans to help each child get a healthy start to life through prenatal care and good nutrition; to promote healthy lifestyles that include good eating habits and physical exercise; to remove the stigma attached to mental illness to ensure that it receives the same priority as physical illness; and to eliminate the disparities in the ways illnesses affect some population groups more than others. He has also expressed his desire to fight suicide, teen smoking, teen pregnancy, drug abuse, violence, and HIV and AIDS. He spent the first few months out of the public eye, becoming familiar with his responsibilities as Surgeon General and Assistant Secretary for Health. Lately he has started spending time on the road, speaking to groups around the country—like an assembly of 1,000 minority high school students in New Orleans who were interested in careers in medicine, and a gathering of middle-school students in Massachusetts who developed a program to keep their classmates from smoking. Describing his role, Satcher said, "I want to be the Surgeon General who reaches our citizens with cutting-edge technology and plain, old-fashioned straight talk. As the Assistant Secretary for Health and the Surgeon General, I want to take the best science in the world and place it firmly within the grasp of all Americans." True to his past, Satcher is determined to reach all Americans. "Whether talking about smoking or poor diets, I want to send messages of good health to our cities and suburbs, our barrios and reservations, and even our prisons."

MARRIAGE AND FAMILY

Satcher has been married two times. While he was attending Morehouse College, he met and fell in love with Callie Frances Herndon, the woman who would become his first wife. Herndon, who was then a student at Spelman College, was also from his hometown of Anniston. Married in 1967, they had four children who are all now in their 20s: their eldest, daughter Gretchen, and three sons, David, Daraka, and Daryl. Callie was diagnosed with breast cancer while she was pregnant with their fourth child, but she couldn't be treated until after the baby was born. She died of cancer just two years later, in 1978. Before she died, she asked her husband for two things. "Callie wanted me to take the children closer to home," he recalls. "She actually wanted me to find somebody who would be a good mother. I told her it was never gonna happen, that I'd never remarry." Her death was very hard on Satcher, and he rarely speaks about it. "That's one of my weaknesses," he says. "I don't talk about it a lot. If I had to do it again, I would do it differently. I would talk about it more with my children."

In the year following Callie's death, Satcher took the job at Morehouse College, moving back down to the south. And in 1979, after 18 months, Satcher married Nola Smith, a poet who had five grown children of her own and who helped raise Satcher's children—the two youngest kids even call her mom. Currently, David and Nola live in a brick home reserved for the Surgeon General on the grounds of the National Institutes of Health in Bethesda, Maryland, outside Washington, D.C. All four of Satcher's children are now grown and no longer live at home.

HONORS AND AWARDS

Watts Grassroots Award for Community Service: 1979
Human Relations Award (National Conference of Christians and Jews): 1985
Founders' Award of Distinction (Sickle-Cell Disease Research Foundation): 1992
American Black Achievement Award (*Ebony* magazine): 1994
Breslow Award for Excellence in Public Health: 1995
Nathan B. Davis Award (American Medical Association): 1996, for promoting "the art and science of medicine and the betterment of public health"
Election to the American Academy of Arts and Sciences: 1996
James D. Bruce Memorial Award (American College of Physicians): 1997
John Steams Award for Lifetime Achievement in Medicine (New York Academy of Medicine)
Surgeon General's Medallion, for significant and noteworthy contributions to the health of the nation

FURTHER READING

Books

American Men and Women of Science, 1998-99
Who's Who in America, 1998

Periodicals

Atlanta Constitution, Apr. 17, 1994, p.M1; Jan. 21, 1996, "CDC at 50: Crusades and Controversies" (Special Section)
Current Biography Yearbook 1997
Ebony, Mar. 1986, p.42; Jan. 1994, p.80

Los Angeles Times, Mar. 1, 1994, p.E1

New York Times, Sep. 26, 1993, Section 4, p.7; Sep. 12, 1997, p.A16; Sep. 13, 1997, p.B1; Feb. 5, 1998, p.A1; Feb. 11, 1998, p.A20; Feb. 14, 1998, p.A7; Apr. 21, 1998, p.F1

USA Today, Apr. 30, 1998, p.D10

Washington Post, Apr. 3, 1991, p.A1; Aug. 24, 1993, Health Section, p.6; Sep. 13, 1997, p.A3

ADDRESS

Office of the Surgeon General
Department of Health and Human Services
200 Independence Avenue S.W., Room 716-G
Washington, D.C. 20201

WORLD WIDE WEB SITES

The web site for the Office of the Surgeon General is currently in development; it's expected to be up and running in late 1998:
    http://www.surgeongeneral.gov

The web site for the Centers for Disease Control and Prevention:
    http://www.cdc.gov

The web site for the Department of Health and Human Services, which includes the Office of the Surgeon General:
    http://www.hhs.gov/

The kids' page of the web site for the Department of Health and Human Services (with links to kids' sites from many government agencies):
    http://www.hhs.gov/kids

OBITUARY

Betty Shabazz 1936-1997

American Activist, Civil Rights Leader, Educator, and
Health Administrator
Widow of the Slain Civil Rights Leader Malcolm X

BIRTH

Betty Shabazz was born Betty Sanders on May 28, 1936, in
Detroit, Michigan. Betty was adopted as a baby and raised by
Helen and Lorenzo Don Malloy. She was their only child.

248

YOUTH

Betty Shabazz was a private person who didn't reveal much about her early life. But certain facts are well known. Her father owned a shoe-repair shop, her mother was a teacher, and Betty grew up in a middle-class family in a thriving Detroit neighborhood filled with black businesses and churches. Her mother was very active in community groups and particularly in their church, Bethel A.M. E. (African Methodist Episcopal).

Betty led a very sheltered life that revolved around family, school, and church. As she once said, "Pick a week out of my life. If you understood that week, you understood my life. I went to school from Monday to Friday. On Friday I went to the movies. On Saturday I was at my parents' store. On Sunday I went to church. Sometimes on Saturday I would go with the young people from church to parties. This was in Detroit, Michigan, which is a Delta [Sigma Theta] town, so in high school I was a member of a sorority called the Del Sprites."

Betty's parents were very protective of their only child. They worked hard to give her a life that was free of worries. As she once recalled, "[Outside the classroom] I didn't have a serious thought in my head. . . . [I] had been adopted by older persons, and their one agenda for me was that I should be happy. If I wanted a new dress or whatever, I got it. I didn't even know how to cook." Betty's parents also worked hard to protect her from the evils of racism. Despite the era in which she grew up, she didn't even know the word until years later, when she was in college. "In many ways, I was a somewhat typical 'lil' African-American girl' shielded from the realities of racism and its outward manifestations," she recalled. "Most black families tried to keep the 'ugly' issue of race from their children, and my early childhood can be summarized as an attempt to keep this issue from me. Thus my elementary schooling was typically American, although I can remember small instances of racial hostility. I had both white and black friends. Indeed, in high school, several of my white classmates were good friends. My racial consciousness was far less developed than my awareness of the 'specialness' of adolescence. After high school, my higher education pursuit was still in keeping with the world view of a middle-class young woman reared to pursue education, a good job and children, a husband and family."

EDUCATION

Betty graduated from Northern High School in Detroit in 1952. She then attended Tuskegee Institute (now Tuskegee University), a historically African-American college in Alabama that her father had also attended. It was her first experience in the South and her first time away from the protected environment of her parents' home, and she had her first experiences with racism there. At Tuskegee, she planned to major in elementary education, but decided to switch to nursing instead. The dean of nursing suggested that she attend a three-year nursing school, so Betty transferred to the Brooklyn State Hospital School of Nursing in New York. There, she earned her certification as a registered nurse (R.N.).

It was in New York that she met her future husband, the civil rights activist Malcolm X. Betty interrupted her education for several years after they got married and started having children. Years later, after the assassination of her husband, she returned to school. She earned her bachelor's degree (B.A.) in public health education from Jersey City State College. She earned her doctorate (Ph.D.) in education in 1975 from the University of Massachusetts at Amherst.

"[The] woman known universally as Sister Betty faced more than her share of trials," according to Ebony *magazine, "but she confronted them all, giving America, and black America especially, one of the great images of the indomitable tenacity of the spirit, and especially the indomitable tenacity of spirit of great black women."*

GETTING INVOLVED WITH THE NATION OF ISLAM

Betty was living in New York and studying at the Brooklyn State Hospital School of Nursing when she got involved with the Nation of Islam. From that time onward her story is intertwined with the history of that complicated and controversial group and its minister, Malcolm X.

The Nation of Islam is one of a number of groups whose members are called Black Muslims. The Nation of Islam combines religion with the ideas of the black nationalist movement. Despite the name, the group is not considered part of the Islamic religion, and its adherents, though called Muslims, are not considered orthodox Muslims. As explained here by Mustafa Malik, director of the American Muslim Council, "To be a Muslim, you have to believe that there is only one God and Muhammad is his last Prophet. The Nation of Islam people believe that Elijah Muhammad is the last Prophet. There is nothing in common except that we call ourselves Muslims and they call themselves Muslims." Another difference is that the Islamic faith, unlike the Nation of Islam, does not judge people on the basis of race.

The Nation of Islam is a fairly recent group. It was founded in about 1930 in Detroit, Michigan, by Wallace Dodd Fard, also known as W.D. Farad

Muhammad, a door-to-door salesman who sold silks. While selling, he spread his message that black Americans should return to the Islamic faith, which was taken from them when they were driven from Africa as slaves. In 1934, he disappeared and was never heard from again. His assistant, Robert Poole, took over, changing his name to Elijah Muhammad.

ELIJAH MUHAMMAD

Elijah Muhammad, who was also known as the Messenger, led the Nation of Islam from 1934 until his death in 1975. He claimed that Farad Muhammad, the founder of the Nation, was an incarnation of Allah (God) and that he, Elijah Muhammad, was Allah's divine messenger, or prophet. Blacks were Allah's chosen people, according to Elijah. He said that black people were part of the tribe of Shabazz, which came from an explosion in space about 70 trillion years ago. White people were created some 6,000 years ago by a mad black scientist named Yacub. Through genetic manipulation, Yacub created the white race, which proved to be defective and inferior — "devils," in Elijah's view. These surprising theories about Yacub and the creation of the races were first proposed by Elijah Muhammad, and they have been embraced by many modern-day Black Muslims as well.

Elijah Muhammad rejected the call for integration and equality that characterized the Civil Rights Movement in the 1950s and 1960s. Instead, he espoused black nationalism, drawing on Marcus Garvey's "Back to Africa" movement from the early 1900s. Muhammad argued for the separation of the races and the creation of a new nation just for blacks. He also advocated black self-sufficiency, saying that blacks should take care of their own community and not expect help from white individuals or the white government. To that end, he created a multi-million dollar business organization that included a bank, a publishing house, a fish import company, apartment complexes, small businesses, schools, and temples.

Elijah Muhammad emphasized self-respect, racial pride, personal responsibility, respect for family, and avoidance of drugs and alcohol. He recruited, in particular, in poor neighborhoods and in prisons, places where his message of self-help was most needed. Members of the Nation became known for their moral behavior, upright bearing, and neat appearance. Expectations for women and men were clearly defined, as Malcolm X himself explained in *The Autobiography of Malcolm X.* "Islam has very strict laws and teachings about women, the core of them being that the true nature of man is to be strong, and a woman's true nature is to be weak, and while a man must at all times respect his woman, at the same time he needs to understand that he must control her if he expects to get her respect." In the Nation, the young women donned modest clothing and joined the Muslim Girls Training Class to learn how to be proper wives and homemakers. The young men joined the Fruit of

Islam. They wore their hair cropped short and dressed in suits with white shirts and bow ties. They took classes in the responsibilities of a husband and father. The Fruit of Islam served several purposes for the Nation of Islam. It was a way for young men to break away from their previous life on the streets, and it served as a security contingent for the Nation.

———— " ————

Shabazz tells about the first time she saw her future husband, Malcolm X. "I looked over and saw this man on the extreme right aisle sort of galloping to the podium. He was tall, he was thin, and the way he was galloping it looked as though he was going someplace more important than the podium. Have you ever seen people who are going someplace and you just know they are focused? Well, he got to the podium — and I sat up straight. I was impressed with him — clean-cut, no-nonsense. I felt that somewhere in my life I had met that energy before. Isn't that strange?"

———— " ————

Stanley Crouch, a prominent black commentator on African-American music and cultural life, reflected on that era in the *Village Voice.* By the 1950s, "Suddenly here were all these clean-cut, well-dressed young men and women — men mostly," Crouch wrote. "You recognized them from the neighborhood. They had been pests or vandals, thieves or gangsters. Now they were back from jail or prison and their hair was cut close, their skin was smooth, they no longer cursed blue streaks, and the intensity in their eyes remade their faces. They were 'in the Nation' and that meant that new men were in front of you, men who greeted each other in Arabic, who were aloof, confidant, and intent on living differently than they had."

MEETING MALCOLM X

One of those "new men" was Malcolm X. Malcolm Little, as he was originally known, had had a tough early life. His house was burned down, his father was killed, his mother suffered a breakdown, and the family was split apart — all by the time Malcolm was 12. He managed for a while, but he eventually dropped out of school and became a street hustler, a drug dealer, and a thief. Arrested for armed robbery, he was convicted and sent to prison in 1946. In prison, he underwent a spiritual awakening and converted to the Nation of Islam. After he was released on parole in 1952, he became an assistant minister for the Detroit Temple. It was then that Elijah Muhammad gave him the last name of X. In the Nation of Islam,

X symbolizes the lost African family name and signifies a rejection of the name given in America by the slave master.

In his work for the Nation, Malcolm gave lectures at the temple and spent time on the streets recruiting new members, first in Detroit and then in Boston. In 1954, he became the minister of Temple Number 7 in Harlem, New York. He later became the national spokesman for the Nation of Islam as well. The best known and most respected of the Nation's ministers, Malcolm was a charismatic and dynamic speaker who spoke powerfully on the issues of self-respect, self-discipline, and self-reliance. Here is how one convert remembered those lectures. "He held me spellbound. Listening to him, I began to understand how empty I was. And he put in me, in place of that emptiness, knowledge. And out of that came self-discovery, and pride." In everything he did, Malcolm X showed that he stood for "fierce pride, unflinching courage, [and] absolute determination to win freedom from injustice," according to Alex Haley, who helped Malcolm write his autobiography and who later wrote *Roots*.

Betty Sanders was one of many drawn into the Nation of Islam by Malcolm. She first became involved with Malcolm and the Nation while she was studying at the Brooklyn State Hospital School of Nursing. A friend from the hospital invited her and her date to dinner, and then urged them to come to a lecture to meet her minister. Betty was really not very interested in going to the lecture or meeting the minister. But her friend was such a good cook that Betty hoped to be invited again for dinner, so she decided to go along to please her.

Here, Betty recounts when she first saw the minister, Malcolm X. "[Our] hostess was sitting behind me and she whispered in my ear, 'The minister is here.' I said to myself, *Big deal*. But then I looked over and saw this man on the extreme right aisle sort of galloping to the podium. He was tall, he was thin, and the way he was galloping it looked as though he was going someplace more important than the podium. Have you ever seen people who are going someplace and you just know they are focused? Well, he got to the podium — and I sat up straight. I was impressed with him — clean-cut, no-nonsense. I felt that somewhere in my life I had met that energy before. Isn't that strange?"

After meeting briefly at the temple that night, Betty next saw Malcolm at a dinner party. They talked about her experiences with racism while attending school at Tuskegee in Alabama: "I told him about living in Alabama and the hostilities I encountered there, and how my parents did not want to deal with it. They though it was my fault. I'm talking about the irritation between the races in the South. Malcolm started talking to me about the conditions of black people. This was the first time I heard the word racism used. He started giving me a history lesson—told me racism was not my fault. I began to see why people did certain things. I began to see myself from a different perspective." For Betty, this was when she first began to develop a broader world view.

Betty returned to hear more lectures from Malcolm X, and gradually she became involved in the Nation of Islam as well. Soon she joined the Nation and took the name Sister Betty X. As a nurse, she started teaching health and hygiene classes to the women. She and Malcolm got to know each other while talking about issues related to their faith. But at that point, Betty didn't think anything of it—Malcolm was very popular with women in the Nation, and she didn't think he was interested in her personally. Although he never admitted any interest, Malcolm started finding more and more reasons to be around her. And over time, they started a sort of courtship. In the Nation of Islam, unmarried men and women do not go out on dates; they go out with a chaperone or as part of a group. Malcolm seemed to find a lot of opportunities to be near Betty. He would drop into her classes, or sit with her at dinners, always as part of a group. This went on for over a year.

MARRIAGE AND FAMILY

Their relationship changed rather suddenly. In January 1958, Malcolm took a trip back to Michigan to visit his family. He drove into Detroit, pulled up to a pay phone, and called Betty. In his autobiography, he described that conversation. "Getting gas at a filling station, I just went to their pay phone on a wall; I telephoned Sister Betty X [at the nurses' residence at the hospital]. . . . She said, 'Oh hello, Brother Minister—' I just said it to her direct: 'Look, do you want to get married?' Naturally, she acted all surprised and shocked. The more I have thought about it, to this day I believe she was only putting on an act. Because women know. They know. She said, just like I knew she would, 'Yes.' Then I said, well, I didn't have a whole lot of time, she'd better catch a plane to Detroit. So she grabbed a plane." She and Malcolm went to stay with his brothers who were also Muslims, and they were delighted by the news. Her parents took it hard, though. As devout Methodists, they were distressed by her decision to become a Muslim and to marry Malcolm X. At the time, her parents sobbed, "What have we done to you to make you hate us so?" With time, though, Betty and her parents were reconciled.

On January 14, 1958, Sister Betty X, as she was then known, married Malcolm X in Lansing, Michigan. They returned to New York, and in time they had six daughters: Attallah, born in 1958; Qubilah, born in 1960; Ilyasah, born in 1962; Gamilah, born in 1964; and the twins, Malaak and Malikah, born in 1965.

Betty and Malcolm were married for seven years. Despite their love for each other, their home life went through some upheavals. Betty continued doing work for the Nation, developing curriculum and setting up classes for women at different mosques. She really wanted to get a paying job, but Malcolm re-

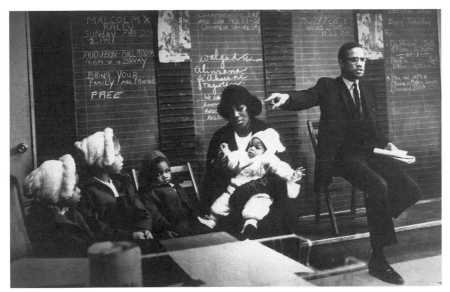

Malcom X with Betty Shabazz and their children announcing a rally at the Audubon Ballroom, where he was killed just a couple of months later

fused to allow her to do any work besides the volunteer work for the Nation. Because he wouldn't allow her to work outside the home, Betty left Malcolm three different times. Each time she went to stay with family, and each time they reconciled after a short time. But life outside their home brought even more upheaval. Malcolm had been a passionate believer in racial separatism as a way of creating equality for blacks. In his fiery and persuasive speeches he freely expressed his hatred of whites, calling them devils. He often used the phrase "by any means necessary," which many people interpreted to mean that he advocated violence as a means to address racial issues. For all of these reasons, he was widely vilified in white communities.

LEAVING THE NATION OF ISLAM

But by the early 1960s, Malcolm was changing his beliefs. He learned that the Nation had been involved in financial wrongdoings that benefitted his idol, Elijah Muhammad, and his family. He also learned that Muhammad had been involved in a series of extra-marital affairs with women from the Nation of Islam and had even their fathered children—in direct violation of the Nation's moral teachings. Malcolm felt personally betrayed by these revelations: "I felt as though something in *nature* had failed, like the sun, or the stars." After a period of increasing suspicion and hostility between Malcolm and other members, he left the Nation of Islam in March 1964. His interest in orthodox Islam grew. He became an orthodox Muslim, made a pilgrimage (or hajj) to Mecca, took the name El-Hajj Malik El-Shabazz, rejected racial separatism, and began to believe in the possibility of brotherhood between blacks and whites. Inspired by his conversion, Betty also left the Nation and became an orthodox Muslim, taking the name of Betty Shabazz.

Malcolm's departure from the Nation of Islam was also the result of a huge behind-the-scenes power struggle. Because of his power within the group he had been the subject of jealousy and hatred. Malcolm wrote about some of the veiled implications he would hear: "For example, it was being said that 'Minister Malcolm is trying to take over the Nation,' it was being said that I was 'taking credit' for Mr. Muhammad's teaching, it was being said that I was trying to 'build an empire' for myself." Malcolm knew that he was in danger—there had even been death threats made against him. In December 1964 Louis Farrakhan [see *Biography Today*, January 1997], who is the current leader of the Nation of Islam, wrote this in the Nation newspaper *Muhammad Speaks*: "Only those who wish to be led to hell, or to their doom, will follow Malcolm. The die is set, and Malcolm shall not escape. . . . Such a man as Malcolm is worthy of death."

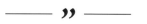

> "Dr. Shabazz's struggle and violent end became, for many African-Americans, a universal allegory of aspirations, perseverance, bitter disappointments, and uncontrollable twists of fate. It also showed how Dr. Shabazz, as the widow of Malcolm X and the stubborn guardian of his legacy, has attained a place among modern African-American trailblazers."
>
> Frank Bruni, *New York Times*

Two months later, during the night of February 13, 1965, Malcolm and Betty's house was firebombed. Someone threw Molotov cocktails through their living room window. They were able to get themselves and the children out safely, but their home and their belongings were destroyed. Just one week later, on February 21, 1965, Malcolm X was assassinated at the Audubon Ballroom in Harlem. He had just begun to speak, with Betty and the girls in the audience, when shots rang out. Betty, who was then pregnant with the twins, threw her four daughters down on the floor and covered them with her own body. By the time she got to her husband, he was already dead. Three Nation of Islam members were eventually convicted of the assassination. Farrakhan later expressed regret that he had contributed to the violent environment in which the slaying took place, but he has denied that he had any role in the actual murder. Yet after more than 30 years, there are still rumors about possible conspiracies behind the assassination.

Many people still question whether the Nation of Islam had a role in ordering Malcolm's death.

CREATING A NEW LIFE FOR HERSELF AND HER FAMILY

The years following her husband's death were hard on Betty Shabazz. Unlike other well-known widows of that era, like Jacqueline Kennedy and Coretta Scott King, she received little emotional or financial support—white people were put off by her husband's inflammatory rhetoric, and black people were put off by his complicated and problematic relationships with the Nation of Islam. Devastated by grief, she looked for a way to rebuild her shattered life. She made a pilgrimage to Mecca, after which she took the name Hajj Bahiyah Betty Shabazz. She found that experience so profound that she wished everyone could make the pilgrimage. "It was one of the ingredients of mental survival for me," she later said. She found great comfort in her Islamic faith.

Shabazz kept a low profile in the years following Malcolm's death, worried that she and her daughters would also be a target of violence. She bought a house in Mount Vernon, a suburb of New York City, and led a quiet life taking care of her children. In the early 1970s she returned to school, earning several advanced degrees. She completed her doctorate in 1975. The following year she took a position at Medgar Evers College in Brooklyn, part of the City University of New York system. She started as an associate professor of health administration in 1976 and later became director of the Department of Communications and Public Relations. In recent years she served as director of the college's Department of Institutional Advancement.

Gradually Shabazz also took on public speaking engagements. She developed a busy lecture schedule, speaking at college commencements, black history conferences, and other events associated with her late husband. She often spoke on her husband's legacy and on issues related to health and education for children. In addition, she was involved in a number of community activities. Her public profile was further enhanced with the release in 1992 of the Spike Lee film *Malcolm X*, which dealt with the slain leader's life and beliefs. This movie created a renewed interest in Malcolm and his widow among many people, especially among the many young people who were too young to have known about them in the 1960s.

FAMILY TROUBLES

Despite her public persona, Shabazz had created a haven of privacy around her family life. This quiet private life was shattered with a series of events in the 1990s. In 1994, on an interview on a TV news program, Betty said that she believed that Louis Farrakhan had something to do with her husband's

Standing, from left, Attallah, Qubilah, and Ilyasah
Seated, from left, Gamilah, Malikah, and Malaak

death. In 1995, her second oldest daughter, Qubilah Shabazz, was indicted on charges of plotting to kill Farrakhan, the leader of the Nation of Islam. Qubilah (pronounced as in Kublai Khan) tried to hire an old friend from high school to kill Farrakhan. But that friend turned out to be a government informer who told the police about the plan. At the time, it was reported that Qubilah and others in her family believed that Farrakhan had been involved in the murder of Malcolm X. Qubilah Shabazz was sentenced to a two-year probationary period, which included psychiatric and chemical dependency treatment in Texas. For much of that time, her son Malcolm stayed with his grandmother, Betty Shabazz, at her apartment in New York.

On the night of June 1, 1997, a fire broke out in Betty's apartment. She was severely burned while trying to escape. She spent three weeks in the hospital in extremely critical condition, fighting to survive. Her daughters, as well as many other mourners, kept a constant vigil at the hospital. Betty Shabazz died on June 23, 1997.

Her grandson Malcolm was soon charged with setting the fire. Reports suggested that he had had a history of emotional problems. Reports also suggested that he was tired of staying with his grandmother. Experts believe that he didn't mean to kill her—instead, he hoped that his problem behavior would force her to send him back to Texas to live with his mother, whom he missed desperately. He pled guilty to second-degree manslaughter and was sentenced to a juvenile detention center, where he will receive psychological counseling.

The traumatic death of Betty Shabazz touched many people, bringing forth an outpouring of sympathy. She was remembered, according to *Emerge* magazine, as "a woman who was committed to public service and, fundamentally, to two things: preserving the memory of her husband and protecting his other legacy—the daughters he left behind." Despite facing one of our nation's great historical tragedies, Shabazz was determined to achieve—to raise her daughters, return to graduate school, earn her doctorate, and devote herself to a career. Betty Shabazz became an important symbol of our age, as Frank Bruni explained in the *New York Times*. "Dr. Shabazz's struggle and violent end became, for many African-Americans, a universal allegory of aspirations, perseverance, bitter disappointments, and uncontrollable twists of fate. It also showed how Dr. Shabazz, as the widow of Malcolm X and the stubborn guardian of his legacy, has attained a place among modern African-American trailblazers." For many, Betty Shabazz was an icon of modern black history.

Yet her many admirers felt a more personal relationship with her as well. They honored her for her courage, modesty, and dignity in the face of overwhelming adversity. Over and over, people praised her tenacity, fortitude, and perseverance, calling her a symbol of strength and pride. "[The] woman known universally as Sister Betty faced more than her share of trials," according to *Ebony* magazine, "but she confronted them all, giving America, and black America especially, one of the great images of the indomitable tenacity of the spirit, and especially the indomitable tenacity of spirit of great black women."

FURTHER READING

Books

Barr, Roger. *The Importance of Malcolm X*, 1994 (juvenile)
Clarke, John Henrik, ed. *Malcolm X: The Man and His Times*, 1990
Davies, Mark. *Malcolm X: Another Side of the Movement*, 1990 (juvenile)
Myers, Walter Dean. *Malcolm X: By Any Means Necessary*, 1993 (juvenile)
X, Malcolm. *The Autobiography of Malcolm X*, 1964 (as told to Alex Haley)

Periodicals

Atlanta Journal Constitution, Sep. 6, 1992, p.A1
Ebony, June 1969, p.172; Nov. 1995, p.62; Aug. 1997, p.138
Emerge, Sep. 1997, p.48
Essence, Feb. 1992, p.50; Oct. 1997, pp. 72 and 74
Look, Mar. 4, 1969, p.74
New York Times, June 2, 1997, pp.A1 and B4; June 3, 1997, p.A1; June 8, 1997, p.1; June 24, 1997, p.A1; June 26, 1997, p.B1; June 30, 1997, p.A1
New Yorker, July 7, 1997, p.4
Time, June 16, 1997, p.48
U.S. News & World Report, June 16, 1997, p.60
Washington Post, June 3, 1997, p.A3; June 7, 1997, p.A1; June 30, 1997, p.A9

Kordell Stewart 1972-

American Professional Football Player
Quarterback/Running Back/Wide Receiver for the
Pittsburgh Steelers

BIRTH

Kordell Stewart was born on October 16, 1972, in Marrero,
Louisiana, which is right across the Mississippi River from New
Orleans. His parents were Robert and Florence Stewart. Kordell
was the youngest of their three children, with one brother,
Robert Jr., and one sister, Falisha.

YOUTH

When Stewart was about 12, his mother died of liver cancer. His father was forced to work several jobs to support the family, including working as a home remodeler, carpenter, painter, and barber. His older brother left college and came home to help out, too. Kordell grew up in a hurry after he lost his mother. He helped out at his father's barbershop, and he helped out around the house by cleaning, doing laundry, and cooking dinner. "From the time my mother passed on, my father treated me like a man," Stewart recalled. "As I look back, I think I needed that discipline. Things got pretty rough down where I lived, and I have to thank Daddy for keeping me in line." Some of his friends became involved with drugs and crime, and one of his cousins was shot to death in New Orleans. But Stewart stayed out of trouble. Instead, he concentrated on his family responsibilities, his schoolwork, and football. Kordell has played football since he was a kid, in fact — his family would push him back into sports whenever it seemed like he might be getting out of line. "The worst thing he ever did," his father remembered, "was come home at five after 12 when I told him to be home at 12."

EDUCATION

Stewart played football throughout his school years, even back when he was attending Ellender Middle School. "I was sort of goofing off in class, too interested in football, when my seventh-grade history teacher made me realize how important schoolwork was," Stewart recalls. "He got his message across. I used to do crazy things, like put a blanket over my shoulders and jump off a roof pretending I was Superman. That history teacher settled me down."

When he got to John Ehret High School in Marrero, Stewart began as a place kicker. Fortunately for him, he was not very good at it. His high-school coach, Billy North, recalled an incident during Stewart's sophomore year that would affect the rest of his playing days: "Our first-string quarterback was holding for him, and Kordell kicked him right in the hand. Broke it. That's how he got in the lineup." But he had to earn his place in the lineup. "He really worked hard in the weight room," North recalls. "He stayed late after practice. When the coaches would go home, we would have to bring him home because he was still out there working." Stewart took over as quarterback and excelled in that position. He was named All-State during his senior year and graduated from John Ehret High School in 1991.

Stewart received a full scholarship to the University of Colorado, where he attended classes from 1991 to 1995. He majored in communications there and played football for the UC Buffaloes. He left the University of Colorado in 1995, just a few credits short of earning his bachelor's degree in communications.

CAREER HIGHLIGHTS

University of Colorado Buffaloes

Colorado became a college football powerhouse during Stewart's years there. He was joined in the backfield by star running back Rashaan Salaam, who was the nation's leading rusher and scorer. The Buffaloes were often ranked among the top teams in the country and were especially known for their high-scoring offense. Though Stewart was generally considered a running quarterback—thanks to his incredible speed—he also became the Buffaloes' career passing leader by completing 456 of 785 passes for 6,481 yards and 33 touchdowns. These impressive totals gave him 7,770 yards in total offense during his college career.

Unfortunately, during his junior year Stewart also gained a reputation as a quarterback who was unable to win big games. His worst performance came during a game against Colorado's biggest rival, the University of Nebraska Cornhuskers, to decide the Big Eight Championship. Rather than remaining calm and depending upon his teammates, Stewart tried to do everything himself and ended up completing only 8 of 28 passes and throwing 3 interceptions in an embarrassing 21-17 loss.

But Stewart managed to turn things around during his senior year thanks to Coach Rick Neuheisel, who joined the team as an offensive coordinator. Neuheisel had been a quarterback himself at the University of California-Los Angeles and had gone on to coach star quarterback Troy Aikman there. "It's just incredible what he's teaching me," Stewart said at the time. "He has made my confidence go so high. I feel like I'm a totally different guy." He possessed the same physical skills, but he was able to use them better as he improved his concentration and maturity. One trick Stewart learned was to cover his head with a white towel while the Colorado defense was on the field to keep from getting distracted. "That towel just puts me in my own world. It keeps me away from everything," he explained. "Other guys get pumped up about what's happening or what's about to happen. I can't get caught up in that. I can lose my concentration."

Stewart demonstrated his newfound mental toughness during a tight game against the University of Michigan Wolverines early in the 1994 season. With his team trailing 26-21 and only a few seconds remaining, Stewart launched a "Hail Mary" pass toward the Michigan end zone. The ball sailed 70 yards in the air, bounced off the hands of two Wolverine players, and was caught in the end zone for a game-winning touchdown by Colorado receiver Michael Westbrook. An ecstatic Stewart ran down the field and kissed his teammates. The incredible play was repeated on sports highlight reels across the country, and many analysts called it "the play of the college football season." Stewart went on to lead his team to victory over Notre Dame in the 1995 Fiesta Bowl

with 348 yards of total offense and to be selected for the All-Big Eight team. He left college early, before completing his degree, in order to pursue a professional football career.

Pittsburgh Steelers

Prior to the 1995 National Football League (NFL) draft, Stewart impressed many professional scouts with his all-around athletic ability. They knew he could be a good NFL player, but they were not certain that he had what it took to be a good NFL quarterback. But Stewart was determined to become a pro quarterback, so he hired agent Leigh Steinberg — whose clients included 23 NFL quarterbacks — to represent him in discussions with NFL teams. Steinberg made it clear to the teams that they should only draft Stewart if they planned to use him at quarterback, as his client was not interested in playing other positions.

The Pittsburgh Steelers finally selected Stewart in the second round of the draft, with the 50th overall pick. It was apparent that many teams would have taken him earlier based on his athletic skills, but were not willing to guarantee that he would play quarterback. "I just don't know why a quarterback has to be 6 feet 8 inches and 230 pounds, with blond hair and blue eyes," Stewart said of the teams' reluctance to draft him. "A team will invest in someone like that and say that he's going to be its quarterback six years down the road. But why can't a team do that with a guy who is 6 feet 1 inch [212 pounds] and black? People still think a black guy isn't going to be a smart quarterback, and that's b.s."

When Stewart first joined the Steelers, he was the fourth-string quarterback on the depth chart. This meant that he was not even on the active roster and could not dress for games. The Steelers already had veteran quarterback Neil O'Donnell as their starter, Mike Tomczak as a backup, and Jim Miller as third string. Stewart moved up to third string for the second game of the season after O'Donnell was hurt. He then got to wear a uniform and pads, but he spent all of his time on the sidelines holding a clipboard for the next six games. At this point, he said he felt like he was "rotting away," forgotten on the bench.

But one day, after several of the Steelers' wide receivers were injured, Head Coach Bill Cowher asked Stewart if he would be willing to fill in at the position during practice. He agreed, and before long he was shredding the first-string defense. "He looked so natural and so effortless doing it that the coaches got the idea we could get him involved as a receiver," said Tom Donahoe, director of football operations for the Steelers. "We didn't think there was any downside to it. We took a player who was just standing around . . . and found a way to get him into the lineup." Though Stewart was not sure he liked the idea, he decided to do what was necessary to help the team. "When [the coach] asked me about playing another position, I wasn't happy because I wanted to play quarterback," he noted. "I was kind of shooting myself in the foot by playing wide receiver. But he told me next year I'd be back at QB."

The "Slash"

In order to make use of Stewart's incredible athletic skills—he was the fastest runner on the Steelers, could throw the football 70 yards, had the soft hands of a wide receiver, and could even punt—the team created a unique role for him that Cowher called a "Slash." "He has a future at quarterback," the coach explained. "But for now, his position for us is quarterback-slash-wide-receiver-slash-running back-slash-punter." Beginning with the seventh game of his rookie year,

"I just don't know why a quarterback has to be 6 feet 8 inches and 230 pounds, with blond hair and blue eyes," Stewart said of the teams' reluctance to draft him. "A team will invest in someone like that and say that he's going to be its quarterback six years down the road. But why can't a team do that with a guy who is 6 feet 1 inch [212 pounds] and black? People still think a black guy isn't going to be a smart quarterback, and that's b.s."

Stewart began seeing limited playing time at each of these positions. He also started to like making a contribution to the team, even if it was not always in the position he preferred. "I'd rather have this 'Slash' role than stay on the sideline," he admitted.

Up to this point, the Steelers' record was a disappointing 3-4. But with Stewart in the lineup, their offense went from predictable to explosive and they won their next eight games in a row. Football analysts initially called him a "novelty" or a "wrinkle," since they thought he was just thrown into the offense once in a while to confuse the opposition. But after he began to demonstrate his abilities, they starting calling him "one of the most dangerous weapons in the league" and saying that he had "revolutionized the science of offense." During the Steelers' winning streak Stewart threw a pass for a touchdown, caught a pass for a touchdown, ran with the ball effectively, and even made a 41-yard punt. He ended up with 23 first downs to his credit (11 rushing, nine receiving, and three passing). No one knew what he would do next.

Opposing defenses suddenly began taking Stewart very seriously. Whenever he ran onto the field, players on the other team would shout out his number—"There's 10, there's 10!"—and desperately try to guess what kind of play the Steelers would run. One time, Stewart lined up at quarterback in a shotgun formation and the opposing defense starting yelling, "Option, option!" They thought he would roll out and either run the ball himself or pitch it to a running back trailing behind him. The only problem was that no running back was lined up in the backfield. "I'm thinking, 'Option?' Who do they think I'm going to pitch it to?" Stewart laughed. "They were so confused. It cracked me up."

Stewart had the best game of his professional career against the Indianapolis Colts in the American Football Conference (AFC) Championship game. During one critical Steelers drive just before halftime, he made three first downs—two lined up as quarterback (on a sneak and an option) and one as a running back (on an end around)—and caught a touchdown pass as a wide receiver. That drive was the Steelers' longest of the season, 17 plays for 80 yards, and helped them defeat the Colts to earn a spot in Super Bowl XXX. "The great thing about it is that we have some plays left [for Stewart]," Cowher said afterward. "We have one more game left, and you haven't seen the last of it."

Stewart also became involved in his first NFL controversy during that game. Television replays showed that he had stepped on the back line of the end zone before catching the touchdown pass. The score could have been called back, because players are not allowed to go out of bounds under their own power and then return to make a play, but the referees did not see the infraction. Stewart claimed that the Colts' defender, safety Jason Belser, had pushed him out of bounds, although he appeared to be two steps ahead of Belser by that point. Belser then said that Stewart had actually pushed him, which he called "a smart play by a savvy receiver." But Stewart responded: "I wouldn't know about that. I'm a quarterback."

Although Stewart put in another solid performance in the Super Bowl—running twice as a quarterback and twice as a running back for three first

downs—the Steelers lost to the Dallas Cowboys 27-17. He finished his rookie season having completed 5 of 7 passes for 60 yards and a touchdown, caught 14 passes for 235 yards and a touchdown, and rushed 15 times for 86 yards and a touchdown.

Recent Seasons

Going into the 1996 season, Stewart had high hopes of finally getting his chance at quarterback, since starter Neil O'Donnell had left the team as a free agent. Unfortunately, the Steelers' coaches felt he was not ready and gave him limited playing time at his preferred position. But Stewart had continued success in his "Slash" role, converting 30 first downs in 36 chances (14 rushing, 13 receiving, and three passing). In 16 games, he completed 11 of 30 passes for 100 yards, rushed 38 times for 179 yards and 5 touchdowns, and caught 17 passes for 293 yards and 3 touchdowns. The Steelers went 10-6 on the year and won their division, but were defeated in the second round of the playoffs by the New England Patriots.

While Stewart was frustrated by not moving on to the quarterback position, he was willing to do whatever he could to help his team win. "My short-term goal is to do what I can to help the Steelers get to the top," he stated. "But my long-term goal is to be a quarterback—and I will be a quarterback." One benefit of his unique role is that it has created an atmosphere of excitement in Pittsburgh and made him very popular with fans. And some analysts feel that playing a variety of positions will help him become a better quarterback someday. "He's getting a chance to see what defenses are doing from a wide receiver's perspective," said Joe Theismann, a former pro quarterback and current ESPN television analyst. "This will enhance his development as a quarterback."

Entering the 1997 season, Stewart was expected to compete with Jim Miller for the Steelers' starting quarterback job. He ended up winning the starting job and playing quarterback in all 16 regular-season games for the Steelers. Stewart completed 236 of 440 passes for 3,020 yards, 21 touchdowns, and 17 interceptions. He also rushed 88 times for 476 yards and 11 touchdowns. The Steelers posted an 11-5 record to win the AFC Central, but they were knocked out in the second round of the playoffs by the New England Patriots.

Stewart appreciates the way he has been allowed to develop with the Steelers. "I was blessed with a lot of talent. They've done a great job getting plays in there for me. I've been put into great situations and just skyrocketed from there," he noted. "I'm having fun—that's what this game is all about. If you get caught up in things and think of football as business—which it is—instead of being fun, it all changes."

HOME AND FAMILY

Stewart, who is single, lives in the Pittsburgh area with his Akita dog, Dice. He remains close to his family, especially his father. "Actually, I'm Slash Junior," he said. "Slash Senior is down in Louisiana. He's a barber-slash-house painter-slash-carpenter. He does more things than I do, believe me. One of my goals is to get him out of that neighborhood and move him out into the country."

HOBBIES AND OTHER INTERESTS

In his spare time, Stewart enjoys playing the drums. He likes all kinds of music and often plays along with his favorite albums. At one time, he gave friends haircuts as a hobby. He learned barbering from working at his father's barbershop as a teenager, and he cut the hair of many of his teammates at the University of Colorado. But so far, he has not performed the same service for the Steelers. "Probably doesn't want anyone to know," his father stated. "They'll never leave him alone. He's real good."

But Stewart has some more serious interests, too. In 1997 he established the Kordell Stewart Foundation, whose primary goal is to fund cancer research. Stewart was inspired to create the foundation in memory of his mother and his sister, Falisha, both of whom died of liver cancer. Falisha died of cancer in 1996, when she was just 29. "People talk about wins and losses as if they were the end of the world," Stewart says. "When you lose a family member, that's 10 times worse. If I lose a game, I'm just going to go back, look at it on the film, and try to understand why I make the mistakes I made. Life is more serious than that."

HONORS AND AWARDS

Pittsburgh Steelers Rookie of the Year: 1995

FURTHER READING

Periodicals

New York Times, Dec. 30, 1996, p.B7; Jan. 2, 1997, p.B9; Jan 5, 1997, p.S1
Sport, Jan. 1997, p.34
Sports Illustrated, Nov. 20, 1995, p.156; Dec. 11, 1995, p.54
Sports Illustrated for Kids, Sep. 1996, p.40

ADDRESS

Pittsburgh Steelers
Three Rivers Stadium
300 Stadium Circle
Pittsburgh, PA 15212

WORLD WIDE WEB SITES

http://www.steelershom.com
http://www.nflplayers.com/players/stewkord.htm

Shinichi Suzuki 1898-1998

Japanese Musician and Teacher
Creator of the Suzuki Method of Instrumental Music
Instruction

BIRTH

Shinichi Suzuki (shi-NEE-chi soo-ZOO-key) was born October 18, 1898, in Nagoya, Japan, to Masakichi and Ryo Fujie Suzuki. Masakichi owned a violin factory, and Ryo was a homemaker. Shinichi was one of 12 children, with six brothers and five sisters.

Shinichi and his siblings grew up playing in their father's instrument factory. At first, they didn't think of the violins as precious instruments to be handled with care. In fact, Suzuki remembered that he and his brothers would chase each other through the factory using the violins to bash each other over the head. Their father, Masakichi Suzuki, had begun his career making traditional Japanese stringed instruments, such as the samisen. But when he heard the violin, he loved the instrument and decided to focus on that. By the early 20th century, when Shinichi was growing up, the Suzuki Violin factory was the largest in the world, making 65,000 instruments each year.

The Japanese way of life was changing enormously when Shinichi Suzuki was young. It wasn't until the late 19th century that Japanese culture opened up to the influence of the rest of the world, through trade and commerce. Up to that point, the country was a closed, feudal society, more like Europe in the Middle Ages than like the U.S. in the late 1800s. As Shinichi was growing up, the old world was vanishing forever. He remembered that he loved to listen to the old violin makers tell tales of ancient Japan. He would sit for hours as the old men made instruments and spun yarns of the brave samurai warriors who had been the "knights" of the formal feudal way of life in Japan.

EDUCATION

Up until the age of 14, Suzuki was educated at home. For high school, he was sent away as a boarding student to a commercial school in Nagoya, where he studied business and prepared to take on a role in the family trade. He was a good student and served as president of his class. He graduated in 1916 and returned home to help out at the Suzuki violin factory.

EARLY WORKING AND MUSICAL LIFE

Suzuki took his place working in the factory, where his older brothers were already employed. Around this time Suzuki had an experience that changed the way he thought of music, and the violin, forever. He had never studied the violin and had not had any formal music education. His family had gotten a gramophone—an early record player—and a recording of violinist Mischa Elman playing Franz Schubert's "Ave Maria." Suzuki was electrified by the music. "The sweetness of the sound of Elman's violin utterly enthralled me. His velvety tone as he played the melody was like something in a dream. It made a tremendous impression on me. To think that the violin, which I had considered a toy, could produce such beauty of tone!

"Elman's 'Ave Maria' opened my eyes to music. I had no idea why my soul was so moved. But at least I had already developed the ability to appreciate this beauty. My profound emotion was the first step in my search for the true meaning of art."

Suzuki's reaction to Elman's playing paved the way for his later revolutionary method of teaching violin. "I brought a violin home from the factory, and listening to Elman playing a Haydn minuet, I tried to imitate him. I had no score and simply moved the bow, trying to play what I heard. Day after day I did this, trying to master the piece. My completely self-taught technique was more scraping than anything else, but somehow I finally got so I could play the piece."

Suzuki continued to teach himself to play while he worked in the factory. After several years, he met a wealthy member of the Japanese aristocracy, the Marquis Yoshichika Tokugawa, whose influence would govern the next years of his life. Tokugawa took an interest in Suzuki, and after hearing him play, approached Suzuki's parents to encourage them to let him study privately. His parents agreed, and at age 21, Suzuki moved to Tokyo and studied with a private teacher. In Tokyo, Suzuki lived with the Marquis, who introduced him to scholars, artists, and the culture of Japan and the Western world.

Traveling Abroad

The Marquis then asked Suzuki to accompany him on a trip around the world. Suzuki got his parents' permission and began his world tour. He only got as far as Berlin, where he stayed for eight years, studying the violin. In his first months in Germany he went to concerts constantly, immersing himself in the Western classical music tradition. At one concert, he heard the violinist Karl Klinger and asked Klinger to take him as a student.

Suzuki studied with Klinger for eight years, playing a wide variety of music from the violin repertoire. Klinger also introduced Suzuki to other musicians and artists living in Berlin. Suzuki also became reacquainted with a family friend, Dr. Michaelis, who had visited the Suzuki home in Japan. Through Michaelis, Suzuki met Albert Einstein, the famous physicist, who was also an accomplished violin player.

MARRIAGE AND FAMILY

In this circle of Berlin musicians, artists, and intellectuals, Suzuki met his future wife, Waltraud Prange, a 17-year-old vocalist and pianist from a German family of musicians. The two fell in love and were married in Berlin on February 8, 1928. They had no children.

BACK TO JAPAN

The couple moved back to Japan, where Suzuki made a career of performing and teaching violin. He and three of his brothers formed the Suzuki Quartet and began giving concerts. Soon, the devastating effects of a worldwide economic crisis changed their lives forever. The Great Depression, which started

Suzuki performing with students

in 1929 and continued for several years, severely damaged the economics of Japan, the United States, Europe, and countries around the globe. Many businesses failed, many people lost their jobs, and poverty became a major problem. Lots of families had trouble finding food, shelter, and clothing, and even people who kept their jobs worried about the future. Suzuki's father, once a prominent, successful businessman, was on the verge of bankruptcy. He was forced to sell off his land and the family home, and he asked his children to make financial sacrifices, too. Suzuki had to sell his precious Vuillame violin, and Waltraud sold her beautiful Bechstein piano, which had been a wedding gift from her family, to help the Suzuki family.

World War II

Bad economic times continued, and in the late 1930s Japan prepared to go to war. World War II began in 1939, when Germany, an ally of Japan, invaded

Poland. In December 1941, the Japanese made a massive attack on Pearl Harbor in Hawaii, in which they nearly destroyed the U.S. naval fleet. The U.S. declared war on Japan. The Suzuki violin factory was converted to war production and produced wooden seaplane floats. Suzuki spent part of the war in the northern provinces of Japan, seeking new sources of wood. His wife, Waltraud, had to live apart from him for years, in a remote, isolated area of Japan.

> *"Right after the war, when there were still many remains of destroyed buildings all over the city, I started this talent education. I started it because I realized how much these innocent children were suffering from the dreadful mistakes made by adults. These precious children had absolutely no part in the war and yet they were the ones suffering the most severely, not only in food, clothing and a home to live in, but also something that was very important, their education."*

As the war continued, food became scarce. At one point, Suzuki had to eat boiled grasses to survive. In August 1945, the U.S. dropped two atomic bombs on Japan. The Japanese surrendered, and the war was finally over. Yet Suzuki and his wife continued to live apart. Waltraud found a job with the American Red Cross in Yokohama after the war. At that time, she was the only member of the Suzuki family with an income, so for several more years she sacrificed a life with her husband to earn money to keep the entire Suzuki family fed.

DEVELOPING THE SUZUKI METHOD: TALENT EDUCATION

In the aftermath of World War II, Suzuki began to develop the method for which he became famous, which he called "talent education." He created the process in part as a response to the destruction of war. "Right after the war, when there were still many remains of destroyed buildings all over the city, I started this talent education. I started it because I realized how much these innocent children were suffering from the dreadful mistakes made by adults. These precious children had absolutely no part in the war and yet they were the ones suffering the most severely, not only in food, clothing and a home to live in, but also something that was very important, their education." He began to teach at a music school founded in Matsumoto, incorporating theories he'd been developing for years.

In his book *Nurtured by Love*, Suzuki outlined his philosophy, making statements that turned traditional educational theories upside down. "Talent is no accident of birth," he claimed. Instead, he believed that talent can be nurtured in every child. Years before specialists began to focus on children's development in their early years, Suzuki used the violin to show that very young children have great learning potential. He began to teach violin to children as young as two and three. Central to his philosophy was the fact that children, from all backgrounds, can learn their mother tongue readily and almost without exception. "Japanese children can all speak Japanese! The thought suddenly struck me with amazement. In fact, all children throughout the world speak their native tongues with the utmost fluency." He blamed the education system for failing children, for labeling them "not very bright" or born with "low intelligence." "How do we account for the splendid capacity of children to speak Japanese, and do we search for a better method of training?"

The "Mother Tongue" Method

Based on his theories of how a child learns language, which he called the "mother tongue" method, Suzuki applied his theory to music. At its simplest, the Suzuki method can be described as "patience and repetition." His method involves having a child learn music by listening to a simple tune, "Twinkle, Twinkle Little Star." That tune forms the basis for all the learning on the instrument. Through repetition, the child learns first to sing the song, then the rhythm and pattern of the song, and then learns to handle the instrument.

Beginning Suzuki students don't start out with a violin, but rather a simplified version of an instrument, like a cigar box with a ruler attached, which replicates the size and shape of a violin. They learn how to hold the "instrument," and they learn the proper way to stand when they play. They learn games and exercises with their fingers and hands that prepare them to hold the bow and violin properly. All of these activities are practiced over and over, repeating the action until it comes naturally. Children are praised for their accomplishments, and correction is handled in a warm, encouraging manner.

After they have advanced to a real instrument, Suzuki students are given a miniature violin—some as small as 12 inches—to begin to play on. Consistent with the mother tongue method, which holds that a child learns to speak through imitation before she or he learns to read, the beginning student is not taught to read music. They are taught instead to begin a piece on a specific string, and to put down a finger at a certain position. Only after years of listening, imitating, and building on what has been previously learned do students learn the names of the notes and how to read music.

Suzuki students all begin with the same song, "Twinkle, Twinkle Little Star." First they learn to play the tune in its simplest form. Then they begin to learn variations on the theme, which help to develop their sense of rhythm and bowing technique. Suzuki instruction is divided into progressively more difficult books of music. After "Twinkle," students learn more complex musical pieces, but they still begin practice with a review of their earlier pieces, using them as building blocks to the more challenging works. Students move at their own pace, memorizing each piece and adding it to their musical "vocabulary." By the end of the first book students are playing the music of such complex musical masters as Bach, Vivaldi, Handel, and Mozart, with ease and facility.

> *Suzuki's concern was with nurturing and educating the entire human being, not with creating musical prodigies. When a parent asked him, "Will my boy amount to anything?" Suzuki replied, "No. He will not become 'something.' He will become a noble person through his violin playing. Isn't that enough?" "I want to tell everyone that this method is not education of the violin. It is education by the violin," Suzuki claimed.*

Parental involvement is central to Suzuki instruction. A parent attends class with a child and basically learns to play the violin with the child. At home, the parent listens to the songs on a tape with the child and supervises practice. Suzuki believed firmly that "the destiny of children lies in the hands of their parents." As he explained, "Children have to adapt to manifold environments and are brought up in superior or inferior surroundings depending on their parents."

Suzuki's concern was with nurturing and educating the entire human being, not with creating musical prodigies. When a parent asked him, "Will my boy amount to anything?" Suzuki replied, "No. He will not become 'something.' He will become a noble person through his violin playing. Isn't that enough?" "I want to tell everyone that this method is not education of the violin. It is education by the violin," Suzuki claimed. He believed that his method introduced not just music but the world to a child, and he believed that some of the world's most beautiful music could provide lessons in character for a child. "We are not only nourishing a child's sensitivity to music but also to humanity. Through Mozart, for instance, he can also learn a high morality."

Mass Concerts

In the 1950s, Suzuki began a series of "summer institutes" to train young players. At the end of the institute, the young students would play their pieces together, in a mass concert format. Viewers were astonished to hear the ability and quality of the music that Suzuki's students, some as young as three, were able to produce. In 1955, Suzuki gave the first of his annual concerts in Japan, in which 1,500 children, ages four to 15, played for an audience that included the Japanese royal family. Members of the international media also attended the performance and wrote of the remarkable spectacle of these very young and very accomplished players.

Demonstrating a correct bow hold

In the U.S., news of Suzuki's methods and success were met with a certain amount of skepticism. Yet when teachers saw a film of the 1955 concert, they were impressed. As one American teacher wrote, "Aside from the sheer weight of numbers and the appeal of cute tots performing seriously, the outstanding features for the string specialists were these: (1) There was not a poor left-hand position or bow arm visible in the entire group. (2) Intonation was good and pleasing tone was modulated expressively. In short, this was not just mass playing of 1,500 children from four to 15 years of age — it was *good violin playing.*"

In 1961, Pablo Casals, world renowned cellist and one of the greatest musicians of the 20th century, came to Matsumoto to visit Suzuki. Four hundred Suzuki students played for him. When they were finished, Casals embraced Suzuki and wept. He had been moved, he said, not just by their accomplished playing, but by the spirit in which they played. He praised Suzuki for training them in music as well as "making them understand that music is not only sound but such a high thing in life that perhaps it is the music that will save the world."

First Tour of the U.S.

In 1964, Suzuki brought a group of students to the U.S. to perform. Ten students, ages six to 13, played concerts in Seattle, Chicago, Boston, and New York City, where they performed at the U.N. and at the famous Julliard

Conducting students

School of Music. Everywhere they played, they astonished their audiences. At Julliard, the distinguished violin professor Ivan Galamian was impressed with their "remarkable training, and a wonderful feeling for the rhythm and flow of music."

Teachers throughout the U.S. rushed to adopt the Suzuki method, and the first generation of American Suzuki students began their training. But there were many would-be Suzuki teachers who began to teach without proper training in the technique. Consequently, there were early reports that the method didn't work.

In response to the lack of proper training of new teachers, Suzuki began a series of workshops in the U.S. in the mid-1960s. These took place at some of the most prestigious music schools in the country, including the Eastman School of Music and Oberlin College. John Kendall of Southern Illinois University, an early follower of Suzuki and later the president of the Suzuki Association of the Americas, became part of the movement to train American teachers in Suzuki's methods.

Growing Success of the Suzuki Method

The movement grew in the U.S. throughout the 1970s, with the numbers of both students and teachers growing at a rapid rate. Before Suzuki methods were adopted widely in the U.S., many American orchestras were desperately looking in Europe for violinists, largely because the traditional way of training string players in the U.S. hadn't produced enough high caliber musicians. As Kendall recalls, "string educators were struggling. Symphony orchestras couldn't find enough qualified players, school orchestras were disappearing, and we were wondering where the next generation of musicians—let alone audiences—would come from." Within 20 years, as a direct result of Suzuki's methods, the quality of American string playing improved enormously.

In 1977, a Suzuki tour of the U.S. included a stop at the White House, where President Jimmy Carter, whose daughter Amy was a Suzuki student, hosted the musicians. On that trip, Suzuki, then 79 years old, spent a good deal of time teaching groups of children. Approaching his eighth decade, Suzuki continued to claim, "the potential of every child is absolutely unlimited. And these children know when you believe that. You can see it in their eyes when we're communicating one living soul to one living soul. I learn so much from them."

Suzuki did have some detractors, who believed that Suzuki students had a difficult time adapting to reading music later in their musical careers. Most teachers dismiss that notion, citing the number of Suzuki-trained musicians who play in some of the finest orchestras in the world. Some critics also stated that children can't appreciate the music Suzuki students play at a very young age. To that, John Kendall of the American Suzuki Association replied, "We certainly know that children are capable of learning a great deal and that meaning becomes more and more a part of them as they mature. Children learn poetry when they're young and remember it all their lives, but that poetry becomes more significant as they become more mature human beings. And the same is true of music."

Throughout the 1980s and 1990s Suzuki continued to travel and give workshops all around the world. By 1998, the Suzuki method had spread to 34 countries. Suzuki continued to travel and teach himself until his late 90s, when he became too weak to leave Japan.

Although he claimed he was so busy he said he couldn't retire "until I am 110," Shinichi Suzuki died on January 26, 1998, in Matsumoto, just nine months shy of his 100th birthday.

LEGACY

At the time of Suzuki's death, there were more than 400,000 music students training with his methods worldwide, three-quarters of them in the United States. The high caliber of string playing in this country and around the world is largely credited to his methods of teaching, which has spread beyond the violin to include instruction in cello, viola, bass, piano, flute, harp, guitar, and recorder. The hundreds of thousands of children around the world who learned to love music and take pride in themselves are a lasting testament to this gentle man, so firm in his convictions that each and every child has within the ability that, once nurtured, can lead to success in music, and in life.

"The destiny of children lies in the hands of their parents. Children have to adapt to manifold environments and are brought up in superior or inferior surroundings depending on their parents."

Suzuki was the recipient of several honorary doctorates, including one from the Eastman School of Music, which characterized his contribution this way:

"Countless small children today on both sides of the broad Pacific know the joy of music, not through passive listening but through skillful performance with their own hands and hearts of the works of the masters. The faith and dedication of Shinichi Suzuki brought about this revolution in the musical education of the young. . . . Beginning with Japanese children, the innocent victims of war, the movement spread to other lands and transformed the lives of thousands of children and their parents. Ever growing, it affords the thrill of real accomplishment and the spiritual and emotional nourishment of great music to all the children of the world."

FURTHER READING

Books

Baker's Biographical Dictionary of Musicians, 1992
Hermann, Evelyn. *Shinichi Suzuki: The Man and His Philosophy*, 1981
Honda, Masaaki. *Suzuki Changed My Life*, 1976
New Grove Dictionary of Music and Musicians, 1980
Suzuki, Shinichi. *Ability Development from Age Zero*, 1969
———. *Nurtured by Love*, 1969
Who's Who 1997
World Book Encyclopedia, 1997

Periodicals

Chicago Tribune, Feb. 5, 1998, Commentary Section, p.21
Cleveland Plain Dealer, Apr. 2, 1995, p.J2; Mar. 24, 1996, p.J2
Independent, Jan. 27, 1998, p.20
Los Angeles Times, Jan 27, 1998, p.B8
Miami Herald, Jan. 27, 1998, p.B4
New York Times, Nov. 13, 1977, p.B1; Jan 27, 1998, p.A21
Philadelphia Inquirer, May 15, 1986, p.H2
Reader's Digest, Nov. 1973, p.269
St. Louis Post Dispatch, Apr. 17, 1997, p.G1
Times Educational Supplement, July 2, 1982, p.32

WORLD WIDE WEB SITE

http://mrdata.com/andrich/eric/suzuki/resources.html

OBITUARY

Mother Teresa 1910-1997

Albanian-Born Indian Roman Catholic Nun
Nobel Prize-Winner Who Served the Poor of Calcutta
for 50 Years

BIRTH

The Roman Catholic religious leader known as Mother Teresa
was born Agnes Gonxha Bojaxhiu (GONE-yah bow-yahk-YOU)
on August 26, 1910, in the city of Skopje (SKAWP-ya), which
was then part of the Ottoman Empire. The area later became
Yugoslavia and is now Macedonia. Mother Teresa's parents

were Albanians living in Skopje. Her father, Nikola, was a building contractor. Her mother, Dranafile, was a homemaker. Agnes was the youngest of three children, with a sister, Age, and a brother, Lazar. As a child, Agnes was called by her middle name, "Gonxha," by her sister and brother. The name means "flower bud" in Albanian. Her brother Lazar remembered that "we thought of her as a rosebud. When she was a child, she was plump, round, and tidy."

YOUTH

Mother Teresa remembered a happy, loving family life in a large, comfortable house. But after her father's death when she was nine, the family's circumstances changed radically. Her father's death was sudden and unexpected, and her mother was overcome with grief. Nikola Bojaxhiu's business partner took all the assets from the contracting business that had provided the family's income, and they were left with only their house and possessions. When Dranafile recovered from her grief, she set about making a living for her family. She began a business producing and selling embroidered cloth, and the family soon got back on its feet.

As Agnes grew up, it was clear that she was drawn to helping the poor. Her mother, deeply religious and devoted to helping others, often took Agnes with her when she distributed food and clothing to the poor and needy. These experiences, combined with her religious education, led her to decide, at the age of 12, that she would become a nun and work with the poor.

EDUCATION

As a child, Agnes attended the local government school. Little is known about her nonreligious learning, or even about her life outside of her strong interest in helping others and her deep Catholic faith. As a young girl, she belonged to a "sodality," a Roman Catholic organization of girls and women, where she developed her interest in foreign missionary work. Through this group, she learned about a group of Catholic missionaries working in India. Agnes had found what she wanted to do. "I had a vocation to help the poor," she remembered. "I wanted to be a missionary." Still a very young girl, she had second thoughts because she didn't want to leave her family. Yet, she said, "the vocation won."

At the age of 18, Agnes Bojaxhiu decided it was time to leave home and begin her life as a nun. She told her mother, who went to her bedroom for 24 hours. When she came out, she was ready to give her youngest child her blessing. Her mother saw Agnes off at the train station in 1928, when she left for Ireland to begin her training. It was the last time she saw her mother.

In Ireland, she studied with a group of Catholic nuns, the Sisters of Loreto, who had a mission in India. She stayed for one year, learning English. Then she was sent to Darjeeling, a city in northeast India, where the nuns ran a school. There, Agnes began the training that would lead to her becoming a nun.

JOINING A RELIGIOUS ORDER

Agnes studied with the nuns for one year, in a training called a "novitiate." During the novitiate, a nun prepares for her vows, her commitment to the Catholic Church and to a life of poverty, chastity, and obedience. In 1929, she took her vows, and the name Sister Teresa. She chose the name in honor of a 19th-century French saint, Therese of Lisieux, a Carmelite nun who died of tuberculosis at 24. She is revered for her courage in facing illness and death at such a young age.

That year, Sister Teresa also began teaching at a girl's school in Calcutta. At St. Mary's High School, she taught geography, history, and catechism, and lived in the convent with the other nuns. Her students were largely the daughters of the middle- and upper-class families of Calcutta. For Sister Teresa, it was a life of some comfort. Happy with her teaching job, she stayed at St. Mary's for 17 years, eventually becoming the principal.

A "CALL WITHIN A CALL"

When a Christian responds to what they believe is the word of God prompting them to a vocation in the Church, it is referred to as a "call." On September 10, 1946, while riding on a train to Darjeeling, Sister Teresa received what she termed "a call within a call." She felt God speaking to her and telling her what to do. "The message was clear," she said. "I was to leave the convent and help the poor while living among them. It was an order."

She appealed to the Catholic authorities and told them what she wanted to do. It took two years for her request to be granted, but in 1948, she began her work as Mother Teresa, in Calcutta. She left the order of the Sisters of Loreto and began what became, in 1950, her own order, the Missionaries of Charity. Leaving behind the habit of the Sisters of Loreto, she adopted the dress she and all the members would wear, a white sari, made of coarse cloth and edged in blue, with a Christian cross on the shoulder.

CAREER HIGHLIGHTS

From the beginning of her work, Mother Teresa's principles were clear and unwavering. Her mission was to help the "poorest of the poor." She asked the Church leaders if she could add an additional vow for members of the

Missionaries of Charity. In addition to poverty, chastity, and obedience, she wanted to add that her order would "devote themselves out of abnegation to the care of the poor and needy who, crushed by want and destitution, live in conditions unworthy of human dignity." Mother Teresa gave her mission its motto: "Let every action of mine be something beautiful for God."

Mother Teresa went directly to the streets of Calcutta to find those she would help. Calcutta is one of the largest and poorest cities in the world. At the time Mother Teresa started her work there, it was also teeming with refugees from the Indian wars of independence and partition that divided the nation in 1948. Many of the poor of Calcutta are homeless and live and die in the streets of the city. Their poverty and deprivation are almost unimaginable to people of the United States. For Mother Teresa, these poor represented "Christ in his distressing disguise." One of the main aims of her mission was to find the destitute and dying and give them comfort in death. In India, poor people who are dying are often left on the streets, sometimes even tossed onto trash heaps. In the first days of her mission, Mother Teresa found one such victim, a woman covered with open sores and already attacked by rats and ants. Mother Teresa tried to find a hospital that would take the woman, but all refused. She stayed with the woman until she died.

On September 10, 1946, while riding on a train to Darjeeling, Sister Teresa received what she termed "a call within a call." She felt God speaking to her and telling her what to do. "The message was clear," she said. "I was to leave the convent and help the poor while living among them. It was an order."

Mother Teresa asked the city of Calcutta to donate space to her so she might help more of the needy, particularly to provide shelter and solace to the dying. The city gave her space next to a Hindu temple, which she opened as the Nirmal Hriday Home for Dying Destitutes in 1952.

The leaders of the Hindu temple were at first wary of Mother Teresa. The majority of the Indian population are either Hindus or Moslems; Christians make up only about four percent of the population. Many Indians are suspicious of Christian missionaries because they have so often been related to the imperialist forces of the British and other Western powers that dominated India for many years. And yet what Mother Teresa and her order brought to Calcutta was different from the very beginning.

The Hindu temple next to the Nirmal Hriday Home is one dedicated to the goddess Kali, the spirit of death and destruction. The Hindu priests complained to the city and asked that the home be moved. But then one of the former Hindu priests, ill with tuberculosis, was denied a place in the local hospital. He was taken to the Nirmal Hriday and taken care of by Mother Teresa. When he died, she delivered his body to the temple for final rites. This began a pattern that has continued at all her missions to this day. A dying person is taken in, given medical attention and comforted. Some recover and leave the hospital. Those who die are given the rites of their own faith—Hindu, Muslim, Christian, or whatever their religion. This commitment to compassion and reverence for all faiths is what created and sustained the strong bond between Mother Teresa's order and the missions she started in Calcutta and throughout the world.

In aiding the dying, Mother Teresa believed that "these people are the body of Christ. Actually, we are touching his body." "My community is the poor," she said. "Their security is my own. Their heart is my own. My house is the house of the poor—not just of the poor, but of the poorest of the poor: those who are so dirty and full of contagious germs that no one goes near them; those who do not go to pray because they are naked; those who do not eat because they do not have the strength; those who collapse on the sidewalks, knowing they are about to die while the living walk by without even looking back; those who do not cry because they have no more tears left."

Mother Teresa believed that to "be able to love the poor and know the poor we must be poor ourselves." She and her order of nuns lived just as their patients did. They had three saris each, "one for wearing, one for washing, one for mending," a pair of sandals, and a bucket to wash their clothes in. In their missions, the sisters rise at 4:30 each day, attend services, then devote themselves to the poor for a total of 16 hours each day. Mother Teresa herself followed this strict schedule daily. She herself scrubbed floors and toilets, tended the sick, ate the food prepared for the poor, and shared in all the tasks performed by the nuns of her order.

The nuns who joined Mother Teresa's order came from India and all over the world. Her first helper was a former student who, as Sister Agnes, began working with Mother Teresa in 1948. In a time when most Catholic religious orders were faced with a declining number of applicants, the Missionaries of Charity were the fastest growing order in the world.

In addition to the homes for the dying, Mother Teresa started schools for poor children, orphanages, and hospitals for lepers and the mentally ill. As the missions grew, she added special homes for AIDS patients, alcoholics, drug addicts, and battered and abused women and children. From the beginning, Mother Teresa refused any kind of regular funding from the government of India. Instead, the work was funded by donations. These came in the form of buildings, food surpluses, and cash gifts. Mother Teresa's work was always under the direct control of the Roman Catholic Church and the pope, who have always supported her mission. In 1964, Pope Paul VI was visiting Calcutta and gave her the white limousine he had used during his visit. Without even taking a ride in it, Mother Teresa auctioned off the car and used the money to start a leper colony in West Bengal. In the 1960s, she also began missions in other areas of the world, including Africa, South America, Australia, and the South Bronx section of New York City.

A Worldwide Reputation

Mother Teresa did these good works in anonymity until 1969. That's when the British journalist Malcolm Muggeridge produced a television special on Mother Teresa entitled *Something Beautiful for God*, which he later used as the basis for a book of the same title. The program was broadcast around the world and introduced her life and work. The outpouring of interest was enormous. People from all over the world volunteered to work with her, and also to help fund her missions. In 1969, the International Association of Co-Workers of Mother Teresa was formed. It is an international, interdenominational organization made up of men, women, and children "who seek to love God in their fellow men through whole-hearted free service to

*Mother Teresa is handed the
1979 Nobel Peace Prize diploma and
gold medal by committee chairman
John Sanness*

the poorest of the poor of all castes and creeds and who wish to unite themselves in a spirit of prayer and sacrifice with the work of Mother Teresa and the Missionaries of Charity." The group currently numbers more than 150,000.

Mother Teresa was famously unconcerned about money, believing always that the "Lord sends it. We do his work; he provides the means." In the early 1970s, Mother Teresa began to receive awards with large cash stipends, including the Pope John XXIII Peace Prize, with a prize of $25,000, and a Joseph Kennedy Jr. Foundation Award, with a prize of $15,000. The money from the Peace Prize went to build a new leper colony and to help rape victims in Bangladesh. The money from the Kennedy prize funded a home for handicapped people in India.

As her reputation grew around the world, Mother Teresa was asked how she saw herself. "By blood and origin I am Albanian. My citizenship is Indian. I am a Catholic nun. As to my calling, I belong to the world. As to my heart, I belong entirely to the heart of Jesus." Many who met her were struck with her resilient personality. Just under five feet tall and seemingly frail, she was not, in the words of British journalist Polly Toynbee, a "Madonna." Instead, she was tough, with a will of iron. Often described as charismatic, Mother Teresa had a powerful personality that drew others to her. "All these girls want to work with *her* and be near *her* as much as possible," said Toynbee of the Missionaries of Charity.

The Nobel Peace Prize

In 1979, Mother Teresa received the Nobel Peace Prize. In awarding her the honor, the Nobel committee said that "poverty and distress also constitute a threat to peace." In the presentation speech for the prize, John Sanness of the Nobel committee said, "Mother Teresa has personally succeeded in bridging the gulf that exists between the rich nations and the poor nations . . . . With her message she is able to reach through to something innate in every human kind — if for no other purpose than to create a potential, a seed for good. If this were not the case, the world would be deprived of hope, and work for peace would have little meaning."

When she learned that she had received the Nobel, Mother Teresa's immediate response was, "I am not worthy." She went to Norway to accept the prize, and took the cash award — $190,000 — to build a new leper colony and homes for the poor. She also asked that the traditional banquet held in honor of the recipient be canceled, so that she could use the money — $7,000 — for her mission.

At the awards ceremony, Mother Teresa gave a speech in which she accepted the award "in the name of the hungry, of the naked, of the homeless, . . . of those who feel unwanted, uncared for." She also spoke out against abortion, a consistent theme that has proven to be her most controversial stance. "I feel the greatest destroyer of peace today is abortion, because it is a direct war, a direct killing," she said.

A Controversial Figure

After receiving the Nobel, Mother Teresa became a famous world figure. She began to draw criticism because of her stand on issues like abortion. Consistent with the teachings of the Catholic Church, she opposed abortion and contraception. In a country like India, whose population numbers some 816 million, overpopulation is a staggering problem. Mother Teresa's response was indicative to some of how out of touch she was with the realities of modern life. She also firmly believed in the traditional women's place in the Catholic hierarchy and in society. She spoke out against nuns who wanted to be ordained priests, and she urged Indian women to be traditional homemakers, leaving men to do "what they do best" — work outside the home.

Such beliefs angered feminists all over the world, which had little effect on Mother Teresa. As recently as 1995, speaking at a prayer breakfast in Washington, D.C., she told a group that included President Bill Clinton, "I feel that the greatest destroyer of peace today is abortion." She repeated that theme as the guest speaker at a commencement at Harvard University. She seemed not to care whom she offended in speaking her mind about her beliefs. She also spoke out against what she saw as the poverty of materialism in the United States. "There are many in the world dying for a piece of bread, but many more dying for a little love," she said. "The poverty in the West is not only a poverty of loneliness, but also of spirituality. There's a hunger for love, as there is a hunger for God."

Another area of controversy involved the sources of money Mother Teresa accepted over the years to fund her mission. In addition to funds from religious and philanthropic organizations, she accepted donations from Jean-Claude (Baby Doc) Duvalier, the former dictator of Haiti, and Charles Keating, the American financier who was accused of losing millions of dollars for investors in the savings-and-loan scandal of the 1980s. Yet she consistently refused to condemn anyone who gave her mission money, saying that she believed she had "no moral right" to refuse money given in the name of the poor.

——— " ———

"My community is the poor. Their security is my own. Their heart is my own. My house is the house of the poor — not just of the poor, but of the poorest of the poor: those who are so dirty and full of contagious germs that no one goes near them; those who do not go to pray because they are naked; those who do not eat because they do not have the strength; those who collapse on the sidewalks, knowing they are about to die while the living walk by without even looking back; those who do not cry because they have no more tears left."

——— " ———

Mother Teresa's achievements have prompted a variety of responses from people all over the world. The American writer Barbara Grizzuti Harrison provided a thoughtful essay on her own ambivalence toward Mother Teresa. She wrote that "women, in particular, have a hard time with the concept of a sacrificial life, because we have so often had sacrificial lives, lives of self-abnegation, forced upon us." Harrison said, "In an age when selfishness is legitimized, a woman who is the antithesis of selfishness elicits our attention, if not our wholehearted affection; in a world devoted to the pursuit of a narrow self-fulfillment, she is balm to the needy, a necessary irritant to the privileged — a saint."

British journalist Polly Toynbee noted that "Mother Teresa's most astonishing and bewildering characteristic is her lack of any sense of indignation." She "reminds one sharply that in the teachings of Christ, there is no rage and indignation, no burning desire to change the horrifying injustices of a society that allows such poverty; like it or not, there is only the injunction to turn the other cheek." And indeed, some of Mother Teresa's detractors criticized her for not becoming involved with the social issues of her chosen home of India. She in turn said, "If anyone feels that God wants him or her to change the structures in society, that is a matter between God and that person. We all have the duty to serve God

Mother Teresa and Princess Diana

where we feel called. I feel called to help individuals, not to interest myself in institutions. I do not feel like judging and condemning." When told that her work represented only a "drop in the bucket" in its attempt to help the world's poor, she replied, "We can do no great things, only small things with great love."

Mother Teresa did sometimes involve herself in international conflict, however. In 1982, she arrived in war-torn Beirut and removed children from a hospital in the middle of the war zone. During the Gulf War conflict in 1991, she wrote letters to both U.S. President George Bush and Iraq's President Saddam Hussein, pleading with them to try to reach a peaceful resolution.

Mother Teresa's most vociferous critic is Christopher Hitchins, a British-born journalist living in the U.S. who co-produced a 1994 television documentary on Mother Teresa called "Hell's Angel." Hitchins's main criticism of Mother Teresa is her anti-abortion stand. He also questioned her handling of her order's finances and brought up the contributions from Duvalier and Keating. Further, Hitchins accused her of wasting money by flying first class on Air India. In truth, Air India gave Mother Teresa a lifelong first class ticket years ago so that she would be free to travel wherever and whenever she wished. In general, most observers see Hitchins as extreme, and he has been widely discredited. As David Warren wrote in *Saturday Night*, "Surely, this man has a strange little hobby."

As Mother Teresa grew old, many observers began to worry about how her mission would continue after her death. Ill with heart disease and bowed by a degenerative bone disease, she resigned as the head of her order in 1990. But the sisters could not agree on a replacement, so Mother Teresa stayed on as director. Finally, in 1997, Mother Teresa did step down as head of the Missionaries of Charity, replaced by another nun, Sister Nirmala.

DEATH

On September 5, 1997, Mother Teresa had a massive heart attack and died in the headquarters of her order in Calcutta. She was 87. Tributes flowed in throughout the world. Coretta Scott King said that "Our world has lost the most celebrated saint of our times," a sentiment echoed by many.

In her adopted nation of India, religious leaders of every order attended her funeral. Throughout her life, she had believed that "If people become better Hindus, better Muslims, better Buddhists by our acts of love, then there is something else growing here. They come closer and closer to God." Representatives of the Hindu, Muslim, Sikh, Buddhist, and Parsee faiths took part in the ceremony marking her death. In the words of one Hindu priest, "We think of Mother not as a Christian but simply as Mother. She was just the mother of us all."

At the time of her death, the number of Sisters of the Missionaries of Charity numbered over 4,500, serving in more than 500 missions in 120 countries. How these missions will fare after her death remains to be seen. Some observers believe that the force of Mother Teresa's personality was the driving impetus behind the mission, and that it will lose its focus and importance now that she is gone. Mother Teresa herself did not fear the end of her life or doubt that her mission would survive. "The world will understand that it is not my work," she said before her death. "It is God's. It will go on."

LEGACY

At the time of her death, Mother Teresa was one of the most honored and respected woman in the world. Yet she represented a response to the misery and deprivation faced by the poor that was for some inconsistent with the temper of the modern world. As reported in *Time* magazine, "Mother Teresa had a faith that was not of this world. She was intent on saving souls in an era that no longer believed souls existed. She confounded and overcame that skepticism with the paradox attributed to St. Francis of Assisi nearly eight centuries ago: in giving we receive; in dying we are born to eternal life. It was not a message the 20th century expected to hear or wanted to learn, and Teresa angered many with her simple, hardheaded adherence to it. But to many others, the rewards of her example were enormous. As hundreds of mourners gathered at Calcutta's mother house, a weeping Muslim driver explained, simply, 'She was a source of perpetual joy,' a holy commodity indeed."

WRITINGS

Gift for God, 1975
Heart of Joy, 1988
Living the Word, 1990
Loving Jesus, 1991
A Simple Path, 1995

HONORS AND AWARDS

Kennedy International Award: 1971
Pope John XXIII Peace Prize (Roman Catholic Church): 1971
Jawaharlal Nehru International Award: 1972
Templeton Prize for Progress in Religion (Templeton Foundation): 1973
Albert Schweitzer International Prize: 1975
Nobel Peace Prize: 1979
Bharat Ratha/Jewel of India Award (Indian Government): 1980
Presidential Medal of Freedom: 1985
Congressional Gold Medal (U.S. Congress): 1997

FURTHER READING

Books

Chawla, Navin. *Mother Teresa*, 1992

Egan, Eileen. *Such a Vision of the Street*: *Mother Teresa — the Spirit and the Work*, 1985

Muggeridge, Malcolm. *Something Beautiful for God*, 1971

Opfell, Olga S. *The Lady Laureates: Women Who Have Won the Nobel Prize*, 1986

Wasson, Tyler, ed. *Nobel Prize Winners: An H.W. Wilson Biographical Dictionary*, 1987

Who's Who, 1997

World Book Encyclopedia, 1997

Periodicals

America, Mar. 22, 1980, p.239; Aug. 23, 1980, p.74

Current Biography Yearbook 1973

Glamour, Aug. 1995, p.92

Good Housekeeping, Apr. 1992, p.108

Ladies Home Journal, Apr. 1996, p.146

Life, July 1980, p.54

McCall's, Mar. 1980, p.73; Aug. 1985, p.8

Nation, Mar. 17, 1997, p.8

New York Times, Sep. 6, 1997, p.A1

New York Times Biographical Service, Dec. 23, 1970, p.3211; Oct. 1979, p.1439; Dec. 1979, p.1744; Mar. 1997, p.390

Newsweek, Oct. 29, 1979, p.60; Sep. 15, 1997, p.70; Sep. 22, 1997, p.22

Reader's Digest, Mar. 1973, p.141; Dec. 1987, p.164

Saturday Evening Post, Sep./Oct. 1996, p.26

Saturday Night, Nov. 1995, p.47

Time, Oct. 29, 1979, p.87; Dec. 29, 1975, p.47; Dec. 4, 1989, p.11; Sep. 15, 1997, p.78

U.S. News and World Report, Sep. 15, 1997, p.12

Vanity Fair, Feb. 1995, p.36

WORLD WIDE WEB SITE

http://www.catholic.net/RCC/People/MotherTeresa

Mike Vernon 1963-

Canadian Professional Hockey Player with the San Jose Sharks
MVP of the 1997 Stanley Cup Championships

BIRTH

Michael Vernon was born on February 24, 1963, in Calgary, in the province of Alberta, Canada. His father, Martin Vernon, is a building contractor, and his mother, Lorraine Vernon, is a homemaker. Mike is the fourth of five kids. He has three older brothers, Terry, Dan, and Kevin, and a younger sister, Rachelle.

YOUTH

As far back as he can remember, hockey was a part of Vernon's life. On wintry Saturday evenings, the entire family gathered around the television to watch Canada's premier sports program. "We'd have dinner at 6 o'clock, just when 'Hockey Night in Canada' was starting," recalls Vernon. "We'd watch the game while we ate, then we all went into the living room to watch the rest of it. It'd be over by 9 o'clock, and then we'd go outside and play under the lights until our mom called us in for bed."

Though his idol was the great Boston Bruin defenseman, Bobby Orr, Vernon loved a different position. "I always wanted to be a goalie," he claimed later in life. "I was caught up with the equipment. I mean, you looked at those pads, the mask, the gloves — who wouldn't want to wear them in a game?" Whether he played hockey in the streets during warm summer days, in the basement during thunderstorms, or on an ice rink in the frigid Calgary winters, Mike volunteered to be the goaltender. "I like people shooting at me and trying to stop them." Mike also realized one other facet to goaltending — while he might not participate in scoring goals, at least he remained on the ice for the entire game. "I wanted to play every minute, and goalies don't sit on the bench."

He first played goalie at age 4, on a team coached by his mother. But Vernon claims his mom "didn't really coach. All she did was change the lines and open and close the gate," he still got a taste of what goaltending was like. From that moment, he was hooked. He absorbed whatever hockey knowledge he could from his mother and father (who also coached), and applied them against his older brothers, who needed little arm-twisting to get on the ice and launch a barrage of hockey pucks at their little brother. Vernon so loved playing his position that, even if he was sick, he climbed out of bed and went to school. "I'd feel lousy during the day," stated Vernon, "but I was able to put on those pads after school and that meant everything." One of the most familiar sights at school was little Mike Vernon walking into the building with his goalie pads.

Vernon played for local teams as soon as he could. At age 6 he received his first goalie mask, and in an attempt to match the mask to his team's colors, he spray-painted it green. The next day he wore it for the game, but when he removed it at game's end he wondered why his teammates laughed so hard. During the contest, the green paint slowly leaked off the mask and onto his face.

When he did not tend goalie for a league team, Vernon rushed down to the local frozen pond to join his brothers and friends for more hockey. The boys shoveled snow around the pond's edges to serve as sideboards, then spent fantastic afternoons and evenings charging back and forth on the solid surface. Since Vernon could not dash around the ice like the other players but had to remain near his net, the cold nipped at his hands and feet much worse than at his companions'. He recalled that "the tears would be coming out of your eyes because everything hurt." Often he was so cold that at intermissions he removed his skates to let someone rub his numbed feet. Then, cradling a cup of hot chocolate to restore warmth to his hands, Vernon waited until the feeling returned to his feet, then lumbered back onto the ice.

Like many young athletes, Vernon experienced disappointment at an early age when his coaches cut him from the midget team. Bitterly hurt at being dropped, Vernon nonetheless attended the team's first game because he wanted to cheer for his friends who had made the squad. His sportsmanship paid off when the scheduled goalie failed to appear for the game. The other players asked if Vernon could play. Though he did not bring his equipment with him, Vernon was happy to fill in. "They found some [equipment] in the back room—pads too big, skates three sizes too large—but I played." Vernon played so well that, following the contest, the other players asked the coach if he could be their goalie. He has never been cut since.

——— *"* ———

Of his trade to San Jose, Vernon says "Any team I've been traded to, there's a missing link or some type of reason why they wanted me. I just hope to bring experience, consistency, and leadership to help this team win."

——— *"* ———

CAREER HIGHLIGHTS

Junior Hockey

Vernon played in junior league hockey's many different levels at the beginning of his career. He traveled all over Canada, playing for different Calgary teams. He played bantam hockey with the Chiefs, midget hockey for the Colts, Tier 2 for the Canucks, and Tier 1 for the Wranglers. In 1981, Vernon was drafted in the second round of the draft by his hometown Calgary Flames of the National Hockey League (NHL).

However, he still had much to learn about the sport and thus spent most of the next four years polishing his goaltending abilities. The clubs of the NHL have different levels of hockey, too, and a player normally spends a few years playing in the farm club leagues until they reach the majors. In 1981, he played for the Alberta Junior Hockey League and set a record for allowing the fewest goals. In 1982 and 1983, he played in the Western Hockey League in Calgary, becoming an all-star goalie and winning the MVP award as most valuable player. In 1984, he played for Denver, and in 1985, played on a team in Moncton, Ontario. Finally, in 1985, he was called up to play in the majors.

One reason for his success was that Vernon loved playing his position. As he explained, "I know hockey is a team sport and it will always be a team sport. But a goaltender has more personal challenges than the other players. That's why my position is so special. They have to beat me before they can put a number on the scoreboard and it is my job to beat them. It is strictly one-on-one in the final analysis, and I like that part of it and I like it a lot. I love playing goal, especially in the big games." Chicago Blackhawks center, Bernie Nicholls, explained what most players think about goalies. "The goaltender is the last straw. We can make a mistake and get away with it. If he makes a mistake the puck's in the net."

Calgary Flames

Vernon's rookie season (1985-86) in the NHL established him as a goalie to watch. His 9-3-3 record helped lead the Flames into hockey's 1986 post-season contest—the Stanley Cup playoffs—where his hot hand at goalie carried the team into the finals against the mighty Montreal Canadiens.

For one of the rare instances in hockey, two rookie goaltenders faced each other in the Stanley Cup Finals—Vernon for the Calgary Flames and the equally intimidating Patrick Roy for the Canadiens. After the Flames won the first game in the best-of-seven series, Montreal swarmed back with four straight wins against Vernon and the Flames, winning three by only one goal. While disappointed, Vernon gained valuable experience from his 21 playoff games, in which he allowed less than three goals per game. Fans in Calgary looked forward to the coming seasons. With their young goalie yielding goals at a miserly rate, a Stanley Cup seemed imminent.

Vernon claimed that the key to being a star goalie was "not being great; the key is being consistent." His record over the next three years illustrated that point when he registered 30, 39, and 37 wins.

After being knocked out in the early rounds of the playoffs in 1987 and 1988, the Flames again reached the Stanley Cup finals in 1989, largely behind Vernon's hot play. In the deciding game of round one, with the Flames on the verge of being knocked out, Vernon twice stopped Vancouver from scoring in overtime. On the first attempt, two Vancouver players skated in alone on Vernon, who blocked a torrid shot from Petri Skriko. A short time later Stan Smyl rushed in on a breakaway, but Vernon made such an acrobatic save to keep his team in the game that the Canadian television program, Hockey Night in Canada, kept replaying the save. The Flames advanced to the Finals, where Vernon again faced the Canadiens and Patrick Roy. This time the Flames triumphed, winning the Stanley Cup in a deciding game played at the Forum in Montreal. It was Vernon's first Stanley Cup win.

Over the next five seasons Vernon established himself as one of hockey's best goalies. His teammates played with confidence because they knew that they could count on him to make the big save when they needed it. He won at least 23 games in each of those seasons, and took his team into the play-offs each year. However, when the Flames failed to advance beyond the first round for five straight seasons, Calgary fans turned on the hometown boy.

Rather than lose the playoffs due to poor goaltending, according to commentators, Vernon was either outplayed by his op-ponent or failed to receive much scoring support from his team-mates. The Edmonton Oilers and their superstar, Wayne Gretzky, especially dominated the Flames. One hockey general manager claimed that Vernon

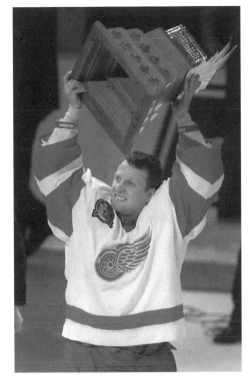

*Vernon holding the Conn
Smythe Trophy, 1997*

was unfairly blamed. "He was a whipping boy of the Calgary fans because of all his losses to the [Edmonton] Oilers in the playoffs. But everybody lost to Edmonton then."

However, Vernon received the brunt of the criticism because he was the hometown kid that Calgary expected would lead them to glory. Instead, for five years the Flames quickly departed the playoffs. Vernon explained that "making the NHL in my home city had both good and bad points. If any-thing, knowing so many people and having my family there pushed me to play well. But it also meant having a lot of questions asked when things did not go so well."

On one occasion Vernon attended a local basketball game and was booed by the fans. To avoid the constant questions and criticisms whenever he ap-peared in public, during playoffs Vernon "would only eat in places where I knew the owner and he could hide me in a back room." Even his father ex-perienced abuse. "If Mike has a bad game, I hear about it all around me. It's hard having a son who is a goaltender. People blame the goalie anytime the other team scores."

Detroit Red Wings

On June 26, 1994, Vernon married Jane Dean in Calgary. To their dismay, three days later Flames officials announced that Vernon had been traded to the Detroit Red Wings for defenseman Steve Chiasson. Vernon mentioned, "This caught me by surprise. The GM (General Manager Doug Risebrough) here was quoted the day before saying he wouldn't trade Mike Vernon. He called today to wish me luck on my marriage and then said, 'By the way, you've been traded for Chiasson.'" Realizing that trades are a part of his professional life, Vernon added that "I suppose it's a little ironic that I wound up with the Red Wings because neither me nor them has been around long in the playoffs." He viewed the move as a positive one, though, stating that "for everyone, this is a clean slate."

The Red Wings needed a veteran goalie to shore up a young, inexperienced Chris Osgood. Though showing flashes of brilliance, Osgood had permitted too many easy goals in the team's humiliating 1994 playoff loss to the San Jose Sharks, a team they should easily have defeated. Wing's coach, Scotty Bowman, explained, "All the Sergei Federovs and Steve Yzermans in the world can't help you win a Stanley Cup unless you have a great goaltender saving you at the other end."

> *For his steady performance, Vernon received the Conn Smythe Trophy as the most valuable player in the 1997 playoffs, but he was more concerned about the Stanley Cup. "I wanted to get rid of it [the Conn Smythe Trophy]. I wanted to get Lord Stanley out there, because that's what we're all here for. The Conn Smythe is a nice little gesture, but it takes a team effort, and everybody is deserving of it."*

Future Hall of Fame coach Bowman, who had won previous Stanley Cup championships with such outstanding goalies as Glenn Hall, Jacques Plante, and Ken Dryden, selected the 5'9", 165-pound Vernon as his man to bring the Stanley Cup to Detroit. Bowman claimed that Vernon "gives us something that will make the other teams stop and think. He is a veteran goaltender, and a good one, and that can give us a big psychological edge. Our opponents will just have to look at us in a different way." His former goalie, Glenn Hall, gushed that in Vernon, "you've got a good one, Scotty. There'll be some nights you won't like the look of some of the goals, but don't worry about it. The guy is a winner. He'll make the plays when they count. He is a champion."

Not only could the veteran Vernon instill confidence in the other players at playoff time, but possibly he could satisfy Detroit's hungry fans, who had suffered through 40 frustrating years without a Stanley Cup championship. Not since the likes of the immortal Gordie Howe and Ted Lindsay in the 1950s had they tasted victory, and their impatience was turning ugly. Since Vernon had handled similar anger in Calgary, maybe he could do the same in Detroit. As the Red Wing general manager, Ken Holland, said, "That he won a [Stanley] Cup was important. But it was how he handled himself when things got bad that impressed us."

Vernon fit into the Red Wing system immediately. Rather than demand that he receive the starting goalie position, as many veterans might have done, Vernon willingly shared the duties with young Chris Osgood. "I was in that situation, too," he said. Vernon went out of his way to impart his experience and knowledge to Osgood, and the two became fast friends. Ken Holland mentioned at the time that "They're inseparable. When you see one of them, you know the other one can't be far behind."

One of the traits he attempted to teach Osgood was the ability to forget mistakes. Errors are a part of any sport, but Vernon tried to explain that if you allow them to bother you, you will make more mistakes. If he allows an easy goal, Vernon says, "I do everything in my power to get ready for the next play. I guess you can say it's like golf. You can't let the bad shots get to you. You have to put them behind you. They scored and I can't take it back. So let's go on and see what happens."

Vernon played in 30 of the 82 regular season games in the 1994-95 season, compiling a 19-6-4 record with a spectacular 2.52 goals-against average. Even though Osgood started the other 52, Bowman went with his veteran goalie in the playoffs. Behind a hot Vernon and a potent offense which featured Steve Yzerman and Sergei Federov, the Red Wings advanced to the Stanley Cup Finals. However, a disastrous four-game sweep by the New Jersey Devils caused rumblings in the hometown fans. As happened in Calgary, Vernon was once again the center of criticism. Typically, Vernon shrugged off the abuse. "That's nothing compared to people who lose their jobs or go on welfare. I don't think you go through a sport or a life without peaks and valleys. It's all part of life."

The fans continued to give Vernon a difficult time during the 1995-96 season, raining down a chorus of boos whenever he allowed a goal. Ken Holland claimed that "I don't even know if he hears that stuff. You can boo until you're blue in the face and it doesn't affect him." The booing became so nasty that a local sports columnist rose to Vernon's defense by stating that the "harassment of Vernon is damaging and dumb. He can't say it, but I can: Back off. You will need him before this season is over."

Again, Vernon remained calm during the turmoil. "Booing is their preroga-tive," he said. "That's the way it is between fans and goaltenders. Patrick Roy was booed, then cheered. Grant Fuhr was booed, then cheered. You deal with it and go on." He never lost faith in his talent or his belief that, sooner or later, he would again experience a championship season. "I don't think I ever doubted myself. During the tough times, I just reflected on the fact that I'd done it before, so why couldn't I do it again? I never had to convince any-body else. All I had to do was convince myself."

Besides, he was simply having too much fun to let criticism ruin it. Not only was he playing the only position he coveted, but he was enjoying all the events that surround professional hockey. "I love hockey and the people in it. I mean, it's game night and you go into the dressing room and there are 25 guys in there all waiting to play. You get some coffee, talk to them, read the paper, joke around, do whatever—and then you go out for practice, come back in, and then play the game. How can anything be better? It is a tremendous life. A fun life. A great life. And I've been privileged to be a part of it." With his ever-present optimism, Vernon relishes new opportunities to excel. "The challenge is what keeps me coming back," he explains. "You have something to prove every day and every year. It's not about yesterday. It's always about today and tomorrow."

Vernon and Osgood combined in the 1995-96 season to win the Jennings Trophy, awarded to the goalie(s) with the lowest goals-against average. With Osgood carrying most of the burden in the playoffs, the Red Wings were again knocked out before reaching the finals.

Vernon played mainly a back-up role during the first half of the 1996-97 sea-son. That quickly changed on March 26, 1997, in a game against the Colorado Avalanche and their outstanding goalie, Patrick Roy. During the first period, two opposing players tangled and began fighting. Before long, a brawl broke out all over the ice. Red Wings enforcer Darren McCarty found Claude Lemieux and pummeled him as a payback for the hit on Chris Draper the year before. When Colorado goalie Patrick Roy tried to help Lemieux, Vernon met him at center ice for a near-comical fight in their thick pads. The Red Wings came out on top in most of the fights and went on to win the brutal game, 6-5, on a goal by McCarty. As a result, the Red Wings erased the painful playoff defeat from their memories and became the dominant team in the rivalry with the Avalanche. "Maybe this is what we needed," Vernon said afterward. "It shows we're willing to go to war for each other. This was the game that brought the Red Wings together. The boys were will-ing to pay the price." From that point on, Vernon played more frequently.

The March 26 game was memorable for more than just the fight. The victory was Vernon's 300th NHL win, making him only the 13th goalie in NHL his-tory to achieve that remarkable plateau. In a classy gesture Patrick Roy, who

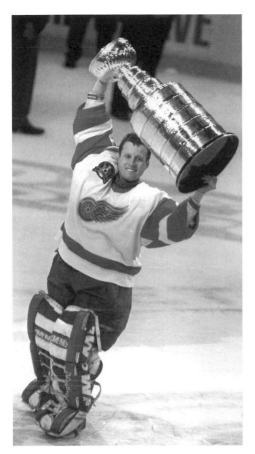

Vernon with the Stanley Cup after the Red Wings win the 1997 championship

had notched his 300th win earlier in his career, shot the game-winning puck down the ice to Vernon so he would have a keepsake. "I wasn't surprised he did it," stated Vernon. "Patrick and I don't know each other that well, but we respect each other."

Stanley Cup Champions at Last

Bowman handed the starting playoff job to Vernon, who responded by playing the best hockey of his career. In 20 playoff games, Vernon allowed only 36 goals in winning 16 contests, three more than he had won during the long regular season. The Wings swept the Anaheim Mighty Ducks in four games — three of which went to overtime — to advance to the conference finals, where they would again face the Colorado Avalanche. The Wings lost game one to their hated rivals and were behind 2-0 in game two when they showed their newfound toughness. The Wings ended up beating the Avalanche in the series, 4-2, to make it to the Stanley Cup finals. Though they faced the Philadelphia Flyers, led by the dominating young star Eric Lindros, the Red Wings would not be denied. Their stifling defense forced the Flyers to make turnovers, and their offense converted them to goals. Best of all, the Red Wings won in a four-game sweep to bring the Stanley Cup to Detroit for the first time since 1955.

For his steady performance, Vernon received the Conn Smythe Trophy as the most valuable player in the 1997 playoffs, but he was more concerned about the Stanley Cup. "I wanted to get rid of it [the Conn Smythe Trophy]. I wanted to get Lord Stanley out there, because that's what we're all here for. The Conn Smythe is a nice little gesture, but it takes a team effort, and everybody is deserving of it." Vernon was once more the darling of the fans, one of whom held up a large sign proclaiming, "VERNON I APOLOGIZE." He earned a $200,000 bonus for being named the most valuable player and enjoyed a whirlwind aftermath of media attention.

Traded to San Jose

Vernon had hardly begun to celebrate his triumph when another of hockey's cruel twists altered his career. Preferring to keep the younger Osgood as goalie, the Red Wings traded Vernon to the San Jose Sharks, where he signed a three-year contract. Though displeased, Vernon understood that trades are a part of his life. "I was a little disappointed in leaving, but I just have to look on to my future and go from there."

By the end of the 1996-97 season, Vernon had compiled an envious record. Of the 42 goalies in NHL history to win 200 or more games, Vernon held the second-best winning percentage, trailing only Montreal's Ken Dryden. His 301 regular season victories and 73 playoff wins rank him with hockey's best.

When Vernon returned to Joe Louis Arena to play against his former teammates for the first time in October 1997, he was greeted with thunderous applause from the fans. He looked up and saw the Stanley Cup banner he had worked so hard to win for his old team. But Vernon harbors no ill-will toward his former team. He's philosophical about his career in hockey, saying "Any team I've been traded to, there's a missing link or some type of reason why they wanted me. I just hope to bring experience, consistency, and leadership to help this team win."

MARRIAGE AND FAMILY

Vernon and his wife, Jane Dean, have one daughter, Amelia. They live in Calgary in the off-season.

HOBBIES AND OTHER INTERESTS

Vernon plays golf whenever he can. He once put a reporter on hold during a cellular interview so he could hit his tee shot.

HONORS AND AWARDS

Western Hockey League's Most Valuable Player: 1981-82, 1982-83
Western Hockey League's Top Goaltending Trophy: 1981-82, 1982-83
Western Hockey League's Player of the Year Award: 1981-182
Western Hockey League All-Star first team: 1981-82, 1982-83
National Hockey League All-Star Game appearances: 1988, 1989, 1990,
    1991, 1992, 1994

Jennings Trophy: 1996, for goalie with the lowest goals-against average (with Chris Osgood)

Conn Smythe Trophy: 1997, for most valuable player in the Stanley Cup playoffs

FURTHER READING

Books

Editors of *Sports Illustrated. Stanley Cup Champions: Detroit Red Wings, 1996-1997*, 1997

Editors of the *Detroit Free Press. Stanleytown*, 1997

Editors of *The Sporting News. The Sporting News Complete Hockey Book, 1995-1996*

Periodicals

Associated Press, May 16, 1989, p.C3

Calgary Herald, May 13, 1997, p.C1; Feb. 12, 1989, Sunday Magazine, p.4

Chicago Tribune, Apr. 14, 1995, p.3

Detroit Free Press, June 30, 1994, p.D1; March 28, 1997, p.F4; May 14, 1997, p.C1; June 7, 1997, p.B1; June 12, 1997, p.D1; August 19, 1997, p.C6

St. Louis Post-Dispatch, Apr. 22, 1997, p.C3

Star Tribune, May 16, 1989, p.C1

The Sporting News, May 22, 1995, p.46

Sports Illustrated, Feb. 20, 1995, p.58; Feb. 21, 1994, p.41; June 16, 1997, p.28

Sports Illustrated for Kids, Nov. 1994, p.66

Toronto Star, May 9, 1995, p.E3

ADDRESS

San Jose Sharks
San Jose Arena
525 W. Santa Clara Street
San Jose, CA 95113

WORLD WIDE WEB SITES

http://www.nhl.com
http://www.sj-sharks.com

Reggie White 1961-
American Professional Football Player and Minister
Defensive Lineman for the Green Bay Packers
NFL Career Sack Leader

BIRTH

Reginald Howard White was born in Chattanooga, Tennessee, on December 19, 1961, to Thelma Dodds and Charles White. Reggie's parents never married. He lived with his mother, but he grew up knowing his father, who was a semi-professional baseball and softball player. When Reggie was seven years old, his mother married Leonard Collier. Reggie had an older brother, Julius, and a younger sister, Christie.

YOUTH

Although White was relatively small as a baby, he grew into a very large boy. He was so big, in fact, that his tee-ball coaches made his mother bring his birth certificate to prove his age. "I didn't like being so big, because the other kids made fun of me and called me names like 'Land of the Giants' and 'Bigfoot,'" White recalled in his autobiography, *Reggie White: In the Trenches.* Sometimes his large size made him a target for other kids who wanted to test his toughness. "Not being a fighter by nature, I was intimidated and scared by all these challenges—and I tended to give in rather than stand my ground," he admitted. But after having a dream in which he stood up to the neighborhood bully, White gained the confidence to do just that. For the most part, however, White worked out his aggressions in less harmful ways. "If I got mad or depressed, I'd grab a stick, go into the woods, and beat on a tree," he explained. "Some people might say that's a terrible thing to do to a tree. Well, maybe so—but I think it's better to take out your frustration on a tree than to take it out on one another."

When White was seven years old, his mother married Leonard Collier, who was in the army and was stationed for a year at Fort Riley, Kansas. White and his brother were given a choice by their mother at this time: they could either live with their grandmother in Chattanooga for a year or go with her to Kansas. The boys chose to stay in a familiar place, though White recalled that "I had always been very close to my mother, and I missed her a lot during that year." Shortly after his mother and stepfather returned to Chattanooga, White began having personality clashes with his stepfather. Collier imposed new rules that his stepson did not always want to follow.

The conflict heightened when, at the age of 13, White had a religious awakening. He had been attending church with his grandmother and was inspired by her spirituality. "Because of her influence, I asked Jesus to come into my life," he recalled. "Instantly, I was saved, I was right with God, my sins were forgiven. There's a saying that Christians aren't perfect, they're just forgiven—and that was me." As a result of his newfound religious beliefs, White became critical of his stepfather's drinking. Collier in turn pointed out what he saw as White's faults. It was not until White was 15 that the relationship began to smooth out and he gave Collier respect as head of the household. "I finally realized that to be a good Christian and to show love and respect for my mother, I needed to respect my stepfather," White noted.

Being a good Christian was a very important aspect of White's youth—every Sunday he would walk five miles to church with his grandmother. The church they attended was an all-black one with a white pastor, Reverend Ferguson, who spent a great deal of time with the children in his community. "By his example, he inspired me to want to serve God, to help people, and to invest myself in the lives of young people," White stated. "From Reverend Ferguson, I learned that it's not enough just to talk about the love of God on Sunday mornings; you have to show people the love of God by spending time with them and getting involved in their lives." The other strong and steady influence during White's childhood was his mother. "My mother taught me to feel secure, capable, and positive about myself," he said. "She taught me to stand on my own two feet, to believe in myself, and to go after my dreams." During his teen years, White revealed to his mother what he wanted to be when he grew up — a professional football player and a minister. Though she was surprised by this combination, White's mother responded, "If that's what you want to be, then work hard to achieve it — and I believe you will."

EDUCATION

Though baseball had been White's sport of choice during his childhood, he changed to football when he was 12. Right from the start, though, White knew that playing offense was not for him. When asked by a friend if he wanted to be a running back, White quickly responded, "Man, I don't want to play offense and get knocked around all the time. I want to play defense. I want to be the guy who knocks those other guys around!" Even though White went on to play football, basketball, and track at Howard High School in Chattanooga, he realized early on that his size and strength, as well as his personality, made him best-suited for football.

White started at center his first year in high school and enjoyed the game, but he still wanted to try playing on the defensive side of the ball. The coach who enabled him to do this was Robert Pulliam, a former defensive lineman for the University of Tennessee. Pulliam possessed a strong understanding of the defensive side of the game and was able to see White's potential early on. One day after a tough practice, Pulliam pulled White aside and told him, "I really believe that you could be the best defensive player to ever play the game of football." And when White assumed the coach was referring to high school football, Pulliam corrected him: "No, I'm not talking about high school. I mean pro football too." Only a sophomore at the time, White's heart swelled at such praise. "To this day, I wonder how he saw that in me," he acknowledged. "But when he said that, he inspired me always to want to be the best."

Coach Pulliam had a plan to help White reach his potential. In order to teach White toughness, Pulliam began pushing, pressuring, and harassing his young player on the field and in the gym. At first, White submitted to the abuse. He finally decided to fight back during his junior year, following a basketball game in which Pulliam deliberately elbowed him in the chest. Leaving in tears and expecting an apology, White was surprised when

Pulliam grabbed the front of his T-shirt and said, "If you think I'm gonna apologize, you might as well go in there and get ready for your next whupping. Until you start fighting me back, I'm gonna keep kicking your butt."

So White began to fight back, giving elbow for elbow. "It was years before I realized what Coach Pulliam was doing in my life: He was building toughness and confidence inside me," White stated. "He knew my goal in life was to play pro football, and he knew that if I was going to achieve that goal I would need to have the physical, emotional, and spiritual hide of a rhinoceros. He was pounding on me to toughen my hide—and it worked." During his senior year White was named All-State in basketball, All-American in football, and Chattanooga's Player of the Year in both football and basketball. He was also honored as the Two-Sport Player of the Year in the nation. He graduated from Howard High School in 1980.

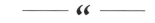

White achieved one of his career goals before he even entered college, when he became a licensed minister at the age of 17. To earn this license, he gave a sermon on forgiveness before a group of ministers at St. John's Baptist Church in Chattanooga. Witnessing the sermon, White's mother told him, "It was so thrilling, watching you up there preaching—it seemed like a heavenly light shone around you."

"My mother taught me to feel secure, capable, and positive about myself," he related. *"She taught me to stand on my own two feet, to believe in myself, and to go after my dreams."*

White's second career goal, to be a professional football player, took another step forward when he received attractive scholarship offers from numerous universities during his senior year in high school, including Alabama, UCLA, Michigan, Ohio State, and the University of Tennessee. After spending a weekend in Knoxville and experiencing the emotion of a Volunteer football game—when 96,000 cheering fans greeted the players as they entered the field—White decided to remain close to home and attend the University of Tennessee. "That settled it," he explained. "From that moment I knew my future was going to take me right through the same tunnel and onto that same football field. I knew I was destined to wear the orange and white of the UT Volunteers."

White attended the University of Tennessee, combining football with his studies in human services. He left Tennessee in January 1984 without earning a degree. He later returned to school and completed his bachelor's degree in human services in 1990.

CAREER HIGHLIGHTS

University of Tennessee Volunteers

White started out playing football at UT in 1980 with a mixture of excitement and intimidation. At this new level he was no longer bigger than everyone else. In fact, there were plenty of guys roughly the same size as him. "Even so," White recalled, "I clearly stood out in a crowd, and because of my size, my classmates and teammates began calling me Big Dog, my nickname ever since." Despite all the work Coach Pulliam had done to toughen White up, he was ready to quit after enduring the physical abuse of his first college football practice. But after his mother encouraged him to never give up and to give everything he had, White settled in and began focusing on his goals — to make All-American and to be the Southeastern Conference (SEC) Player of the Year.

Although White performed well during his first two seasons, he truly became a star in 1983 with the help of the team's new defensive coordinator, Larry Marmie. Under Marmie's direction, the Volunteer defense climbed from last place to first in the SEC in total defense. White led the way with 15 sacks and more than 100 tackles, earning him the nickname "minister of defense." This phenomenal season ended with White reaching his goals: he was chosen for the All-America team and named the SEC Player of the Year. He also made the list of four finalists for the Lombardi Award, given annually to the nation's outstanding college lineman. In 1991, when the Volunteers celebrated their centennial football season, White was named to the school's all-time team. Despite having played in several team uniforms since, White noted that "I still have a deep and lasting affection for the Big Orange of Tennessee."

United States Football League

In January 1984, White left school to begin his professional football career with the Memphis Showboats of the short-lived United States Football League (USFL). "I was finally a pro," he recalled. "My dream was coming true in a big way. I would not only be playing professional football, I'd be playing close to home where my family and friends could come watch me play." Success came quickly for White. His 11 sacks that first year earned him a spot on the league's all-rookie team. During the 1985 season, he finished third in sacks with 12.5 and became a first-squad selection for the All-USFL team. During his two years with the Showboats, White started 34 games, made 193 tackles (120 of which were solo stops), tallied 23.5 sacks, and forced a total of 7 fumbles.

White enjoyed his time in the USFL because he liked his teammates and coaches, the fans, and the freedom that the league enjoyed. With the league struggling financially, though, he saw the end coming months in advance and got out while he could. The Philadelphia Eagles bought out the rest of his contract with the Showboats and signed him to a four-year contract. He began to play with them during the fall season of 1985.

Philadelphia Eagles

White made his NFL debut in the fourth game of the 1985 season, against the New York Giants. He gave fans a glimpse of the future by making 2.5 sacks and deflecting a pass that was intercepted by a teammate and returned for the Eagles' only touchdown in a 16-10 loss. Eagles head coach Marion Campbell made White a starting defensive end the very next week, and he finished the season by posting the fifth-best sack total in the league (with 13). He was also named to the NFL's All-Rookie Team and voted Defensive Rookie of the Year. "I was thrilled to be in the NFL," White remembered, "but I had no idea what lay ahead. My years with the Eagles were destined to be the stormiest, most troubled years of my career."

At the end of the 1985 season, Campbell was replaced as head coach by Buddy Ryan, the former defensive coordinator for the world-champion Chicago Bears. "I was excited that Buddy was coming to coach us, because I knew he had an extremely aggressive style of defense," White related. He flourished in the team's new attack-oriented defense, emerging as one of the league's leading pass rushers with a team record 18 sacks during the 1986 season. Making his first trip to the Pro Bowl that year, he sacked the AFC quarterbacks a total of four times and was named the game's most valuable player. "Sacks are fun, man," White observed. "There's nothing like throwing a quarterback down for a big loss. But there's a whole lot more to being a great defensive lineman than sacking the quarterback. You have to play the run as well as the pass."

The 1987 season was shortened due to a players' strike, but White continued to dominate the league with 21 sacks in only 12 games, falling short of the single-season league record by just one. For his efforts, he was named the NFC Player of the Year by United Press International and unanimously selected to the All-NFL team. By this time White had gained a reputation as one of the toughest and most feared defensive players in the league. Ryan took advantage of the intimidation factor by starting his star player in a variety of different positions. "That way," Ryan told *Sports Illustrated,* "we can scare . . . a whole bunch of people instead of just one."

The season ended on a rocky note, however, because White's contract was up for renegotiation. "Sure, I was happy to be in Philly, I loved the fans and the team, I loved Buddy Ryan, and I really wanted to finish my career in an Eagles uniform," he explained. But he was unhappy with his contract and

with the approach team management used during negotiations. "I had been developing a sour feeling in my stomach about [Eagles' owner Norm] Braman for some time," White admitted. As the negotiations began, White's new agents discovered an option year written into his original contract which allowed the Eagles to either play him for a fifth year at just 10 percent more than his fourth-year salary, or to release him and owe him nothing. White felt that he had been cheated, and consequently the negotiations with Braman lasted over a year and a half. During one heated discussion, Braman told White that he should not care about money because he was a Christian. White replied, "I work just as hard as the wicked man does. I deserve just as much as he gets. If I'm the best at my position, then I'm going to demand what I think I deserve, whether I'm a Christian or not."

The 1988 season began with the contract negotiations still underway. The Eagles got off to a poor start, losing three of their first four games, but turned it around behind White and quarterback Randall Cunningham. They defeated the Dallas Cowboys to claim the NFC Eastern Division championship, but were eliminated from the playoffs by the Chicago Bears. "A loss to Chicago wasn't the way we wanted to end the season — but there was no denying it had been a great year," White observed. "It had taken him three years to do it, but Coach Ryan had finally built the team he wanted. . . . Clearly, Buddy's loyalty to his players inspired the best effort from his team, and we kept getting better and better." For his part, White racked up a league-leading 18 sacks and added 133 tackles during the season. Continuing to earn the respect of his opponents with his deadly combination of speed and strength, he was voted NFL Player of the Year.

In the course of his long negotiations with the Eagles, White ended up filing a lawsuit against his former agent, Patrick Forte, which would result in his contract being dissolved if he won. It was in the Eagles' best interest to settle the contract dispute, which would enable White to drop his lawsuit. White had grown increasingly frustrated with team management, and by this time the only reason he was willing to re-sign with the Eagles was because of Coach Ryan and his teammates. "I was hopeful that the public would understand that I wasn't trying to take the Eagles for everything they had," he stated. "I was just asking for what I thought was fair." In late August an agreement was finally reached. White got three years guaranteed with a signing bonus, and at the end of the three years he would be a free agent. He went on to play with the Eagles for four more years.

In 1989, the Eagles' defensive unit tallied up a team record 62 sacks, 11 of which belonged to White. But the Eagles finished second in their division to the Giants and were eliminated in the first round of the playoffs by the Los Angeles Rams. In 1990 White continued to lead the Eagle defense with 14 sacks, which placed him second in the NFC and fourth in the league. He also got his second career interception during a game against the Washington Redskins and returned it for 33 yards. Unfortunately, the Eagles again finished second in their division and were knocked out in the first round of the playoffs.

This turned out to be Ryan's last game as head coach of the Eagles, as Braman fired him a few days after the playoff loss. "I was not happy about the loss of Buddy Ryan," White recalled. "I was not happy about a lot of things in the Philadelphia Eagles. I didn't think it could get any worse than this." Offensive coordinator Rich Kotite was named head coach after Ryan's departure. During the first regular season game, however, starting quarterback Randall Cunningham was injured and unable to play for rest of the season. The Eagles proceeded to go through three more starting quarterbacks that year. Although the team failed to make the playoffs, the defense was strong throughout the year, led by White's 15 sacks and 100 tackles.

Between the 1991 and 1992 seasons White and the rest of his teammates suffered a difficult loss when defensive lineman Jerome Brown died in a car accident. "Every day I suited up, I was reminded of Jerome. His locker was right next to mine, and we left it exactly as he had left it," White stated. "The heart had been ripped out of our team, and we all knew it." Despite this tragedy, the Eagles performed well in 1992, ending their playoff drought with a victory over the New Orleans Saints in the first round. But they were defeated by the Dallas Cowboys in the second round. This ended a season in which White had posted 14 sacks—the eighth consecutive seasons he had recorded more than 10 sacks.

Free-Agent Pioneer

Off the field, White's involvement with legal issues continued as he became the lead plaintiff in a class-action suit brought by the players against the NFL for antitrust law violations. The players wanted an unrestricted free agency system, which would give a player who had completed his contract with one team greater freedom to offer his services to other teams in the league. But the team owners feared that such a system would lead to a bidding war for top players that could bankrupt the sport. After legal arguments for both sides were presented, a United States District Court Judge ordered those involved to resolve their differences or be faced with a court-imposed labor settlement. In early 1993, the owners and the players' union worked out an agreement that instituted free agency with a cap on players' salaries. A writer for the *Sporting News* observed that "20 years from now White . . . will be remembered not only for his Hall of Fame skills, but also for his role as a free-agent pioneer who paved the way for non-quarterbacks to finally get their due."

Braman's vehement opposition to the agreement left White searching for a new team at the beginning of the 1993 season. "If the man had dealt with us on the basis of win-win, mutual respect, and trust instead of on a basis of confrontation and I-win/you-lose, he could have built a tradition of winning *and* a healthy bottom line," White contended. Before long, every team in the league was competing for White's attention. He went on a 37-day tour of NFL cities in order to decide where to play. Vince Aversano of *Inside Sports* described how White was received on this trip: "He was greeted at airports by marching bands—even was introduced to the mayor in some cities—and was wined and dined by team presidents and general managers in the hopes that the best defensive lineman in pro football would sign his name on their dotted line. Press conferences were held just to announce that Reggie was in town *thinking* about playing for the local team." White recalled his feelings about receiving the star treatment: "After the eight years I had spent being embattled and underappreciated in the Eagles organization, it was an incredible feeling to have . . . teams rolling out the red carpet and saying, 'We want you.' I was amazed at how many teams understood what I was truly looking for—not just more money but a place to win a championship and a place to carry out my ministry."

Green Bay Packers

Many people were surprised when White chose to play for the Green Bay Packers. The Packers were not perceived as a Super Bowl contender, and Green Bay was a small city. In fact, the Packers were not even on White's list when he started out. He was leaning toward San Francisco, where he thought God was telling him to go, until he finally realized that God was in fact referring to Green Bay, "the San Francisco of the East." White was impressed with the city ownership of the team, the history of football in Green Bay, and Coach Mike Holmgren, so he accepted the Packers' offer of a four-year contract that gave him a large portion of his $17 million salary right away. He thus became the highest paid defensive player ever in the NFL.

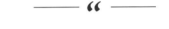

"Please, just one Super Bowl before I retire, I prayed as I trudged off the field. Not two or three, I ain't greedy. Just give me one."

White was welcomed with open arms by the people of Green Bay, who considered him something of a football savior. One local paper even depicted him as Moses, parting the sea of NFL competition to lead his team to the promised land of the Super Bowl. White, too, was confident that the Packers would win soon and that God had sent him to Wisconsin for a reason. "I truly believe that God is bringing a spiritual revival to America, and that Wisconsin is going to play a major part in that revival," he maintained. White soon came to appreciate Packers fans, who turn out in the thousands even for practices and scrimmages, and the entire Packers organization. "The moment I joined the team, I discovered that the chemistry on the Packers team, throughout the organization, and across the community is something special, something I had never experienced before," he noted. "I quickly became aware that I was part of one of the most close-knit, least ego-fractured teams in the NFL."

The season before White arrived, the Packer defense had ranked 23rd in the league in yards allowed per game. But in 1993, with White as their defensive end, the unit jumped quickly to second. Although the team's young quarterback, Brett Favre, had an erratic year, everyone on the team, including White, knew that if they were going to win it would be with Favre. "We all understood our roles," White stated. "As a minister and a football player I'm a leader — but I'm not the field general of the Green Bay Packers. That's Brett's job. He's the man." Though the Packers started off the season with a 1-3 record, they managed to turn it around and ended the season at 10-7. White tied for the NFC lead in sacks with 13. Reaching the playoffs for the first time in 11 years, the Packers defeated the Detroit Lions in the first round but lost to the Dallas Cowboys in the second. "Earlier that season, I had told my team that losing makes me mad and it makes me cry," White recalled. "That's exactly how I felt when that game was over. We had come a long way just to have the dream trampled into the artificial turf at Texas Stadium. *Please, just one Super Bowl before I retire,* I prayed as I trudged off the field. *Not two or three, I ain't greedy. Just give me one."*

Before the start of the 1994 season, White was one of only five active players named to the NFL's 75th Anniversary All-Time Team. Although 1994 saw the first decline in White's numbers (8 sacks and 59 tackles) when he suffered an elbow injury late in the season, the Packers finished 9-7 and earned another trip to the playoffs. They experienced another frustrating loss to the Cowboys, but it was clear they were on their way back to being one of the elite teams in the NFL. By the end of the season, White had tackled more quarterbacks behind the line of scrimmage than any other player in NFL history. And he recorded many of his 145 career sacks despite being double- or triple-teamed. When he was selected for the Pro Bowl that year, he became the first defensive end to earn the honor for nine consecutive years.

Late in the 1995 season, at a time when he was leading the NFC with 12 sacks, White suffered a torn hamstring and missed a game for the first time in his pro football career. The Packers announced that he would be out for the rest of the season, but the next day White showed up for practice claiming that his injury had been healed by a divine hand. White played an increasing number of snaps each game and inspired his teammates with his courage. "All you can say is that it's very unusual how his body reacts to injury," Coach Holmgren noted. "You can't deny that." The Packers ended the 1995 season by claiming their first outright NFC Central title since 1972. The team's success continued in a commanding post-season victory over the San Francisco 49ers, which meant they would face the Dallas Cowboys again for the NFC Championship and the right to go to the Super Bowl. On the flight home from San Francisco, White sat down next to Holmgren and said, "Coach, I've never been this far. I just want to thank you." The two men sat in silence for a moment, and then Holmgren responded with a good punch line: "Nice try. But you still can't have my Bud Light."

Shortly before the NFC Championship game with the Cowboys, White learned that the Inner City Community Church in Knoxville, Tennessee, where he served as assistant pastor, had been burned to the ground in a hate crime perpetrated by racist arsonists. "It's time for us to stop sweeping this under the rug and saying that we've made progress," he stated. "Progress hasn't been made. Until whites and blacks start working together and fight this, we're going to continue to have problems, and people are going to continue to die. Thank God no one was in the church when this happened." White suffered another blow when the Packers gave up a lead with 10 minutes to go and lost the conference title to the

A Campbell's soup can shown with a "cheesehead," a joking reference to the Green Bay fans

Cowboys. On the trip back to Green Bay, he and his teammates made a pact that next time they got to that position, they would do whatever was necessary to win.

Following the defeat, White shifted his focus back to the Inner City Community Church. By June, the people of Green Bay and other cities had responded to the crisis by donating over $250,000 to rebuild the church. "One boy sent us 92 pennies taped to a piece of cardboard," White recalled. "Those people forgot about me being a football player and said Reggie White, the man, needs our help. They revived me, to be honest." The public outpouring of support was so great that it made White change his mind about retiring when his contract expired at the end of the 1996 season.

As soon as that season got underway, it became clear that the Packers were a driven team. White and his teammates roared through the regular season to claim another NFC Central title and earn home field advantage in the playoffs. This time, the Cowboys would have to come to the "frozen tundra" of Green Bay's Lambeau Field to stop the Packers from making it to the Super Bowl. But the fateful meeting that both the Packers and their fans sought was not to be. The Carolina Panthers upset the Cowboys to make it to the NFC Championship Game, where the Packers defeated them 30-13. As Favre jogged triumphantly to the sidelines with three minutes left in the game, White gave his quarterback a 1996 NFC Championship hat and a big bear hug. Then, as Michael Silver described it in *Sports Illustrated,* "The big man lost it. Steam rising from his head and tears running down his cheeks, the 35-year-old, 300-pound White turned into a bundle of mush."

White was now one step away from the Super Bowl ring he had come to Green Bay to win. The Packers were favored going into Super Bowl XXXI against the New England Patriots, and they did not disappoint. They posted a 35-21 victory over the Patriots and brought the Super Bowl trophy back to Green Bay. White helped cement the victory with three timely and overpowering sacks in the second half. "This is a team that plays together, and for that reason we deserve this," tight end Keith Jackson said afterward. "Nobody is more important than anybody else, whether you're Reggie White or Brett Favre or a guy blocking on special teams. . . . I wish every junior high and high school team could be around this and sniff this and sense what it's like to be a champion."

Now that he has a Super Bowl ring, White's football career is nearing its conclusion. Looking ahead to what retirement will bring, White noted that "When I left Philly, I really missed the guys. So now I know how it'll feel when I retire, missing your buddies. In the last few years, I've contemplated retiring . . . but God won't let me go. I know he's preparing me for something great when I get out of the game."

The Packers have a chance to repeat their Super Bowl performance in 1998. At the end of 1997, they were trying for a playoff berth, and White was posting another outstanding season. Whether it will also be his last season in the NFL remains to be seen.

White has contributed off the playing field in an unusual way during the 1997 season. He is appearing on special cans of Campbell's soup to raise money for charity. Over the course of the 1997 season, Campbell's has donated 20,000 cans of soup for every tackle and 50,000 cans of soup for every sack made by White to food banks all over the country.

White's Legacy to the Game

White's impact on football will not soon be forgotten, as Johnette Howard explained in *Sports Illustrated:* "He's the league's career sack leader. He'll be remembered as the biggest star to attach his name to a 1992 lawsuit that helped revolutionize free agency in the NFL. Players and coaches will recall his 4.6 speed in the 40 and the python embrace he clamped on ball carriers. They'll laugh about his Herculean strength, which allowed him to toss aside a 320-pound lineman with one arm, and his habit of helping up the same foe with a reminder that 'Jesus loves you.' He'll leave the game an authentic hero, an overused phrase in sports that truly applies to him."

HOME AND FAMILY

In January 1985, while he was preparing for his second season with the Memphis Showboats, White married Sara Copeland. The couple first met when she was a 16-year-old college freshman at East Tennessee State in Knoxville and he was a 19-year-old sophomore at the University of Tennessee. A mutual friend, who knew that they were both devout Christians, set up a meeting between the two at church. Although Sara was not impressed with White at first, he was convinced that they would get married one day. They maintained a friendship throughout college, and White finally made his move after starting his professional football career. "And we've been in love ever since," he stated.

> *Now that he has a Super Bowl ring, White's football career is nearing its conclusion. "I know how it'll feel when I retire, missing your buddies. In the last few years, I've contemplated retiring . . . but God won't let me go. I know he's preparing me for something great when I get out of the game."*

"Sara is a great support to me in everything I do," White continued. "Before the games, she gives me prayer, encouragement, and confidence. After a big win, she shares my triumph. After a loss, she is patient with me and comforting, and she helps me to restore my emotional edge." The couple has two children—Jeremy, who was born in 1986, and Jecolia, who was born in 1988. White claims that his family often helps him put his football career into perspective. After a tough loss in the playoffs, he remembered, "I went home real discouraged. I was laying on the bed with the lights out, my feelings really hurt. Then I heard something behind me. I turned and my daughter Jecolia said, 'Dad, I just want you to know that I love you.' That ended it all, put it all into perspective. I knew then I was taking [the loss] too seriously."

When he retires from football, White plans to spend more time with his family and also concentrate on his preaching and community work. He accepts his responsibility as a role model and leader, and wants to use it to make a difference in the world. "I want to have leadership. People respond when you do something positive. You've got to give people opportunity. You've got to put them to work when they need jobs. I do my best to lead by example to the point where if I've got to put my money where my mouth is, then I will."

HOBBIES AND OTHER INTERESTS

White and his wife spent many hours on inner-city streets during their time in Philadelphia, talking to youths about the dangers of alcohol and drugs and the importance of remaining in school, and they continue to do so in Green Bay. In 1991, they opened a residence — known as Hope Palace — on their Tennessee property for new mothers and unmarried pregnant women. They also established the Knoxville Community Development Bank with the mission of revitalizing Knoxville's inner city by giving business and personal loans to those considered too risky by other banks. "The only way you can have an effect on people is to get down in the trenches, go where they are," White stated. "Until we do that — and I'm talking about the masses — we're not going to solve these problems."

WRITINGS

Reggie White: In the Trenches, 1996

HONORS AND AWARDS

All-American College Team: 1983
Southeastern Conference Player of the Year: 1983
USFL All-Rookie Team: 1984
All-USFL Team: 1985
NFL All-Rookie Team: 1986
NFL Defensive Rookie of the Year: 1986
Pro Bowl: 1987-95
Pro Bowl MVP: 1987
NFC Player of the Year (United Press International): 1988
All-NFL Team: 1988
NFL Player of the Year (Washington Touchdown Club): 1989
NFL Best Defensive Player (*Sports Illustrated*): 1989
Byron White Humanitarian Award (NFL Players Association): 1992
NFL 75th Anniversary All-Time Team: 1994
NFL Career Sack Leader: 1994

FURTHER READING

Books

Gutman, Bill. *Reggie White: Star Defensive Lineman,* 1996
Information Please Sports Almanac, 1996
White, Reggie. *Reggie White: In the Trenches,* 1996
Who's Who among Black Americans, 1994-95

Periodicals

Christianity Today, Oct. 24, 1994, p.94
Current Biography Yearbook 1995
Inside Sports, Aug. 1993, p.26
Jet, Feb. 10, 1997, p.51
New York Times, Jan. 26, 1997, p.S1
Sport, Dec. 1995, p.45; June 1997, p.86
Sporting News, July 8, 1996, p.40; Feb. 3, 1997, p.8
Sports Illustrated, Nov. 27, 1989, p.64; Sep. 2, 1996, p.140; Jan. 20, 1997, p.28;
    Feb. 3, 1997, p.30
Sports Illustrated for Kids, Jan. 1997, p.24
Time, Jan. 27, 1997, p.56

ADDRESS

Green Bay Packers
P.O. Box 10628
Green Bay, WI 54307-0628

WORLD WIDE WEB SITES

http://www.nfl.com
http://www.reggie-white.com
http://www.packers.com

Kate Winslet 1975-

British Actress
Star of the Hit Film *Titanic*

BIRTH

Kate Winslet was born in Reading, England, on October 5, 1975. Her parents are Roger Winslet, an actor, and Sally (Bridges) Winslet, a nanny. Kate is the second of their four children. She has an older sister, Anna, a younger sister, Beth, and a younger brother, Joss.

YOUTH

Winslet grew up in a modest rented house on a busy street in Reading, a small town in the south of England, between London and Oxford. Her father was a struggling actor who never got a big break. "A brilliant actor and wonderful man," she says, "he just did not get the right opportunities." Money was always a bit tight in their family, and the household could be a bit hectic, with a couple of extra screaming kids around that her mom was watching. But Winslet never expresses any regrets about her childhood. In fact, she always raves about how lucky she was, growing up in what she describes as "a very strong, loving, secure environment." To this day, she talks about how much she cares about her family and how much emotional support they still give her.

Kate's father wasn't the only actor in her extended family. In fact, she has been surrounded by acting all her life. Her father's side of the family included twin sisters who were part of a vaudeville troop. In the late 19th and early 20th century, vaudeville was a type of variety show on stage that featured songs, dances, magic acts, and humorous skits. On her mother's side, her grandparents were Oliver and Linda Bridges, who ran a repertory theater in Reading, where they presented musicals and plays; her uncle was Robert Bridges, who appeared in the original production of the musical *Oliver!* In the Winslet family, memorizing lines and going on auditions were normal, daily activities. "It wasn't necessarily that I knew acting was what I wanted to do,"

"It wasn't necessarily that I knew acting was what I wanted to do," Kate says. "It's just that I knew it's what I would end up doing."

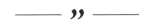

Kate says. "It's just that I knew it's what I would end up doing." In fact, Winslet started acting early. Her first starring role came at age five when she was cast as Mary in the school Christmas play, "a deeply serious event that made me want to cry because I was so happy," she recalls.

EDUCATION

Winslet started out attending public schools in England. After she was rejected by her chosen comprehensive (upper school) because she lived outside of the area, she enrolled at Redroofs, a private school that specializes in performing and acting. Her grandmother paid the tuition there for two years, but after that Winslet was on her own financially. She had to get acting jobs to pay her way through school. Her first paid job came when she was 13, when she appeared in a television commercial for cereal. "I got a Sugar Puffs advertisement for 60 pounds (about $100) at the age of 13 and began earning regularly, with ads and voice-over work — some paid 150 quid (150 pounds, or almost $250) for the day — to see myself through. I knew, right from the start, that it was not a matter of putting on red lipstick and tying your hair in bunches and saying, 'I want to be a star.' As much as I love acting, I always realized it was bloody hard work."

Winslet finished the equivalent of her high school education at Redroofs at age 16, but she decided not to go on to college or drama school. "Since I was 13 or 14, I've always felt older than I actually am," she explains. "Most of my friends are older than I. So I didn't want to stay on at school. I wanted to act, to get on with life, to be in the world of the working. And since then, I've had the most extraordinary education anyone could have — the places I've been to, the people I've seen. It's been amazing."

FIRST JOBS

By the time she finished at Redroofs, Winslet had already started her acting career. In her first series of jobs, she appeared in a variety of British television shows. She had walk-on parts and recurring roles in both situation comedies and dramatic series, including "Dark Season," "Get Buck," "Shrinks," "Casualty," and "Anglo-Saxon Attitudes." It was while appearing in the latter show that she faced a moment of truth.

On the series "Anglo-Saxon Attitudes," she played the daughter of a 300-pound woman. One day on the set, the director walked by the two of them and said, "God, the likeness is extraordinary." Winslet was shocked, and she decided right then to change. Kate, whose childhood nickname was "blubber," had been heavy through most of her childhood, as she explains here. "I was chubby as a child. When I was 16, I was *fat*. It was a family thing. We're all big eaters. My uncle is a chef. My mother is a fantastic cook. Kind of unavoidable." Winslet went on a sensible diet using Weight Watchers, learned to control her eating habits, and lost the extra weight. Within a year, she was down to her current size.

CAREER HIGHLIGHTS

After appearing in various British TV series, Winslet next went on to acting in feature films. Her first film was *Heavenly Creatures* (1994), which was based on a true story that happened in New Zealand in the 1950s. Winslet first read a synopsis of the story when she was in the car with her father. Although she had no movie experience and had never even auditioned for a film, she was determined to win the role. She said, "Dad, listen to this, listen to this: I've got to do this, I've got to do this. I've got to do it." He just said, "You will."

Emma Thompson and Kate Winslet in Sense and Sensibility

With Winslet as Juliet Hulme and New Zealand actress Melanie Lynskey as Pauline Parker, *Heavenly Creatures* shows two girls in an intense, exhilarating, and exceptionally close friendship that soon spirals dangerously out of control. When Juliet's family decides to move, the girls feel threatened by the upcoming separation. Despite their pleas, Pauline's mother says that Pauline can't go with Juliet. So Pauline and Juliet, who were about 15 at the time, devise and carry out a vicious and brutal plan to murder Pauline's mother. In real life, the girls were sent to prison for five years and released on the condition that they never see each other again. On film, it was considered a powerful and deeply disturbing work. Both Winslet and Lynskey gave extraordinary performances, making their terrifyingly realistic characters seem sympathetic. *Heavenly Creatures* won rave reviews and an Oscar nomination for best screenplay, boosting Winslet to the front ranks of young actresses.

After *Heavenly Creatures*, Winslet appeared in the children's film *A Kid in King Arthur's Court* (1995). In this retelling of the story of King Arthur, a boy from the modern era is magically transported back to the Middle Ages. There, he introduces 20th-century creations like bubble gum, roller blades, and rock and roll to the king and his daughters.

Taking on Historical Roles

Winslet went on to act in several period pieces, taking roles in film versions of some of the greatest works in the history of English literature. Her big break-through role came in *Sense and Sensibility* (1995), an adaptation of the 1811 Jane Austen novel. The film, like the novel, focuses on the loves and heart-breaks of two sisters, showing the social climate of early 19th-century England. Winslet played Marianne Dashwood, opposite famed English actress Emma Thompson as Elinor Dashwood. Elinor, who represents sense in the title, is dignified, pragmatic, and restrained, while Marianne, who represents sensibility, is impetuous, headstrong, and flirtatious. Winslet's enthralling performance as Marianne won her nominations for both the Golden Globe and the Oscar for best supporting actress. Although she won neither award, she wowed critics and audiences alike with her captivating portrayal of Marianne's vulnerability, impulsiveness, and romantic intoxication.

"I knew, right from the start, that it was not a matter of putting on red lipstick and tying your hair in bunches and saying, 'I want to be a star.' As much as I love acting, I always realized it was bloody hard work."

Winslet next appeared in *Jude* (1996), an adaptation of the 1895 novel *Jude the Obscure* by Thomas Hardy. *Jude* is the tragic story of an ill-fated romance between two cousins. Jude Hawley (played by Christopher Eccleston) is a stonemason who wants to become a scholar but who can't break free of his peasant origins; his cousin, Sue Bridehead (Winslet), is an intelligent, headstrong, and rebellious woman who refuses to conform to the social and religious restrictions of the Victorian era. Film critic Richard Corliss had this to say about her performance: "Winslet is worthy of . . . the camera's scrupulous adoration. Her teasing sneer of a smile makes her a very contemporary presence. So she's perfect for Sue, a modernist ahead of her time. Take Gwyneth Paltrow's elegance, mix in Drew Barrymore's naughty wiles, and you have a hint of Winslet. She is a star of her time. And *Jude* is a handsome showcase for her gifts."

In 1996 Winslet also appeared in *Hamlet*, a four-hour film version of the early 17th-century play by William Shakespeare. Winslet plays Ophelia, beloved by Hamlet, the prince of Denmark, who is melancholy after the death of his father, the king. The king's brother (and Hamlet's uncle), Claudius, has married his mother, Gertrude, and assumed the throne. After his father's ghost appears and says that he was killed by Claudius and demands revenge, Hamlet spends much of the play in an agony of indecision about how to proceed.

Kenneth Branagh, who both acted the role of Hamlet and directed the film, came in for some criticism. There are multiple versions of many of Shakespeare's plays, and some critics have questioned the authenticity of the version used by Branagh. In addition, some disagreed with his decision to change the play's setting to the 19th century. Yet there was widespread praise for Winslet's interpretation of the role of Ophelia, particularly her haunting depiction of madness.

Titanic

Winslet spent the next year working on *Titanic* (1997), directed by James Cameron. The most expensive movie ever made, *Titanic* tells

Kate Winslet as Ophelia in Hamlet

the tragic story of the ocean liner that left Southampton, England, on April 10, 1912, on its way to New York City with 2,223 people aboard. The ship struck an iceberg in the North Atlantic during the early morning hours of April 15, 1922. Although it was considered unsinkable, it quickly sank to the bottom. More than 1,500 men, women, and children plunged to their death. At 3 hours, 14 minutes, the movie *Titanic* lasts just slightly longer than the 2 hours, 50 minutes it took for the real boat to sink.

Titanic the movie is a sweeping romantic epic. Winslet plays the part of Rose DeWitt Bukater, a wealthy and haughty first-class passenger who is returning home to Philadelphia with her mother (Frances Fisher) and her rich, arrogant fiance (Billy Zane) to make final preparations for her wedding. On board, Rose meets and falls in love with Jack Dawson (Leonardo DiCaprio), a young penniless artist who has just spent several years in Europe and who wins his passage back home in a poker game. He is traveling in steerage, the section of the ship with the cheapest tickets and the poorest passengers. The story explores the effects of class and money on these two young lovers. Told from the point of view of Rose, it also details her gradual transformation, with the help of her lover, from a dependent young woman tied to the conventions of her era to someone who is strong, independent, and free-spirited.

The story of the *Titanic* has become a legend, featured in movies, songs, and even a recent Broadway musical. "The tragedy of *Titanic* has assumed an almost mythic quality in our collective imagination," Cameron has said. "But the passage of time has robbed it of its human face and vitality. I hope that Rose and Jack's relationship will be a kind of an emotional lightening rod, if you will, allowing viewers to invest their minds and their hearts to make history come alive."

Preparing for and filming *Titanic* was quite an ordeal. The film makers spent five years doing research to ensure the historical accuracy of each detail—the layout and design of the ship, the carpeting and chandeliers, the furniture and china, the clothing and luggage, even the manners and behavior. Filming took place in Baja California, in Mexico, where a nearly life-size replica of the ship was built at the edge of the ocean. The replica was 775 feet long—only 10% smaller than the original ship. It floated in a huge tank that held 17 million gallons of water. The camera operators rode on cranes suspended high about the set of the ship.

> *Winslet describes her experiences filming the special effects sequences in* **Titanic** *as terrifying. "We were in body harnesses, we were safe as houses, but I was so scared, I was absolutely freaking out. You just turn around and look at the sky and go, Dear God, just keep it going for one minute longer, [the director's] got to get just one more take. . . ."*

There were many difficult sequences to shoot. For example, the set for the First Class Dining Saloon and the Grand Staircase was built on a hydraulic platform at the bottom of a 30-foot deep tank. It was designed to be angled and flooded with 5-million gallons of filtered seawater. For the final stages of the disaster, the ship was separated into two pieces. At one point, right before the boat goes down for good, the bow of the ship descends into the water, sending the stern straight up in a vertical position. To recreate this, they built a deck on a special tilting platform—a giant seesaw—at the edge of the tank.

Here, Winslet's co-star DiCaprio describes one experience in filming these special effects. "I remember how they got one scene ready in about two hours, and all of a sudden I'm being, like, towed up on the back of a poop deck with a harness around my waist. There's like, 200 extras ready to fall off and hit the cushioned girders. And then there's three cranes around us with huge spotlights. Kate and I just looked at each other, like, 'How did we get here?'" Winslet describes these experiences as terrifying. "We were in body harnesses, we were safe as houses, but I was so scared, I was absolutely freaking out. You just turn around and look at the sky and go, Dear God, just

Winslet and Leonardo DiCaprio in Titanic

keep it going for one minute longer, [the director's] got to get just one more take. . . ." The resulting visual effects shots were tremendous, giving audiences a vivid feeling of what it must have been like to have been trapped on the doomed ship. Computerized special effects were also included to augment the real shots. These digital sequences were integrated into the finished film so seamlessly that it's impossible to tell what was real and what was created on computer.

Ultimately, all the hard work paid off. *Titanic* garnered four Golden Globe awards, including Best Picture, Best Director, Best Original Score, and Best Original Song. The movie also garnered 14 nominations for Academy Awards (Oscars), including a Best Actress nomination for Winslet (who didn't win). The movie won 11 awards, including Best Picture and Director, plus nine more awards for technical achievements in the areas of art direction, costumes, sound effects, visual effects, editing, cinematography, and music. With 11 Academy Awards, *Titanic* tied the record held by the 1959 movie *Ben Hur*. Among audiences, the movie has become a phenomenon. The love story between Jack and Rose has attracted legions of devoted fans who have seen the film many times each. And the special effects of the sinking ship keep them on the edge of their seats. By July 1998, the movie had made over $1.8 billion worldwide—with profits totaling an incredible $1.5 billion. It has surpassed *Star Wars*, *E.T.: The Extra-Terrestrial*, and *Jurassic Park* to become the highest-grossing film ever. *Titanic* is now the biggest money-maker in movie history.

Current and Future Projects

Since *Titanic*, Winslet has been involved in a couple of upcoming projects. Her next film after *Titanic* was *Hideous Kinky*, a low-budget English film based on the autobiographical novel by Esther Freud. Winslet plays a rebellious young hippie mother who packs up her two kids and takes them to live in Marrakesh. She shot that film on location there in late 1997, while fighting a difficult bout with amoebic dysentery. She has also made plans to appear in *Holy Smoke*, a film about cult deprogramming in which she plays a religious cult member. The film co-stars American actor Harvey Keitel and is directed by Australian film maker Jane Campion, who directed the critically acclaimed film, *The Piano*.

MARRIAGE AND FAMILY

Winslet, who is unmarried, lives in England. She has spoken with great feeling about her first love, Stephen Tredre. They met in 1991, while both were appearing in a children's science fiction series called "Dark Season." She and Stephen were involved for about four-and-a-half years, and they remained very close friends after they split up in 1995. "He was the person most important to me in my life, next to my family," she says. "I spoke to him every day."

Tredre was diagnosed with bone cancer a few years ago, and he died just 11 days before the opening of *Titanic*. For Winslet, it was a tremendous loss, but one that seems to have strengthened her. "[Stephen] was such an energized human being, such a big part of my life for such a long time, that I'm going into this year with an extraordinary sort of gusto. I feel that I'm taking on board all of the strength that he ever gave me and really living every moment, which is what he absolutely did, all the time, until the very second he died."

FILM CREDITS

Heavenly Creatures, 1994
A Kid in King Arthur's Court, 1995
Sense and Sensibility, 1995
Jude, 1996
Hamlet, 1996
Titanic, 1997

HONORS AND AWARDS

Best Supporting Actress (Screen Actors' Guild): 1996, for *Sense and Sensibility*
Best Supporting Actress (British Academy of Film and Television Arts): 1996, for *Sense and Sensibility*

FURTHER READING

Books

Marsh, Ed W. *James Cameron's Titanic*, 1997 (photography by Douglas Kirkland)
Who's Who in America, 1998

Periodicals

Cosmopolitan, Oct. 1996, p.182
Entertainment Weekly, Jan. 26, 1996, p.32
Harper's Bazaar, July 1997, p.90
New York Times, Dec. 10, 1995, p.H15
Newsweek, Feb. 23, 1998, p.58
People, Feb. 23, 1998, p.52; Mar. 16, 1998, p.52
Premiere, Feb. 1997, p.76
Rolling Stone, Mar. 5, 1998, p.44
Times (London), Sep. 28, 1996; Jan. 18, 1998
USA Today, Oct. 16, 1996, p.D3
Vogue, Mar. 1997, p.270

ADDRESS

William Morris Agency
151 El Camino Drive
Beverly Hills, CA 90212

WORLD WIDE WEB SITES

http://www.titanicmovie.com

Photo and Illustration Credits

Bella Abzug/Photos: AP/Wide World Photos; UPI/Corbis-Bettmann; Collections of the LIBRARY OF CONGRESS; UPI/Corbis-Bettmann.

Kofi Annan/Photos: UN/DPI Photo.

Neve Campbell/Photos: Kimberly Wright; Andrew Eccles/FOX.

Dalai Lama/Photos: AP/Wide World Photos; David Sasson/Corbis-Bettmann; UPI/Corbis-Bettmann; AP/Wide World Photos.

Diana, Princess of Wales/Photos: AP/Wide World Photos.

Leonardo DiCaprio/Photos: Merie W. Wallace; Etienne George.

Walter Diemer/Photo: Fleer Corp. from *The Great American Chewing Gum Book.*

Ruth Handler/Photos: AP/Wide World Photos; Copyright © Allan Wright.

Hanson/Photos: Copyright © 1997 Michael Lavine; Copyright © 1997 Marina Chavez; Copyright © 1997 Danny Clinch.

Livan Hernandez/Photos: Denis Bancroft/Florida Marlins; AP/Wide World Photos.

Jewel/Photos: Copyright © 1998 by Brigette Lacombe; AP/Wide World Photos.

Jimmy Johnson/Photo: AP/Wide World Photos.

Tara Lipinski/Photos: J. Barry Mittan; AP/Wide World Photos.

Jody-Anne Maxwell/Photos: AP/Wide World Photos.

Dominique Moceanu/Photos: Copyright © Dave Black; AP/Wide World Photos.

Alexandra Nechita/Photos: Copyright © Dan Snipes.

Brad Pitt/Photo: AP/Wide World Photos.

LeAnn Rimes/Photos: John Chiasson; Tom Queally/ABC.

Emily Rosa/Photos: AP/Wide World Photos.

Appendix

This Appendix contains updates for individuals profiled in Volumes 1, 2, 3, 4, 5, 6, and 7 of *Biography Today*.

* YASIR ARAFAT *

During 1998, Palestinian leader Yasir Arafat continued to work on the issues of Palestinian autonomy and control of specific territories such as the West Bank. After 19 months of a stalemate between Israel and the Palestinians, Arafat met in Washington, D.C., with President Bill Clinton and Israeli Prime Minster Benjamin Netanyahu in October 1998. At issue is the implementation of a full peace agreement between Israel and the Palestinians by May 1999. Speaking before the United Nations General Assembly in September 1998, Arafat asked for the help of the organization in his quest for peace and for a Palestinian homeland. "I would like to call upon all of you, from this place, the source of international legitimacy and peacemaking, the guardian of freedom, security and stability, and the source for the achievement of justice and prosperity for humankind to stand by our people, especially as our people demand of us to shoulder our responsibilities, and they await the establishment of their independent state."

*AUNG SAN SUU KYI *

In September 1998, Aung San Suu Kyi and a group of opposition politicians challenged the ruling military government of Myanmar by declaring that they would act as the country's legitimate parliament. Aung San Suu Kyi's group, the National League for Democracy, won election in 1990 in the former Burma, but were barred from taking office by the military government. In response to her recent initiative, the military began mass arrests of pro-democracy advocates. Still, many foreign observers believe that the National League for Democracy has more support than ever before, among Buddhist groups, retired military officers, ethnic groups, and students. Yet in deciding to take on the military government, Aung San Suu Kyi has put herself at great personal risk. One specialist described the political atmosphere in Myanmar as "the most volatile and unpredictable moment in the last 10 years."

* LARRY BIRD *

Larry Bird, who retired from professional basketball in 1992 after 13 legendary seasons with the Boston Celtics, returned to the game in 1997 as the coach of the Indiana Pacers. During the 1997-98 season, Bird proved to be an exceptional coach, leading his team to a 58-24 season, their best since the Pacers joined the league in 1977. Bird's coaching led the team as far as the Eastern Conference finals, where they lost to the Chicago Bulls. For his efforts, Bird was named Coach of the Year for the National Basketball League. The year brought further honors as Bird was inducted into the Basketball Hall of Fame on October 2, 1998, his first year of eligibility for that honor.

* BOUTROS BOUTROS-GHALI *

After serving as Secretary General from 1991 to 1996, Boutros Boutros-Ghali stepped down from the head post at the United Nations in December 1996. It became clear to Boutros-Ghali that the United States would not support him in his effort to continue in the position. He has since moved to Paris, where, in 1997, he was elected head of La Francophonie, an organization of 49 states and regions of the world that describes itself as "the community of countries which have the French language in common." The group was founded in 1986 by former French President Francois Mitterand to "defend French culture and language." Over the years, the organization's mission has changed to focus on forging economic and political alliances among the nations, which include Romania, Bulgaria, Egypt, and Vietnam.

*BILL CLINTON *

For Bill Clinton and for the nation, the year 1998 has been dominated by the scandal involving Monica Lewinsky. Lewinsky was a former intern who worked at the White House in the mid-1990s. In December 1997, Lewinsky was subpoenaed to appear as a witness in a sexual harassment lawsuit brought by Paula Jones against President Clinton. In sworn testimony, Lewinsky said that she had not had a sexual relationship with the president. Clinton also gave testimony in the case, and he, too, denied any sexual relationship.

That testimony was challenged by Kenneth Starr, the independent counsel who has been gathering evidence for years in the Whitewater inquiry involving both Bill and Hillary Clinton. In January 1998, Starr said that he had evidence that contradicted Clinton's testimony. He said the evidence indicated that Clinton and Lewinsky had had an affair, and that Clinton had urged Lewinsky to lie about it under oath. Starr's evidence had come from Linda Tripp. A former friend of Lewinsky, Tripp had secretly taped telephone conversations in which Lewinsky discussed her relationship with the president and her testimony, and then had given those tapes to Starr.

Clinton vehemently denied any wrongdoing. Over the next eight months, he continued to proclaim his innocence, and Starr continued to gather evidence. In June 1998, Lewinsky agreed to testify before a grand jury called by Starr to further investigate the matter. Lewinsky was granted immunity from any prosecution for her testimony, meaning that she could testify without having to worry that she might be punished if she admitted to any wrongdoing. Clinton was also called to testify before the grand jury, which he did on videotape from the White House.

Finally, in August 1998, Clinton admitted that he and Lewinsky had had "an improper relationship." He made his admission in a televised broadcast to the nation, in which he also stated that he felt that the matter was private, between him and his family, and that he should be left alone.

Yet his confession did not make the scandal go away. In September, Starr released a lengthy report delineating the evidence against Clinton. The report was released over the Internet, and people everywhere read the evidence of the president's relationship and learned that he had lied to the American public for months to cover up the scandal. He may have also lied to the grand jury investigating the case while he was under oath. In our legal system, lying while under oath is considered perjury, a very serious offense. Starr delivered his documents and a report to the Congress outlining what he called impeachable offenses.

Next, the U.S. Congress began its own investigation into whether or not to begin impeachment proceedings. In an impeachment, the president is charged with wrongdoing by the Judiciary Committee of the House of Representatives. The Judiciary Committee draws up its charges, and then turns the matter over to the full House of Representatives. The House then votes on whether the president can be charged with wrongdoing. If the House votes to impeach, the president then faces a trial in the Senate on the charges outlined in the House's articles of impeachment. If the Senate finds the president guilty, he must leave office.

On October 10, 1998, for only the third time in the nation's history, the House Judiciary Committee voted to begin an inquiry into the impeachment of a president. The House will be in recess until after the November elections. According to the chairman of the Judiciary Committee, Henry Hyde, they hope to complete their investigation by the end of 1998. Yet many observers believe that the impeachment proceedings will drag on for months and possibly years.

MARJORY STONEMAN DOUGLAS

Marjory Stoneman Douglas, staunch defender of the Florida Everglades, died on May 14, 1998, at the age of 108. Although she had been in poor health for years, her commitment to the preservation of the Everglades was lifelong. Her 1947 book, *The Everglades: River of Grass*, brought the plight of the area to the public's attention. For many years, citizens were oblivious to the dangers of overdevelopment and poor land management to the fragile wetlands of south Florida. She made many realize that those policies were causing the destruction of the area's fresh water resource, and a beautiful, irreplaceable national treasure. In her book, she wrote that "perhaps even in this last hour, in a new relation of usefulness and beauty, the vast magnificent, subtle and unique region of the Everglades may not be utterly lost."As recently as her 100th birthday, in 1990, when asked if she thought the Everglades would survive, she claimed: "I am neither an optimist nor a pessimist. I say it's got to be done." That determination led Roderick J. Jude, the head of Florida's Sierra Club, to claim, "The Everglades wouldn't be there for us to try to continue to save if not for her work through the years."

* BILL GATES *

Bill Gates was in the news this year when his company, Microsoft, was sued by the U.S. Justice Department and 20 states for unfair business practices. They allege that Microsoft had included the Internet Explorer web browser with the newest release of their operating software, Windows 98. That did not allow other web browsers, such as Netscape Navigator, to compete fairly for its share of the ever-increasing Internet market. Further, the Justice Department and the 20 attorneys general representing the states in the suit allege that Microsoft has developed licensing practices that favor only Microsoft products. That is, because 90% of all PCs sold use the Microsoft operating system, Microsoft has an unfair advantage and puts pressure on PC makers to include only its products on new PCs. Also, the suit claims that Microsoft has coerced PC manufacturers to use only its initial user interface—that's the screen that a user first sees when starting a computer. As head of Microsoft, Bill Gates himself has been called to testify in the case. The company's lawyers have tried to have the case thrown out of court, claiming that Microsoft is just being competitive in a competitive market. However, the judge in the case has dismissed their claim, and the case is scheduled to begin on October 15.

* AL GORE *

After being cleared by Attorney General Janet Reno in December 1997 in regard to an earlier investigation into alleged campaign finance abuses, Vice President Al Gore was once again named as the focus of a campaign finance investigation. On August 26, 1998, Reno ordered a preliminary investigation into whether Gore lied to Justice Department prosecutors and FBI agents during an interview in November 1997 regarding possible campaign finance abuses. The focus of the interview was whether or not Gore told the truth to prosecutors when he discussed the type of campaign funding for the major media effort for the Democratic Party in the 1996 campaign. There are two types of campaign financing. "Soft money," which is not strictly regulated by federal campaign law, can be used to fund only the general activities of a political party, such as issue advertising. "Hard money," which is very strictly regulated, can be used for political campaigns for individual candidates. According to published reports, Gore stated that during the fund-raising calls he made from the White House, he asked contributors only for "soft money." Yet some of the money he raised wound up in accounts for "hard money."

Gore has insisted he is innocent of the charges. Reno and the Justice Department will decide by the end of the year whether or not the charges warrant further investigation.

* FLORENCE GRIFFITH JOYNER *

Florence Griffith Joyner died suddenly on September 21, 1998. She was 38 years old. Griffith Joyner was found by her husband, Al Joyner, on the morning of September 21, "unresponsive and not breathing." After an autopsy in September, the cause of death was still not determined. Griffith Joyner had suffered a heart seizure on an airplane in 1996, but no cause or heart disease was ever found. Possibly because of her youth and the unknown nature of her death, some sources raised the rumors that her death might have been linked to steroid use, a charge that she had always vehemently denied and that had never been substantiated.

Then, on October 22, medical authorities released the final results of their inquiry into Griffith Joyner's death. She had died after suffering a seizure that caused her to suffocate while she slept. The seizure was caused by a blood vessel abnormality. The family took the opportunity to lay to rest the rumors suggesting drug use. "The coroner's investigation was very thorough," said Al Joyner. "My wife passed the ultimate drug test."

"Flo-Jo," as she was known to her many fans, is remembered as "the world's fastest woman." In the 1988 Olympics, she became the first American woman to win four medals in one Olympics, taking home three gold and one silver medal. She is still the world record holder in the 100-meter and 200-meter. She is also remembered for her flamboyant sense of fashion, with her six-inch fingernails and vivid running outfits. After her retirement from competition in 1989, she worked with disadvantaged children and was part of the President's Council on Fitness.

* JACKIE JOYNER-KERSEE *

Jackie Joyner-Kersee, called "the world's greatest athlete," retired from competition in July 1998. She competed in her final Goodwill Games, where she won her signature event, the heptathlon. Then, she went home to East St. Louis, Illinois, where she competed in an event called "Track and Filed's Farewell to Jackie Joyner-Kersee." She did the long jump one last time, ending in sixth place, but that didn't stop the crowd of supporters and well-wishers from cheering her for her outstanding career. She retires from the support as "the greatest female athlete of her generation, the first lady of track and field," according to Jere Longman of the *New York Times*. In a career that spanned two decades, Joyner-Kersee won six Olympic medals, always competing with graciousness, with "class and style," as she described her approach. "All we ever wanted was respect for what we were trying to do," she said at a press conference marking her retirement. "That's what's happening now. It's OK for girls to play soccer or softball or football and not be criticized or thought of as different."

Joyner-Kersee has now begun a career as a sports agent, representing players in the National Football League. She hopes to be a role model for women in the business of professional sports. She also continues to work for her foundation in East St. Louis that helps underprivileged kids.

Sadly, Joyner-Kersee was in the news again in September 1998, when her sister-in-law and close friend, Florence Griffith Joyner, died suddenly.

* JANET RENO *

In 1998, Attorney General Janet Reno has been involved most prominently with ongoing investigations into alleged campaign finance abuses by the 1996 Clinton-Gore reelection campaign. The head of the FBI, Louis Freeh, and the former head of Reno's campaign finance task force, Charles G. LaBella, both submitted memos to the attorney general arguing that an independent counsel should be appointed to fully investigate the case. In August and September 1998, Reno announced three separate preliminary investigations into the case. One opened a preliminary investigation into allegations that President Clinton oversaw a plan to violate spending limits in the campaign. The second investigation, which focuses on Vice President Gore, will determine whether he lied to Justice Department officials during interviews in November 1997 regarding possible campaign finance abuses. The third investigation involves former deputy White House chief of staff Harold Ickes and whether or not he told the truth in earlier campaign finance inquiries. Based on the findings of these inquiries, Reno will decide whether or not to appoint an independent counsel to investigate the case.

And on September 22, 1998, Republican Representative Dan Burton called for the House to hold Reno in contempt of Congress because she refused to turn over internal documents related to the campaign finance case.

* JERRY SEINFELD *

After nine seasons with one of the top-rated shows on television, Jerry Seinfeld left the world of prime-time with a flourish in May 1998. His last show, "Seinfeld," received the third-largest audience ever for a series finale, as 76.3 million viewers tuned in for a final look at Jerry, Elaine, Kramer, and George. Seinfeld went on to do a Broadway show based on his comedy routine, which was also filmed as an HBO special, entitled "I'm Telling You for the Last Time."

* DR. BENJAMIN SPOCK *

Dr. Benjamin Spock, whose book *Dr. Spock's Baby and Child Care* influenced several generations of parents, died on March 15, 1998, at the age of 94. He had been in declining health for some time. He is remembered for his role in redefining child rearing in the U.S., with the first edition of his book, which appeared in 1946 as *The Common Sense Book of Baby and Child Care*. His message to parents was simple: trust yourself, you know more than you think you do. T. Berry Brazelton, a leading pediatrician of the current era, remembered him this way: "He said 'Trust your instincts,' and no one had done that before. He turned parenting back to parents."

Spock's interest in children's well-being extended to politics, too. He was part of the protests against the Vietnam War and against the proliferation of nuclear weapons in the 1960s and 1970s. Even in his last book, *A Better World for Our Children: Rebuilding American Family Values*, he continued to speak on behalf of the plight of children in our culture. "When I look at our society and think of the millions of children exposed ever day to its harmful effects, I am near despair." He felt our society was "simply not working," in part due to "the progressive loss of values in this century." He said that "Our greatest hope is to bring up children inspired by their opportunities for being helpful and loving."

*BORIS YELTSIN *

As 1998 draws to a close, Boris Yeltsin is losing his hold on power in Russia. The Russian economy is on the verge of collapse. In August 1998, the Russian government could not pay the interest due on a loan of $50 billion dollars financed by the International Monetary Fund. The Russian unit of currency, the ruble, has been devalued, which means it has a fraction of its former worth, and people cannot buy staples, such as food and clothing. The Russian government owes its workers more than 77 billion rubles in back pay, and it does not have the money to pay them; in non-government businesses, employers owe their workers $70 billion. Throughout the crisis, Yeltsin has been seen as weak and ineffectual. As David Remnick wrote in *The New Yorker*, "The spectacle of Yeltsin's disintegration—his erratic gestures and misbegotten policies—is pathetic." Earlier this year, the Russian parliament, called the Duma, twice refused to appoint his choice to the position of Prime Minister, and calls were made for Yeltsin to resign. There was even a move to impeach him from office.

In October 1998, the Communist party called for a general strike in Russia. Although most of the Russian people do not want the Communist party back in control of their country, they came out to demonstrate to show their anger and disappointment in Yeltsin and his policies. Russia is in economic and political turmoil, and its future, as well as that of its embattled leader, is uncertain.

Guide to the Indexes

Each volume of *Biography Today* contains four indexes: Name Index, General Index, Places of Birth Index, and Birthday Index. Each index is fully cumulative, covering both the regular series and the special subject volumes of *Biography Today*.

The **Regular Series** of *Biography Today* is denoted in the indexes with the month and year of the issue in which the individual appeared. Each individual also appears in the cumulation for that year.

Albright, Madeleine . . . . Apr 97
Dion, Celine . . . . Sep 97
Ford, Harrison . . . . Sep 97
Jordan, Barbara . . . . Apr 96
Reeve, Christopher . . . . Jan 97
Robinson, David . . . . Sep 96
White, Jaleel . . . . Jan 96

The **Special Subject Volumes** of *Biography Today* are each denoted in the indexes with an abbreviated form of the series name, plus the year of that volume. They are listed as follows:

Adams, Ansel . . . . Artist 96   (Artists Series)
Dahl, Roald . . . . Author 95   (Authors Series)
Gibbs, Lois . . . . Env 97   (World Leaders Series: Environmental Leaders)
Mandela, Winnie . . . . ModAfr 97   (World Leaders Series: Modern African Leaders)
Sagan, Carl . . . . Science 96   (Scientists & Inventors Series)
Woods, Tiger . . . . Sport 96   (Sports Series)

Updated information on certain individuals appears in the **Appendix** at the end of the *Biography Today* Annual Cumulation. In the indexes, the original entry is listed first, followed by any updates:

Gore, Al . . . . . . Jan 93; Update 96; Update 97; Update 98
Myers, Walter Dean . . . . . . Jan 93; Update 94

Name Index

Listed below are the names of all individuals profiled in *Biography Today*, followed by the date of the issue in which they appear.

General Index

This index includes subjects, occupations, organizations, and ethnic and minority origins that pertain to individuals profiled in *Biography Today.*

371

Places of Birth Index

The following index lists the places of birth for the individuals profiled in *Biography Today*. Places of birth are entered under state, province, and/or country.

Birthday Index